"Jenny Mosley's deep insights into relational practices in school matter more than ever ... I have to say that the overarching focus on kindness adds a distinctive depth to the work ... perhaps, most importantly to me, this thoroughly revised edition orients the reader to the collective ... and she encourages us to be flexible and responsive in nurturing the strengths within our communities."

Robin Banerjee, *Professor of Developmental Psychology and Founder of the Sussex Centre for Research on Kindness, University of Sussex*

A Circle Approach to Boosting Emotional Wellbeing and Relationships in the Secondary School

This timely resource presents Jenny Mosley's acclaimed Circle Time model specifically adapted for secondary education, offering a structured, powerful and compassionate approach to rebuilding human connection among teenagers. In an era of increasing digital isolation and mental health challenges, Mosley provides educators with practical tools to create spaces where students feel truly seen, heard and valued.

Building on decades of pioneering work in both primary and secondary schools, inside this book you will find:

- A complete framework for implementing Circle Time in secondary settings – from Year 7 through to Year 11.
- Practical, age-appropriate activities, games and discussion prompts that engage even the most reluctant teenagers.
- Behaviour strategies rooted in restorative practice – helping students take responsibility and rebuild relationships.
- Tools to build a positive school ethos, improve classroom climate, and boost mental health and motivation.
- Real-life examples and success stories that show the power of Circle Time in action – from disengaged teens becoming peer mentors to entire year groups forming tighter bonds.

Endorsed by empirical research which links social-emotional learning to academic success, the approach balances emotional literacy with practical skill development. Jenny Mosley doesn't just offer a programme – she offers a philosophy: one where students are not just taught but truly seen, where emotional literacy is not a luxury but a necessity, and where schools become safe spaces for teenagers to grow into capable, compassionate adults.

This essential guide is invaluable for heads of year, form tutors, PSHE leads and classroom teachers committed to nurturing both academic achievement and emotional development. School counselors, educational psychologists and wellbeing coordinators will also find practical strategies they can immediately implement to support teenagers in developing the communication skills and emotional resilience needed to thrive in today's complex world.

Jenny Mosley is a renowned UK education expert and consultant, best known as the founder of Jenny Mosley Training Consultancies and the creator of the widely acclaimed "Quality Circle Time model."

Marilyn Tew was a Circle Time consultant and now works to support children, young people and adults as a psychotherapist.

A Circle Approach to Boosting Emotional Wellbeing and Relationships in the Secondary School

Making Time to Listen
Third Edition

Jenny Mosley and Marilyn Tew

LONDON AND NEW YORK

Designed cover image: J Steer

Third edition published 2026
by Routledge
4 Park Square, Milton Park, Abingdon, Oxon, OX14 4RN

and by Routledge
605 Third Avenue, New York, NY 10158

Routledge is an imprint of the Taylor & Francis Group, an informa business

© 2026 Jenny Mosley and Marilyn Tew

The right of Jenny Mosley and Marilyn Tew to be identified as authors of this work has been asserted in accordance with sections 77 and 78 of the Copyright, Designs and Patents Act 1988.

All rights reserved. No part of this book may be reprinted or reproduced or utilised in any form or by any electronic, mechanical, or other means, now known or hereafter invented, including photocopying and recording, or in any information storage or retrieval system, without permission in writing from the publishers.

Trademark notice: Product or corporate names may be trademarks or registered trademarks, and are used only for identification and explanation without intent to infringe.

For Product Safety Concerns and Information please contact our EU representative GPSR@taylorandfrancis.com. Taylor & Francis Verlag GmbH, Kaufingerstraße 24, 80331 München, Germany.

First edition published by Routledge 2000
Second edition published by Routledge 2013

British Library Cataloguing-in-Publication Data
A catalogue record for this book is available from the British Library

ISBN: 978-1-041-15475-4 (hbk)
ISBN: 978-1-041-15473-0 (pbk)
ISBN: 978-1-003-67961-5 (ebk)

DOI: 10.4324/9781003679615

Typeset in Galliard
by Deanta Global Publishing Services, Chennai, India

Contents

Acknowledgements	ix
Foreword	xii
Introduction	1

PART I
The Circle Time Vision   7

1	Why Do We So Desperately Need Circle Time Now?	9
2	Circle Approaches in Action	13
3	Circle Time and the Social and Emotional Aspects of Learning (SEAL)	21
4	The Circle Time Approach and Ofsted	28
5	The Whole-School Quality Circle Time Approach: Introducing an Ecosystemic Model	35
6	Unlocking the Whole-School Quality Circle Time Model for Wellbeing	41

PART II
Putting Circle Time into Practice   49

7	Setting Up Three Listening Systems – An Overview	51
8	Establishing Codes of Conduct – Are They Clear, Kind and Consistent?	60

9	Creating and Embedding Incentives – Are They Kind, Considerate and Community-Based?	63
10	Creating and Implementing Consequences – Are They Fair and Feasible?	71
11	Setting Up Lunchtimes that Enhance Wellbeing	77
12	Supporting Dysregulated Pupils	82
13	The Containment Stage or How Do We Cope When Nothing Works?	90
14	Achieving the Biggest Impact with Circle Time	92

PART III
Activities, Games and Resources — 97

15	The Five Step Structure of Quality Circle Time	99
16	Glimpses of Circle Time Practice, Followed by a Case Study	106
17	Introduction to Circle Plans	132
18	Game Ideas for Step 1 and Step 4	198
19	Step 2 – Rounds	228
20	Step 3 – Open Forum Drama and Role-Play Ideas	231
21	Step 5 – Calm Down Ideas	237

The Last Word — *253*
Training Available from Jenny Mosley Consultancies — *254*
Index — *256*

Acknowledgements

I am sure this will be the last book I write on secondary schools, although I would be happy to support anyone else if they would like to! Consequently, it's a precious book – and I am going to irritate many readers who bother with this Acknowledgement section by giving it far too much attention. I love the thought of being really old and reading through these memories. Do you know that memories activate similar neural reward pathways and release the same positive chemicals that you originally experienced (Novotney, 2023). I now understand why Reminiscence Therapy is so important.

I haven't referred to it in this book but Leeds Local Authority was once a huge supporter of my work, and we did many exciting projects together. Sean Duggan, one of Leeds' wonderful learning mentors published Building Bridges – a project with KS3 students going into older people's homes and working with them through the Quality Circle Time model. I would be thrilled if I was in one of those homes and the children brought the circle in for me to join in games and have a good laugh!

Firstly thanks must go to Marilyn Tew, my co-author on the original 1999 book. I met Marilyn when she was a Masters student when she signed up for my module. From the start she was captivated, enthusiastic and incredibly diligent. I used to encourage all my students to write assignments for me that could, with only a little extra work, be submitted to be published. Marilyn's first article was published in *Pastoral Care in Education* 1998: "Circle Time: A Much Neglected Resource in Secondary Schools." A natural scholar, she gained her PhD in 2002. So thank you Marilyn for helping to get this book to the stage where I finally had some time to rework, research and record all of the current developments. Well done to you too for forging a career that could create a bridge between counselling and education. When, in this book, you see a name next to a case study or a short, personalised paragraph – you and I know (I was once a secondary teacher) how hard it is to push back the waves of demands and try something new. Teachers are unsung heroes and I sincerely thank all of you who are mentioned in this book.

Helen Sonnet, a long-time friend and a great Nurture Group teacher who has just re-released the four *101 Games* books with me as a co-author (Taylor & Francis).

Maddie McMahon, my brilliant university student from "up the road", was conscripted in for days on end to help me organise far too much material. I feel the experience of working with this older, crankier model of myself has equipped her to conquer the world of work. Any company would be lucky to have her!

Alison Foyle – senior editor at Taylor & Francis – is gentle, warm, passionate and firm. I did not want to write a new edition. I came up with great excuses. Eventually we met up – toasted the education world with good wine and I'm in! It's almost been too hard a journey – because of other work and family commitments, but unexpectedly I found myself getting very excited about the new possibilities and then dashed against the rocks when my research revealed that previously committed schools had let go of some of our key projects. Alison leads a great, well woven together team who all work seamlessly together to create wonderful books.

My energy for this book grew as the project continued. I realised as time went on how in the last decade, whilst I had been into schools regularly, I hadn't been to large conferences and universities as I used to, where I met inspiring people and would share ideas. So, it has been great to link up, even lightly, with Professor Robin Banerjee – who could not warm to an understanding, talented, positive academic who led the world's largest survey on kindness: The Kindness Test. We have not met – but Robin has just gone the extra mile now and read my first raw-edition and agreed to write its Foreword. I am deeply grateful and honoured as I truly admire his work.

Maya Menon created The Teacher Foundation (TTF) in Bangalore, India. Maya attended a Train the Trainers with me in the UK – her vitality, deep intelligence, and sheer energy and vision meant that afterwards I agreed that TTF could become the sole accredited provider of Quality Circle Time (QCT) in India and have partnered her ever since. For the past 25 years, I have been visiting India to support her work. With her own teachers she has developed two books of QCT lesson plans. When I finish this book, I will be going straight over to work for six weeks with her once more. It's hard for Indian schools to get training for all their teachers in the social and emotional areas of education, so sometimes I have up to 1000 teachers a day – a logistical nightmare that only Maya could handle! Busy people always make time for others is a very true aphorism. Maya has contributed four lesson plans to this book. She always follows the Five Step QCT structure which means that her lesson plans are safe and accessible.

Stamatina Kalyveza was also one of my Master's students – who also galloped past me academically, off to do a PhD in Greece. Her doctoral focus was on how high-functioning adolescents with autism, when given experience of being in a mainstream secondary school Circle of Support can really thrive. It boosts their social and emotional competencies and self confidence in being able to form peer-friendships. My other new book also coming out in 2026 – *Early Intervention Through Circles of Support: An Inclusive Approach to Building Self Confidence, Communication Skills and Peer Relationships* – discusses the importance of offering young people with certain challenges the experience of being included in a smaller Circle of Support attended by peers who wish to become kinder and more friendly. Professor Jonathan Glazzard gave this book (and myself) a huge boost by also writing an incredibly thoughtful, wise and knowledgeable Foreword for it. I loved his opening words "this is a brilliant book …" So, Matina's work is so timely and I am thrilled to know that she is working on her own book in Greece.

Thanks to years of working closely with Ian Read (Headteacher of Watercliffe Meadow Primary School) and all his positive, enthusiastic and kind-hearted staff – Sheffield LA are now supporting Ian and I to create a truly unique training experience. We will roll out the Whole-School QCT model (as developed in this book and its mirror primary book) through a day a month for seven months so they can build on what they have learnt and embed it before being introduced to the next section of the model. Why it's unique is because the course is set in Ian's school, so not only will he and I do the training but we will also involve many of the children and staff in training the delegates too. They embedded my model 22 years ago with the constant use of Plan, Do and Review. This course will include primary and secondary heads and hopefully once we have learnt more ourselves from the delegates we will keep rolling out this course – if any of you enthusiastic readers want to join us. I am really excited by this shared vision – it's the best outcome I could hope for in a 50-year-old career in education. If I can, like I have in the past, light up like-minded colleagues to carry on the torch of connection, belonging, openness and fun in all areas of communication, then I am indeed, as I always have been, a very very lucky person.

To learn more about the courses that I run and the training we offer, visit www.circle-time.co.uk

Reference

Novotney, A., 2023. *Feeling nostalgic this holiday season? It might help boost your mental health.* American Psychological Association, 18 December. Available at: https://www.apa.org/topics/mental-health/nostalgia-boosts-well-being [Accessed: 26 September 2025].

Foreword

Almost exactly 30 years ago, I was undertaking my doctoral research into how children navigate their social relationships, and I had a particular interest at that time in children's growing attention to the impressions they make on one another. This developmental process, it turns out, involves a remarkably complex interplay of social behaviours, psychological goals and motivations, patterns of thinking about oneself and about others, and keenly felt emotions. How do I look? What do they think of me? Do I belong?

During that early period of my research, I had increasingly started to focus on different practices in the school context that could support children's relationships, and Jenny Mosley's work jumped out. Her 1996 book on Quality Circle Time (QCT) still sits proudly on my bookshelf, and it was what inspired a small (but for me highly influential) piece of pilot work that I undertook immediately after my PhD. With the invaluable guidance offered on QCT, I carried out a series of Circle Time activities in a local school focused around the theme of being in new social situations.

I was fascinated at the time to find that the Circle Time activities led to reduced concerns among children about changing themselves in order to fit in. Indeed, as I summarised to school leaders at the time, "the Circle Time discussions showed that children were increasingly able to recognise the positive value of having varying personalities, opinions and behaviours in peer interactions," and with this greater social confidence came reductions in social anxiety.

The realisation that these kinds of classroom practices can have such specific impacts on how children and young people think, feel and behave was enormously impactful for me, and led to a whole career focused on how different aspects of social experiences can play a role in child development, from the importance of the peer context for young people's "social and emotional learning" to the development of a "whole-school approach" to mental health.

And now, Jenny Mosley's deep insights into relational practices at school matter more than ever. I was delighted to be asked to write the foreword for this new edition of her work on Quality Circle Time in the secondary school, because I've seen firsthand from my own practice in classrooms what a difference it makes. And I'm also aware that this is a critical time for all of us working in education to shine a light on what we know helps to nurture young people's understanding of themselves, each other and the world.

Jenny has updated her tried-and-tested guidance to take into account the rapidly changing landscape of social life, considering the backdrop of social media, the COVID-19 pandemic, increased prevalence of mental health difficulties and more. She has also taken in new insights from her work across cultures, with a range of inputs from her ongoing collaborations in India. And I have to say that the overarching focus on kindness adds a distinctive depth to the work. This is not a soft and fluffy extra, a nice-to-have when the core business is done. When human beings are involved, kindness *is* the core business!

The whole-school QCT ecosystemic approach that Jenny sets out – which "involves all members of the school community and every part of the school day" – draws upon both established theoretical frameworks and the latest research insights at the intersection of educational practice, social relationships and psychological development. Kindness, as a fundamental dimension of human beings' wellbeing and life satisfaction, is at the heart of this approach and underpins the ethos and value system that knits together **listening, trust** and belonging. Crucially, Jenny has provided compelling **demonstrations** of how these qualities can be cultivated in secondary school **settings, where** respectful and empathic listening has such a critical role to play in **support**ing the development of adolescents and fostering a climate for truly engaged learning at school.

Perhaps most importantly for me, this thoroughly revised edition – rich with examples of successful QCT in action – orients the reader to the collective. Work in schools on the social and emotional dimensions of our lives should never be reduced simply to a focus on which individuals have got problems, and what needs to happen to them. Of course, individualised support may often be essential, but the context needs to be one where we are thinking about "us" – can we create an environment that works for all of us, where we can trust each other, where we all have a voice, where we listen and reflect, and where we find solutions together?

Jenny's new book is not a rigid set of instructions, but rather encourages us to be flexible and responsive in nurturing the strengths within our communities. Whether your immediate focus is on the transition to secondary school, on specific RSHE topics or simply on working towards more harmonious lunchtimes, what I hope will inspire you most is this overarching drive to create an educational context of kindness, listening and trust – as much for the adults in the school as it is for the children and young people.

Robin Banerjee
Professor of Developmental Psychology and
Founder of the Sussex Centre for Research on Kindness,
University of Sussex

Introduction

This Introduction to the third edition highlights that mental health challenges among young people are at an all-time high and teacher wellbeing is increasingly strained. Drawing on over 50 years of experience, the author reflects on the evolving educational landscape and argues for the urgent need to embed the "Circle Approach" more deeply into school life. This Introduction uses evidence from recent research and personal practice to demonstrate the power of structured circle sessions in boosting emotional resilience, strengthening relationships, and creating kind, inclusive school communities. A section on "How to Use the Book" is included with tailored advice for how people with different roles could best utilise the book. Finally, there are some technical clarifications about the language used in the book.

Introduction – Why We Need This Third Edition – A Personal View

Since writing the second edition over a decade ago, the world of education has become even more complex – and, in many ways, more wounded. Mental health is no longer a quiet concern on the margins; it is at the centre of daily headlines. NHS England (2023) reports that one in five young people is now living with mental health challenges. MIND (2025) found that 78% of the 1271 young people aged 13–25 in their survey said that school had made their mental wellbeing worse – bullying being one of the main factors.

Yet, there is hope. MIND (2025) also highlighted that "resilience interventions consistently help pupils manage daily stressors, develop emotional intelligence, and improve academic performance."

Pupil voice is a concept schools often aspire to, but achieving it meaningfully is a different matter. Research shows that when schools truly listen to and act on the opinions and feelings of their pupils, it leads to transformative change. In my 50 years in education, I remain convinced that the Circle Approach is the most powerful tool we have to bring pupil voice to life.

DOI: 10.4324/9781003679615-1

However, its effectiveness depends entirely on how well it is implemented – on the training of the facilitators, the structure of the sessions, and crucially, the systems in place to support the teachers themselves.

In education, we rarely talk about group supervision for staff. Yet today's educators are dealing with increasingly challenging individuals and issues. If staff aren't being listened to themselves, how can we expect them to open up spaces where young people feel heard, especially when those conversations might uncover more trauma, more problems, and more emotional weight, with nowhere to take it?

We, the adults, also need safe, regular spaces for support, reflection and shared understanding.

Early in my career, I worked in a neglected part of London, in an all-through school for children with emotional and behavioural difficulties. One of the most profound experiences we had as staff was a weekly circle session, facilitated by a trained therapist. The therapist set clear boundaries: confidentiality, one voice at a time and active listening. Because we followed those guidelines, we built trust and began to speak more honestly.

I still talk in training about the day I finally asked that circle for help. A red rash spread across my neck with nerves, but I said it:

"I need help, because I have a child in my class ... and I don't like him."

It felt like an unforgivable admission. Here I was, a privileged adult, his teacher, disliking a child who had clearly endured so much in life. But the group listened. One colleague gently offered, "Would it help to know this about his grandmother?" It did help. Another said, "He's very motivated to help younger children," and suggested I let him support some younger children in his class as a reward. They even offered to mentor that arrangement.

And so, the circle became our circle, and the child became our child, not just mine. The stress I'd been carrying alone lifted. I was part of a team.

Professor Robin Banerjee, a leading researcher in social and emotional development, argues that mental health difficulties are too often seen as belonging to the individual, rather than being rooted in relationships. As reported in 2021

> Banerjee's research illuminates the relevance and value of peer group processes as a window into children's mental health and wellbeing ... (his) peer reviewed publications have demonstrated systematic connections among these cognitive, affective, behavioural and social-relational variables, showing that greater peer acceptance is linked to a more sophisticated understanding of emotions.

A weekly circle session builds those connections for both children and staff. When schools invest in regular time for listening, reflection and peer support, children interpret it as proof that peer relationships really matter. As friendship is one of young people's most important concerns, they can see the school as being kind, empathic and caring.

Of course, Circle Time is not magic. If it's poorly facilitated, it can feel awkward or even harmful. That's why this book includes structured session plans, supported by years of experience and training. But beyond a good handbook, what educators really need is ongoing support: real training, regular supervision through the circle approach, and senior leadership that understands and actively backs up this approach in their whole-school policies.

Relationships are not always about deep conversations. In fact, joy and shared presence are essential. Every circle session I've ever run or written includes both playful games and mindful stillness, weaving groups together through shared laughter and shared silence. Never has joy been more important in education than it is today.

My hope is that this third edition inspires educators to return to what matters most: building strong, trusting relationships that support not only pupils but also the staff who care for them. Use these session plans as a launchpad. Be brave. Adapt them. Build your own. But remember if you yourself are not getting the support and group supervision that you need, you can quickly get run down yourself.

Senior leaders must prioritise time, space and emotional backing, not just for pupils, but for the staff around them. Only then can we truly build the connected, kind and resilient schools our children need.

How to Use This Book

It's a great privilege to revisit this book for a third time. Since it was first published, many teachers have used it and thankfully commented on its usefulness. Has the educational landscape changed? Are schools now more concerned to build in proactive circle approaches to support relationships, resilience and reconciliation? To be honest, it all still feels very "patchy."

I genuinely do believe there is a movement, a zeitgeist, happening which is propelling education to find ways to strengthen young people's emotional wellbeing through creating circle opportunities to engage with face-to-face interaction. Many of you currently reading this book are coming from a whole range of roles and responsibilities:

- Subject Specialist
- PSHE Specialist or Tutor
- Head of Year
- Teaching Assistant
- SEN Teacher
- Educational Psychologist
- Teacher Training Student

Forgive me if I have missed any of you out!

You can all make a difference with your enthusiasm and passion. Trawling through the book, you may find a case study, a project or a section that is just right for you. Some of you just want to get on and "have a go" at running circles. There is a huge section of practical circle times for you to engage with. However, just pushing back tables and creating the circle is a challenge. Getting management to support your vision might take time and energy too, but don't let that stop you! Go straight to the second half of the book, pick up some practical session plans and just do the simplest ones first.

Maybe before you start, you could ask your class how they feel about sitting in a circle, playing games and talking to each other. Some of them will say things like: "it's too babyish," "it's boring," etc. Just accept what they say and ensure all the comments are written down. They will form part of your pre-action research questionnaire. When you have done half a term of circles, give them exactly the same written comments and see if they still feel the same way. You have now got some positive "evidence" to take to management – hopefully.

If you are a manager looking at the whole-school ethos, then the first half of the book is best for you. It is rich with examples of schools engaging at all levels with a proactive ecosystemic approach to connectedness, belonging and wellbeing. It explores the growing trends of vertical tutoring and smaller circles and involving all adults.

As managers, you may be more interested in the theory behind circle approaches and how to create policies that align with a school committed to kindness and enhancing staff and student morale and wellbeing through inclusive practices. When I am training, I always say that around every school there needs to be an invisible Circle of Respect, and we need to hold up every policy to its light to check that each policy genuinely shows respect and care for the individual.

All educational changes involve personal courage. After 50 years in education, I still get nervous running training days for adults or circles of children with adults observing. Do you remember that rallying call from Susan Jeffers (no, you're too young!) *Feel the Fear and Do It Anyway* (Jeffers, 2007). Just do it!

Why Do You Keep Using the Word "Circle" in Different Ways?

I understand it might be irritating, but the fact is that this term "circle" has been used in so many different ways over the years that it has become ubiquitous and therefore has lost some of its meaning. So, please bear with me; I use the words Circle Approach, active groupwork, and Circle Time. There are a range of other circles, e.g. community circles and coaching circles – the context that you're reading from will illuminate each meaning. However, I tend to use "Circle Time" to refer to my Five Step model that is part of my Quality Circle Time Whole-School Approach to Wellbeing – what a mouthful! It is necessary though, as the whole book is concerned with unravelling the whole model. There is no point in having circle sessions of respect if the policies in the school are at all disrespectful. Everything needs to feed in and relate to each other. I do hope by the very end of the book this makes sense.

Just a quick note here – the fact that I apply the word "Quality" to my model does not mean that I think my work has more quality than others, it's just that I have been using the term for 40 years now. Initially, I was influenced by my reading of the 1960s development in Japanese industry of Quality Circles and their attempt to make huge faceless corporations become more human. Normally small in size, the circles would consist of shop floor workers and senior managers. They met regularly and were free to select any topic they wished, based on the premise that an employee doing a certain task is the most informed on that certain task. By getting together in a circle, different status employees were encouraged to speak and listen. To me, "the most informed person" in a school is the one living its policies – therefore we must listen to students.

Postscript

Another irritating thing I do in this book is to one minute say "we" and then another say "I." This is because the original script was written with Marilyn and it was a "we" and, of course, some of the original book is in this book. A lot is new, however, so I also use "I."

References

Jeffers, S., 2007. *Feel the Fear and Do It Anyway*. London: Vermilion.

Mind, 2025. Managing stress and building resilience. *Mind*. Available at: https://www.mind.org.uk/information-support/types-of-mental-health-problems/stress/managing-stress-and-building-resilience/.

NHS England, 2023. Mental health of children and young people in England, 2023 – wave 4 follow up to the 2017 survey. NHS England Digital, Leeds. Available at: https://digital.nhs.uk/data-and-information/publications/statistical/mental-health-of-children-and-young-people-in-england/2023-wave-4-follow-up.

Part I

The Circle Time Vision

Chapter 1

Why Do We So Desperately Need Circle Time Now?

So Why Do We So Desperately Need Circle Time Now?

Our young people have inherited a vast, fast-paced technological digital world. We can't undo the massive force now in operation – but we can ensure that young people at least have experience of engaging in active communication with each other with only their full selves present. They need to experience the potential positives of emotional and social live engagement to realise what it has the power to offer.

Researchers suggest that excessive screen time is damaging. Birmingham University found that spending longer on social media was linked to lower grades, poor sleep and disruptive behaviour (5 February 2025, *Lancet Regional Health Europe*). There is a surge of newspaper reports ranging from the Australian decision to ban phones in schools to articles devoted to the fact that Gen Z no longer want to even speak to service people and prefer to order and pay on mobile apps, even whilst in a restaurant (*The Times*, 25 August 2024).

This whole area is currently being explored – but what is not being explored is how we can give adolescents alternative, genuine experiences of enjoyable live communication with their peers – so that they themselves can make positive choices for the future.

So, What Is a Circle Approach?

Simply, it is a weekly opportunity for young people to sit in a circle, look at each other and engage in debating and talking about issues that matter to them, led by a calm, sensitive yet firm facilitator. Human beings need to feel part of a group. They need to feel respected, valued and heard. They need to know their views, thoughts and feelings matter. They need the opportunities to learn how to cooperate with small numbers and large numbers of people.

> The value of thinking together aloud lies in the joint construction of knowledge through speaking and listening. Such conversations create shared

memories, enable groups to work together to solve problems and distribute the task of further learning by making everyone aware of ideas, reasons, explanations, queries and suggestions in the classroom.

(Alan Howe, Oracy Cambridge, 12 November 2024)

My Experience

I have spent my whole teaching life working in circles. In 1972 I was a secondary teacher in a secondary modern boys' school – who were very angry to be made to stay on at school an extra year – due to the government's decision to raise the school leaving age. I ended up, with a musician artist, running action groups for all the Local Authority's bored teenagers – I ran community circles for the Manpower Services Commission for disengaged, disillusioned, unemployed young people. I then went on to develop "Circle Time," a whole-school model, and managed to get it onto some early emerging PSHE curriculum in primary schools in the late 1980s and later, particularly through SEAL, into secondary schools. I taught part-time "Active Groupwork and Creative Arts" at Bristol University, where for a decade my teachers ran action research projects investigating the impact of listening and creativity on the emotional health and wellbeing of young people. So, in fact, I have spent the last 50 years promoting active groupwork through published books, training, consultations and endless demonstrations with children whilst teachers observe.

So, Why, After All This Time, Does Circle Time Regularly Fade Away and Then Fire Up Again?

The problem lies with underfunding and sometimes short-term vision for education by successive governments. One government will ignore other governments' well-thought-through plans – for example, SEAL (Social, Emotional Aspects of Learning) was never built on. There appears to be little coherent, joined-up understanding of what human beings need and only a thin allegiance to any psychological theories that explain the needs that schools must meet. For example, William Glasser (Choice Theory, 1998) has never been fully embraced by UK academics, and yet I think it is probably the most important theory of human needs as it highlights the crucial role of fun and joy in learning. Circle Time weaves in all the important factors of engagement through games, exercises and activities which encourage relaxation and laughter.

Maybe the most pernicious problem lies with teacher training. There used to be a time when personal development and teambuilding and active groupwork were part of the methodology for training teachers. I constantly have new teachers in my audiences, when training whole schools, who have been training for four years, and they come up and say they have never heard any of the ideas that I have just demonstrated proposed by their tutors. How can young potential teachers, who have not been part of any active groupwork circles themselves, train their students in this methodology?

One primary school, Watercliffe Meadow in Sheffield, ensures that the adults in their school have Circle Time once a week based entirely on the belief that this experience will then motivate them to want to keep it going with their own classes. For 22 years now they have had weekly Circle Time.

Circle Time Now – Why We Need It

Strong Social and Emotional Learning skills (SEL) correlate with academic success (Langreo, 2023). Interestingly, the same study found that SEL skills may act as a "protective factor" for some students performing below the academic standards, meaning that students' social and emotional strengths could be used to boost their academic achievements.

A deeper concern, however, is the use of social media by adolescents and their impact on mental health and psychosocial functioning.

> As a species we are highly attuned to reading social cues … there is no question that children are missing out on very critical social skills. In a way, texting and online communicating puts everybody in a context where body language, facial expression and even the smallest kind of vocal reactions are rendered invisible.
>
> (C. Steiner-Adair, The Big Disconnect)

If young people aren't getting enough practice related to others and getting their needs met in person and in real time, many of them will grow up to be adults who are anxious about our species' primary means of communication – talking.

MIND (2021) reported that 96% of the young people they surveyed said their mental health had affected their schoolwork at some point.

- 78% of young people said that school had made their mental health worse.
- 56% of school staff identified that young people who didn't receive support self-harmed.
- 48% of young people told us they had been punished at school for behaviour that was caused by their mental health problems.

Anxiety among young people has become a pressing concern in recent years. A 2025 article (Anderson et al., 2025) highlights how Gen Z are more susceptible to anxiety due to their increased exposure to social media. However, despite the barriers to circle approaches just listed – take heart – the next chapter identifies some positive movements that have been quietly growing in strength.

References

Anderson, T.L., Valiauga, R., Tallo, C., Hong, C. B., Manoranjithan, S., Domingo, C., Paudel, M., Untaroiu, A., Barr, S. and Goldhaber, K., 2025. Contributing factors to the rise in adolescent anxiety and associated mental health disorders: A narrative review of current literature. *Journal of Child and Adolescent Psychiatric Nursing*. doi: 10.1111/jcap.70009.

Glasser, W., 1998. *Choice Theory: A New Psychology of Personal Freedom*. New York: HarperCollins.

Langreo, L., 2023. What new research shows about the link between achievement and SEL. *Education Week*, 07 July. Available at: https://www.edweek.org/leadership/what-new-research-shows-about-the-link-between-achievement-and-sel/2023/07.

Mind, 2021. Improving mental health support for young people. *Mind*. Available at: https://www.mind.org.uk/news-campaigns/campaigns/children-and-young-peoples-mental-health/improving-mental-health-support-for-young-people/.

Chapter 2

Circle Approaches in Action

An Overview of Some Circle Approaches Currently Being Used in Schools

Some Key Theoretical Models Informing These Circles

Right now, in the times we live in, it's the inequalities of life that concern educators most, leading as they do to a society that is riven by mental health issues, poverty, violence and trauma. Psychologists have, for years, been developing theories on how we can meet human needs so that all individuals have the opportunity to reach their potential. Only then can we hope to engage in real change. We are inherently social creatures. If our needs are met we don't feel powerless, lonely or depressed, and then we can we make healthy connections with others.

Rather than "compare and contrast," I am drawn to looking at the threads that these theories share. It has always felt to me that participating in a circle regularly to support, reflect and move forwards was pure common sense – and that the theories that motivate and attract us are those that are straightforward and whose tenets make immediate sense. So first I will just refer very briefly to the models that prompt these circle approaches – I cannot do justice to the wealth of literature that they draw upon here. I will then look at the commonality of the claims they share.

Maslow's Hierarchy of Needs Model (1943)

I have always admired Maslow – most professionals working with children are introduced to his work in their training. The simplicity of his assertion that our basic physiological, emotional and physical needs for safety must be met before we can possibly learn, relate or self-actualise, i.e. to fulfil our inner potential, has always resonated with educators.

DOI: 10.4324/9781003679615-4

Glasser's Choice Theory Model (1998)

Glasser shares a very similar vision to Maslow. He believes that we are internally motivated to fill our basic needs and all our behaviours are a choice we make to satisfy those needs. He identifies needs in the same way as Maslow – i.e. survival, belonging, power, freedom … but why I *love* William Glasser is because he is the only psychologist I know who puts *fun* at the top of his pyramid of human needs. Human beings do need joy, pleasure and laughter to feel happy and alive and capable of connecting.

Restorative Justice Model (2000s Onwards)

Evolving from Restorative Justice, restorative practices became embedded in many schools (McCluskey et al., 2008). Initially they were strongly influenced by schools needing to deal with conflict positively and to create a peaceful ethos where individuals could grow and be themselves. Its practices focus on how to change the school context to one of more transparency, where trusting relationships can be built. One of its key practices was to use circles to focus on issues that concern or worry those within that circle – thereby building a sense of community. Now it too promotes active circles to create the ethos in which peaceful relationships can flourish.

Trauma-Informed Model

Trauma-informed approaches in education, particularly post-COVID-19, recognise the impact of trauma and adverse childhood experiences (ACEs) and rely on schools to integrate a knowledge of trauma-informed psychology into their training, policies and classrooms. They do not specifically recommend circles – but knowledge of their principles would certainly benefit circle facilitators. Trauma-informed approaches require that all adults engage in training that increases their compassion and understanding of young people (Culshaw & Bodfield, 2024).

The Secure Base Model (2009)

This model is rooted in Attachment Theory (Schofield and Beek, 2014). It aims to create a supportive and nurturing environment for all children and caregivers. Schools that are inspired by this model aim to give all their students the experience of being able to build relationships with adults and peers that are safe, predictable, regular and small. Community circles are run often tri-weekly by adults who are trained to be empathetic, accepting and motivated to develop positive relationships for the young people in their care.

The Quality Circle Time Model (1980s Onwards)

A discussion of this model is developed throughout this book. The first book I wrote, *Turn Your School Round* (1993), emphasised the need for every adult and child to belong to regular circles. Currently, in a nutshell, the model promotes three safe listening systems for all children and adults: weekly Circle Time (group listening), Chat Time (one-to-one listening) and Non-Verbal Listening, e.g. drawing, writing. This model is backed up by a set of Golden Rules created and shared by the students and adults, community incentives and consequences, and the organisation of fun, sociable and interesting times, i.e. playground breaks. Extra Circles of Support need to be run for children needing more intense help – all backed up by regular circles for staff reflection. All policies need to be formulated and developed in focused circles of adults.

A Quick Sketch of Shared Beliefs That Underpin All These Models

Emotional and Psychological Safety

If the ground rules of behaving respectfully to each other are embedded, if the circles are seen by the school to be important and very rarely get cancelled, if the adults are trained well to always stay calm and non-judgemental – then the participants relax into a feeling of safety and security.

Positive Relationships and a Sense of Belonging

Just the experience of others in the circle actually listening to you without interrupting is very validating. If the others in the circle not only listen but support you, then you are learning what empathy feels like. We can't ask children to be empathetic if we've never experienced it. If the circle participants see the same people regularly and are always welcomed, you begin to feel a sense of inclusion, shared identity and belonging.

Autonomy and a Sense of Agency

All circle approaches encourage the participants to express themselves. Students are asked to think of ideas to help others and systems within the school. I don't know enough about the other circle approaches, but in our Quality Circle Time model we always recommend that at the end of each circle they sum up the issues. There are issues that we can act on ourselves to make positive changes, and there are institutional issues that need to be taken to a School Council, which would then send back their response to the request or problem. It's not enough to have a "voice" – their voices need to be acted on.

Restoration, Repair and Growth

All approaches aim to "repair" harm, rebuild trust and support and help every person grow in confidence, self-knowledge and resilience to cope with life.

Circles and Spirituality

Before closing this section on the power of circles to support us all emotionally, I also want to briefly explore the connection between circles and spirituality.

We should not forget that Circle Time is as old as the hills that many circles of people once sat on. No one person invented Circle Time. Human beings who want to connect, discuss problems and ways forward also want to be in each other's presence, scanning faces as well as listening to what others are saying.

Looking at the wisdom of Native Americans, beautiful nuggets of truth shine strongly:

> the circle has healing power. In the circle we are all equal. When in the circle, no one is in front of you, no one is behind you, no one is below you. The circle is sacred because it is designed to create unity.
>
> (Lowe et al., 2024)

It's the word "sacred" that somehow resonates. When you're in a circle you have a strong feeling of our common humanity and our bonds with it. Over the years, especially in my early years, I participated in a range of weekly circle groups. If run by sensitive, thoughtful and clear facilitators, over a period of time you feel a sense of unity "we're all in this life together" and you begin to feel a sense of love – love for those who are emotionally holding you safely and responding to you with empathy and warmth.

For a deeper discussion, in "Intertribal Talking Circle," Lowe et al. (2024) explain that

> Native Americans have long used the circle to celebrate the sacred inter-relationship that is shared with one another and with their world. [This] ... refers to knowing the spirit in everything, including themselves, so that the connection becomes known in all aspects of their lives.

So, we are looking here at the spiritual dimension of the circle. Our Western culture pays less attention to spirituality but concentrates more on the psychological healing properties of circle approaches. Maybe one day we too will explore its spiritual benefits!

Spirituality and Students

I am always amazed by how students, when given the safety of well-run circles, show a spirituality that is breathtaking. Young people who have been hurt and bullied by others in their circle will go beyond these factors to support them if they request help. Often the child who hurts others is a person badly treated by life, and deep down even the ones hurt by them know this. The vulnerability of that person asking for help moves them, and they will often volunteer a "Would it help if I/we ... invited you into our group? Told the person on duty when people are deliberately winding you up? Notice when you are staying calm so that we can award you one of our Community Class Certificates?" This is spirituality in action!

Two Examples of Schools Who Share a Commitment to School-Based Community Circles

A Case Study of Carr Manor Community School

I am so glad I agreed to update this secondary book – otherwise I would not have discovered Carr Manor Community School, an all-through school in Leeds with over 1500 pupils and 200 staff. The school has developed systems that enable strong, consistent relationships to flourish across the community. I was put in touch with Tom Shaw, the Director of Character, who is rightfully passionate about their Community Coaching Circles.

I personally needed, at this stage of my career, a surge of optimism and excitement about secondary schools embracing circles. I had discovered that a few of my case studies in the original book had let go of their commitment to the circle pedagogy. Staff leaving, COVID-19 and "no time" were among the reasons given.

Yet here was a school that first started running circles in 2005 and hasn't stopped since. They would probably cite Restorative Practice as being a philosophical force and the implementation of the Safe Base Model as the psychological driver that framed the practical implementation of their coaching circles (Hibbin, 2024).

- Every single adult from teaching to non-teaching staff leads timetabled circles tri-weekly. Monday – Check In; Wednesday – Check Up; Friday – Check Out. Each circle lasts between 30 and 45 minutes.
- Each circle has 8–12 pupils gathered from vertical year groups: Years 1–6 and Years 7–11.
- "These check-ins provide the opportunity to get to know one another, and share targets, worries and achievements, while mid-week sessions explore topics such as careers and financial education, health and wellbeing, and citizenship, while building resilience and independence" (Children and Young People's Mental Health Coalition, 2023, p. 86).

- What the school strongly claims is that their coaching programme has had a deep, long-lasting impact by embedding strong relationships across the year groups, staff and families.

What they are proud of is that these small circles run by committed, trained adults have meant that they can be responsive to how children are in the moment. Face-to-face interaction is incredibly important. You can read facial expressions, tension in the body, the sound of the voice, the silences that speak louder than the words. They are all clues as to what is going on for this child in addition to what is actually being said. The Circle Coach, if concerned, can then refer the child on to the school support teams for inclusion, safeguarding and SEND, or work out with the team whether to get support from the team to help deal with the issue themselves.

These words from a Year 11 student at Carr Manor somehow capture the ethos of the above:

> It's hard to explain what a coaching circle is if you haven't done it. It becomes a kind of place where you feel steady, you can just be how you are – even if you're not feeling great, someone will notice, someone will listen.

I have been helped to understand this model through email conversations and articles shared with me by Tom Shaw. He also introduced me to a school with which I have not had any direct engagement but does share the same vision of a school that puts compassion, empathy, kindness and safety, through listening, at its heart.

Trafalgar School

Trafalgar School in Portsmouth is a comprehensive school with 1000 pupils aged between 11 and 16. This school, led by Executive Headteacher Claire Copeland, has strong links with Carr Manor. They follow a similar practice and the same philosophy of creating an ethos of empathic, enduring relationships.

Their community circles take place in every vertical tutor group on Mondays and Fridays – a Check In and a Check Out. Again, every adult in the school, regardless of their role, is a form tutor, which puts the pastoral system at the centre of everything (Children and Young People's Mental Health Coalition, 2023, p. 86).

With these systems in place in both schools, how would school appear to children from their point of view? This exceptional commitment sends a powerful message to students that every adult cares. It tells children that adults value listening and speaking – that relationships are supported more strongly once you're in a circle. The fact that issues can be brought to that circle and they will be helped allows them to think of circles as a safe, solution-based forum. My hope is that in the future, young people will gravitate towards this way of relating with their friends and family, thus stemming the tide of individuals being in their own digital bubble.

Theories of self-esteem (Burns, 1979) emphasise the human need for others to reflect back our worth, competence and value. When individuals lack supportive relationships such as those with emotionally absent or unloving caregivers, they can struggle with low self-esteem and self-doubt throughout their life. Research shows that a consistent caring circle facilitated by a positive adult and attentive peers can significantly build self-esteem, as the group is functioning as a "generalised other" (Mead, 1934) providing the same restorative power that a significant individual in your life might offer.

How Do We Know They Are Working?

Carr Manor Community School would point you to the fact that they have no permanent exclusions, lower fixed-term exclusions, high staff retention and low staff absence (Shaw, 2019).

As 12% of mainstream secondary schools have moved over to vertical tutoring (Education Observatory, 2021) – it would make sense to research how many of them are using community and coaching circles. It would also make sense if the government could commission some thorough research into how young people feel about vertical tutoring with circles and without.

References

Burns, R.B., 1979. *The Self-concept: Theory, Measurement, Development and Behavior*. London and New York: Longman.

Children and Young People's Mental Health Coalition, 2023. *Behaviour and Mental Health in Schools: Full Report*. London: Children and Young People's Mental Health Coalition. Available at: https://cypmhc.org.uk/wp-content/uploads/2023/06/Behaviour-and-Mental-Health-in-Schools-Full-Report.pdf.

Culshaw, A. and Bodfield, K., 2024. Trauma-informed education: A case for compassion-focused teaching? *Pastoral Care in Education*, 17 February. https://doi.org/10.1080/02643944.2024.2318776.

Education Observatory, 2021. *Vertical Tutoring: Will It Work at Your School?* London: Education Observatory. Available at: https://educationobservatory.co.uk/wp-content/uploads/2021/03/PPP-VerticalTutoring.pdf.

Glasser, W., 1998. *Choice Theory: A New Psychology of Personal Freedom*. New York: Harper.

Hibbin, R., 2024. Relational responsibility, social discipline and behaviour in school: re-orienting discipline and authority through a distributed network of relational accountability. *Pastoral Care in Education*, 42(4), pp. 492–512. https://doi.org/10.1080/02643944.2023.2263453.

Lowe, J., Brooks, J., Lawrence, G., Baldwin, J.A., Kelley, M. and Wimbish-Tompkins, R., 2024. Intertribal talking circle for the prevention of alcohol and drug use among native American youth. *Research in Nursing & Health*, 47(2), pp. 234–241.

https://doi.org/10.1002/nur.22372. Available at: https://www.ncbi.nlm.nih.gov/pmc/articles/PMC11967442/.

Maslow, A.H., 1943. A theory of human motivation. *Psychological Review*, 50(4), pp. 370–396. Available at: https://psychclassics.yorku.ca/Maslow/motivation.htm (first published in *Psychological Review*, 1943; posted on PsychClassics August 2000).

McCluskey, G., Lloyd, G., Stead, J., Kane, J., Riddell, S. and Weedon, E., 2008. 'I was dead restorative today': From restorative justice to restorative approaches in school. *Cambridge Journal of Education*, 38(2), pp. 199–216. https://doi.org/10.1080/03057640802063262. Available at: https://www.pure.ed.ac.uk/ws/portalfiles/portal/14215678/McCluskey_Lloyd_et_al_2008_I_was_dead_restorative_today.pdf.

Mead, G.H., 1934. *Mind, Self, and Society: From the Standpoint of a Social Behaviorist*. Edited by C.W. Morris. Chicago: University of Chicago Press.

Schofield, G. and Beek, M., 2014. *The Secure Base Model: Promoting Attachment and Resilience in Foster Care and Adoption*. London: BAAF.

Shaw, T., 2019. You want to cut exclusions AND maintain staff morale? *Tes Magazine*, 8 November. Available at: https://www.tes.com/magazine/archive/you-want-cut-exclusions-and-maintain-staff-morale.

Chapter 3

Circle Time and the Social and Emotional Aspects of Learning (SEAL)

SEAL was a brilliant UK government initiative, headed up by Jean Gross and introduced in the early 2000s. Its key aims were: to promote positive self-awareness, managing feelings, motivation, empathy, and social skills; to support pupils' emotional wellbeing and mental health; to improve behaviour, relationships, and academic performance; and to help schools create a positive learning environment.

Aligned with Goleman's emotional intelligence framework. It covered five areas: self-awareness, managing feelings, motivation, empathy and social skills. I was invited to write the Circle Time guidance for early years, primary and secondary SEAL.

The investment in training and resources was extraordinary and whilst it is no longer a formal national strategy, many of its principles are embedded in educational practice ("SEAL Community" is still accessible online).

Two research projects were commissioned to evaluate its impact and both are only lightly sketched here to pique further interest. Wigelsworth et al. (2011) conducted a quasi-experimental evaluation of SEAL in secondary schools comparing 22 schools with 19 matched comparison schools and found marginal non-significant improvements in socio-emotional skills which had no effect on pro-social behaviour.

Interestingly, Robin Banerjee's (2014) research came out at a similar time. He conducted a cross-sectional observational study in 49 primary and secondary schools. They focussed on, among others, an association between the whole-school approach, school ethos and pupil social experience. The wider lens of Banerjee's study highlighted that a whole-school approach is significantly linked to positive outcomes in school ethos, attainment, student social interaction and reduced absence.

On Kindness

At this point in my tentative, over-simplified exploration, I was immediately grateful that Banerjee celebrated his SEAL findings that kindness, both giving and receiving, benefits our link to the wellbeing of the individual and that

DOI: 10.4324/9781003679615-5

mental health difficulties should be seen as connected to the relationships and attainment.

Professor Banerjee then went on to research and publish significant research highly relevant to today's society on kindness and its impact on wellbeing. Funded by the Sussex Centre for Research on Kindness, Sussex University and Kindness UK (2007), Banerjee and his team undertook the Kindness Test, a large-scale public study involving 60,000 people. When the data was analysed, amongst the findings, they posited that kindness has a positive impact on mental wellbeing and can increase happiness. Kindness UK, a non-profit organisation, is dedicated to making kindness a part of everyday life (Kindness Day is 13 November 13).

I had a searing moment of clarity when hearing the Dalai Lama respond to the question "What is your religion about?" and he replied "My religion is very simple. My religion is kindness" (Roos, 2021).

Among its physiological benefits are lower cortisol, increased oxytocin and enhanced social connection. So, we have a triple whammy – kindness benefits the human beings who both give it and receive it and it enriches them:

- Physically
- Emotionally
- Spiritually

I am not being facetious, but perhaps we should be viewing all person-centred interventions, including circle approaches, through the lens of whether they are "Kindness in Action" projects or not?

Perhaps life is much simpler than we all thought. To young people, adults who stop their busy day to sit close, listening and responding to them and are concerned to hear their views, who set up communication avenues between you and your peers and who are prepared to get help for you if life is being unkind to you, who turn up every week because you matter to them and they are not put off by your needs, habits or weaknesses, who champion your cause – isn't this the essence of kindness?

So How Does Circle Time Fit in with RSHE Right Now?

In July 2025, Department of Education (DfE) released statutory guidance for Relationships, Sex Education and Health Education (RSHE) for secondary schools.

This new guidance is addressing the current issues affecting young people. There is a stronger focus on tackling misogyny, incel culture and how they shape attitudes to girls and women and the pernicious effects of pornography, knife crime, AI literacy, deepfake images and personal safety. It also tackles menstrual and gynaecological health, mental health and bereavement.

In its response to this report, the PSHE Association (RSHE guidance, 2025a) said "on balance ... the guidance feels safe and positive ... and includes the importance of engagement with pupils, positivity, careful sequencing and skilled delivery and participative education." Excited, I rushed back to the RSHE guidance to do a search ... but no mention of any circle approaches to build safe forums for the sensitive "participation" to take place in.

Relationship Guidance is a core element of the broader PSHE curriculum. Schools are expected to incorporate these updated requirements into their existing PSHE programmes by September 2026.

Secondary schools use different models to deliver PSHE. The PSHE Association (2025b), part funded by the government, categorically states "the most effective model of delivery for PSHE education is a sequenced, spiral programme, building on prior learning ... and like any other curriculum subject, it needs at least an hour a week."

They are categorically against delivering PSHE through "vertical tutoring groups" "whilst there are compelling arguments in favour of vertical tutoring, for pastoral tutoring, we would never advocate it as a model for PSHE lessons." They make it quite clear that a school can only deliver PSHE through a form period, and pupils from a vertical tutoring system need to be allocated to different groups on that day to be with pupils only from their own year group. "It could be harmful not to be in an age-appropriate group; many schools are choosing to deliver relationships or sex education as part of a timetabled PSHE programme" (PSHE Association, 2025).

Is the Above Discussion Pointing the Way Forward in the Use of the Circle Approach in PSHE?

With all its emphasis on the emotional safety needed for young people to discuss PSHE issues within their own age groups, surely the DfE would be asking schools to consider circles? The answer is "no" ... and to me, it just doesn't make sense not to use a circle approach for the process of relating to, thinking about, discussing with and debating through with your peers so that you can gauge and "read" other people's reactions.

A circle time, well facilitated, surely must be the only way forward. The "product" i.e. the information, can be presented in many ways: PowerPoints, worksheets, visiting lecturers, paired work and homework – but the emotional response needs to be part of the whole process of relationships that they are learning about in that lesson. If I can't learn to be in warm, trusting relationships with my peers, how can I, in the future, conduct my own personal or professional relationships, which depend on face-to-face dialogue and response.

I remember being so incensed about this that my irritability communicated itself so strongly that one of my Master's students wrote an assignment which was published in the *Pastoral Care Journal* 47 years ago: "Circle Time:

A Much-Neglected Resource In Secondary Schools" (Tew, 2005). Then later, the same student, Marilyn Tew, helped me co-write this original book in 1999.

For over 50 years, I have campaigned, lobbied, and ran week-long training courses in schools by facilitating circles with full classes, so their teachers could observe. And yet, still, circle approaches flourish and then fade away. They have not yet embedded as a pedagogical strategy.

Scattered throughout our UK Teacher Training courses are references to circle practices as being useful teaching strategies for PSHE, and there are anecdotal references to them in the PSHE Association guidance, but no statutory training or guidance recommends them.

I regularly work in secondary schools, both for INSET closure days and working in school days. I have never met any secondary teachers who have experienced the circle approach within their own teacher training. I would be very happy to be contradicted – anybody reading this, who has a different experience – please write to us and we will include your views in the next edition!!

Is There a Tension Between the Pastoral Activities of Tutor Groups and the Need for PSHE to Also Be at the Heart of a Schools Relational Policy?

The success claimed by secondary schools that have vertical tutoring has resulted in a growth of secondary schools taking this on. It makes total sense to have small groups and a family ethos where younger and older students are together, listening and talking, and hopefully caring for and looking out for each other. This experience can only enrich children's personal growth and development.

However, we need the same feeling of belonging and connection also to be able to deliver RSHE effectively. We need the process of relationship building to help them explore a range of very sensitive topics. Am I being myopic, or wilfully thoughtless? Would it be at all possible to have the same tutoring principle applied to the same year groups – horizontal tutoring?

I suspect that this statement will incur the wrath of those wonderful schools who are having much success with their virtual tutoring. I think probably, what is needed is more widespread research.

To Recap the Current Situation

I am certainly no education expert – I am merely a long-time enthusiast. There appears to be a range of implementation factors regarding circle approaches which can sour teachers' goodwill and kindness output. A quick résumé of what a whole-school pastoral structure could look like if circles were embedded:

- *Vertical tutoring* – tri-weekly community circles, 100% committed to by senior managers with a vision of whole-school kindness as a strong driver.
- This is doable because it's easier to make smaller circles once you involve every adult in the school.
- Teams are set up and are available for adults to support the children who need extra help.
- With ongoing training and, most importantly, ongoing staff focus circles, they too feel listened to. In addition, they are re-energised regularly with new ideas and an implementation booklet.

PSHE is currently delivered in many different ways:

1. Regular timetabled 50-minute lessons
2. Off timetable "drop down" days
3. Form tutor time – 20–30 minutes
4. Rolling lessons
5. Occasional one-off lessons and talks delivered by speakers
6. Solely through other subjects

It is now challenged by the latest guidance to deliver a range of even more intense, sensitive subjects.

What Are the Drawbacks to My Vision of a Regular Weekly Circle Approach to Deliver PSHE?

- Teachers have had no in-depth training on how to run safe, vibrant Circle Times.
- Some teachers are reluctant to do PSHE and have had very little PSHE training and don't feel confident enough to present the information, let alone run a process of Circle Time where children can debate and reflect on the information.
- The classroom can't accommodate large circles.

What Some Teachers Are Doing to Ensure PSHE Circle Times Run Smoothly

Some, still passionate, PSHE teachers, with their students, do an army-like exercise with numbers written under the tables corresponding with a floor plan, so they know exactly where to put them around the edges of the classroom.

Pushing tables back is easier when you only have 12–15 chairs, so, logistically, would it be possible to run fortnightly PSHE for smaller circles once the whole class has experienced and learnt more about the current topic?

Some schools with falling rolls have spare classrooms and have purchased piles of cheap, stackable stools that are easily put in a circle.

A secondary school in Peckham brought a very big comfortable yurt with seats around the edge for circle time. Sometimes drama studios or halls can be timetabled if the senior management are behind you.

To be honest, I don't know how to make these circles happen in your school. In any "revolution" you need to lobby, activate and demonstrate your passion until the senior management are prepared to explore your ideas. Maybe, even more wonderfully, they already believe in them and are lobbying you?

Since we know that 12% of all secondary schools are now running vertical tutor groups and more are coming on board – would it be possible to learn from the administrative knowledge that these schools have gained from setting up these circles and applying it to the pastoral system to same-age circles for RSHE to be linked to the key topics.

Is this final paragraph the last straw for teachers who are very happily moving towards vertical tutoring? If we can't create circles for PSHE students, what is the answer then? Maybe in light of the current problem of our culture, we have to get in "Think Tank" circles and hold a talking stick, say our piece, listen and find ways forward. Equally, we cannot teach children the most important lesson in the world, RSHE, which deals with how they can navigate safely the culture around them without giving them a safe circle forum to debate, discuss, reflect and disagree with their peers whilst supported by an empathetic, well-trained adult.

I feel this Circle Time is a great idea, when we have time to talk and just let go of all the things we're holding inside us, without someone breathing down our necks to try and shut us up, it first calms us down and second we can think better.

(Rishabh, 13 years old)

Being in a circle makes you feel you're not the only person with worries about yourself. It makes you have more confidence, more self-esteem. Before, I felt "Oh, I don't like my face. Wish I could change this and that," but when you actually speak about things like that in a circle you realise other people have the same worries and you're not abnormal.

(Kay, 12 years old)

How can we present RSHE topics, however fascinatingly, on what matters most to children, if they can't reflect later in a circle?

References

Banerjee, R., Weare, K. and Farr, W., 2014. Working with "social and emotional aspects of learning" (SEAL): associations with school ethos, pupil social experiences, attendance, and attainment. *British Educational Research Journal*, 40(4), pp. 718–742.

PSHE Association, 2025a. *RSHE Guidance 2025: What You Need to Know.* Available at: https://pshe-association.org.uk/news/rshe-guidance-2025-what-you-need-to-know/.

PSHE Association, 2025b. *Models of Delivery for PSHE Education: KS3–5 Guidance.* Available at: https://pshe-association.org.uk/guidance/ks3-5/models-of-delivery.

Roos, D., 2021. 5 Spiritual lessons from the Dalai Lama. *HowStuffWorks.* [online] 9 September 2021. Available at: https://history.howstuffworks.com/historical-figures/dalai-lama-quotes.html.

Tew, M., 2005. Circle time: A much-neglected resource in secondary schools? In: J. Wearmouth, T. Glynn, R.C. Richmond and M. Berryman (eds.) *Addressing Pupil's Behaviour* (1st ed.). London: David Fulton Publishers, p. 16. doi: 10.4324/9780203064153.

Wigelsworth, M., Humphrey, N. and Lendrum, A., 2011. A national evaluation of the impact of the secondary social and emotional aspects of learning (SEAL) programme. *Educational Psychology*, 32(2), pp. 213–238. Available at: https://research.manchester.ac.uk/en/publications/a-national-evaluation-of-the-impact-of-the-secondary-social-and-e/.

Chapter 4

The Circle Time Approach and Ofsted

In *Ofsted's Education Inspection Framework* (Ofsted, 2023), they now look at how schools are:

- setting clear routines and expectations for the behaviour of pupils across all aspects of school life, not just in the classroom
- creating an environment in which pupils feel safe, and in which bullying, discrimination, sexual harassment, sexual abuse and sexual violence – online or offline – are not accepted and are dealt with quickly, consistently and effectively whenever they occur
- promoting equality of opportunity so that all pupils can thrive together, understanding that difference is a positive, not a negative, and that individual characteristics make people unique. This includes, but is not limited to, pupils' understanding of the protected characteristics and how equality and diversity are promoted
- ensuring an inclusive environment that meets the needs of all pupils, irrespective of age, disability, gender reassignment, race, religion or belief, sex or sexual orientation, and where no discrimination exists, for example in respect of wider opportunities for pupils

When schools take on an approach such as Circle Time, the staff have regular, timetabled opportunities to hear pupil voice and to "tune in" to students' thinking and responding. Each student has a regular opportunity to voice their concerns, to work out their differences and to think in depth about issues that affect them personally and collectively.

We cannot transmit moral codes through insisting or cajoling young people into becoming good citizens. Instead, we need to provide them with a range of different opportunities to explore their feelings about how they live their lives and how they engage with other people and the improvements they would like to see happen. As a group process, Circle Time helps to generate a sense of "belonging" which encourages individuals to become active members of the class and school community. In my ideal world – at the end of the weekly Circle Time, the group will decide if any of the issues raised need to

DOI: 10.4324/9781003679615-6

be taken by two self-elected members to their School Council. Again, School Councils were once strongly promoted; however, School Council UK was disbanded in 2013. If Circle Time issues relating to weak school systems (dining halls, toilets, corridors, lunchtimes, discipline systems) cannot be fed back into an official mechanism for dealing with them – how can young people really believe that schools want to make life better for them? I remember once a student coming up to me at the end of a Circle Time session and saying, "There seems to be lots of listening around but no one is doing anything about it." This participation in the democratic process in the microcosm of the classroom or school helps to develop individual and corporate responsibility and hopefully, better citizens of the wider community.

Ofsted's Current Emphasis on Safety and Behaviour

Safety and behaviour are now a separate strand in the *Inspection Framework* for Ofsted, but there is nothing new in this emphasis in schools. The issue of pupil safety has become an increasingly, important consideration as it encompasses a growing list of concerns. In addition to long-standing issues such as neglect, abuse and bullying, current concerns include:

- online abuse such as cyberbullying and sharing inappropriate content
- radicalisation and extremism
- hate crime
- female genital mutilation
- gangs, gang culture and knife crime
- child trafficking

Given that safety and behaviour are now their own Ofsted strand, the discussion above in Circle Time and Ofsted is hugely relevant, so please bear with the arguments in the book. We have started the rationale section with the process schools need, i.e. face-to-face talking and communication, and how key concerns of young people should be reviewed in a school council type meeting with adults to support it.

Behaviour is seen to contribute to inspectors' evaluation of students' SMSC (Spiritual, Moral, Social and Cultural) development. Clearly, therefore, safety and behaviour are much more than the behaviour policy of a school. This is about the ways in which a school structures its environment, hears its students' perceptions, looks after its staff and so much more. It is interesting to note that part of the Ofsted evaluation of safety and behaviour is "the extent to which leaders and managers have created a positive ethos in the school." We would want to ask about the structures, processes and procedures that create the positive ethos.

There is strong evidence that a proactive, positive and supportive approach to behaviour will benefit all pupils, boost attendance and can reduce the challenging behaviours. This includes:

- Encouraging and rewarding positive behaviour.
- Explicitly prompting, modelling and reinforcing positive behaviours.
- Understanding reasons behind pupil behaviour and addressing these where possible.

(Education Endowment Foundation, 2024)

Gregory, Cornell and Fan (2011) looked at school discipline and its connection to school ethos and found that the most effective discipline had two major strands: "responsiveness" or social support and "demandingness" or structural systems. The first is measured by how adults and peers respond to the emotional and social needs of students, particularly how warm, caring and accepting they are perceived to be. The second is defined in the clarity of behavioural expectations – fair rules and their equally fair enforcement. The Quality Circle Time model helps a school to address both aspects of creating a supportive and safe ethos. It addresses the relationship building that is fundamental to "responsiveness" and also provides for the development and evaluation of structural systems that expect and require cooperative and responsible behaviour.

So, we can conclude that really not much has changed since the "spot on" observations that Lord Elton made over 30 years ago. He highlighted the role of positive relationships in the teaching and learning environment.

> "To be fully effective ... teachers need ... the ability to relate to young people, to encourage them in good behaviour and learning, and to deal calmly but firmly with inappropriate or dysregulated behaviour." As a useful shorthand we refer to it in our report as "group management skills."
>
> (Department for Education and Science, 1989)

Teachers with good group management skills are able to establish positive relationships with their classes based on mutual respect. They can create a classroom climate in which pupils lose rather than gain popularity with their classmates by causing trouble ... Good group managers understand how groups of young people react to each other and to teachers. They also understand and are in full control of their own behaviour. What education needs now is proper training for teachers in actual groupwork circle approaches.

In many secondary schools, tutors are often required to deliver the PSHE or pastoral programme as part of their role. Unfortunately, they have little training for this task. As subject specialists, they have a knowledge base and have learned how to plan and deliver lessons according to subject requirements. All too frequently, they have received little or no training in any other form of working. They could have limited knowledge of child development, the processes of learning or the group management skills essential for experiential teaching and learning. Consequently, they fall back on delivering information about PSHE issues (e.g. drugs, hygiene, vaping, online abuse, study skills) without entering into processes that might develop relationships and moral values, or encourage students to examine attitudes, develop empathy or draw on peer support. They are also used to being judged against targets and attainment levels, whereas the work of the Circle Approach is more about processes of building relationships and social and emotional competencies.

A Further Look at Why or How the Circle Approach Has the Potential to Deepen Relationships

> I liked passing the egg around and voicing our opinions. I thought it was cool how people had different opinions about different things.
> (Sarah, 12 years)

The games and strategies of Circle Time mix up the friendship groups in a fluid, non-confrontational way. The framework of sitting within a circle, taking a turn to speak and joining in all the activities conveys important messages regarding authority and control to all the participants. The teacher's role is facilitative, encouraging pupils to feel that they too have the authority and self-control to attempt to solve the behaviour, learning and relationship problems that concern them. By contributing to this problem-solving process, individuals are motivated to take more individual and collective responsibility.

> It was instantly obvious that both their concentration and honesty improved dramatically once they were integrated randomly into a circle. They seem to interact to other peers who aren't their friends much better as a result of Circle Time. It has helped tremendously with the less confident members of the tutor group and it is a much more interesting way for the teacher to deliver the content of the curriculum. I don't honestly know yet, whether I can claim it is raising self-esteem, but at least they'd rather stay in the circle than go anywhere else and it gives me the opportunity to know their strengths and weaknesses much better than I would with work sheets and course books.
> (Dominic Salles, Year 8 tutor)

The debate over pupils' ability to regulate their own behaviour has long continued. The question asked is whether people are free agents, with self-determined behaviour, or whether forces outside themselves control them. Some people see their behaviour and environment as under external control, e.g. by luck, chance, or other people. Others believe they have internal control via skill, ability, experience, and inherent potential to control behaviour and influence events.

Rotter (1966) used the term "locus of control" to describe individuals' assessments of the power they can exert over their lives. Those with an inner locus of control are less anxious about their ability to learn, are more confident in social and learning situations, have more self-control, are more likely to delay gratification, are more likely to ask questions of people, are better at retaining information and have superior academic achievement.

Those with an external locus of control are inclined to say things like "He made me do it," "It wasn't my fault, she started it," "I can't do it because I haven't got a ruler/pen, etc." These people have more difficulty with interpersonal relationships and learning situations. They tend to be less self-accepting than those with inner locus of control and are more likely to give the "Yes, but ..." response to new ideas.

The circle encourages pupils to reflect on their behaviour; they offer and receive an array of advice and suggestions as to how they might change unsatisfactory behaviour. They identify personal targets for improvement and support each other in attempts to reach those targets. They recognise the achievements of their peers and praise them accordingly. There is a gradual shift of the onus of responsibility for discipline from the teacher to the young people themselves. They begin to learn and understand the consequences of their behaviour and take responsibility for themselves and others.

> This will help the student–teacher relationship become stronger and closer ... this 30 minute period can have an effect on our entire lives.
>
> (Nizia, 14 years)

Does My School Need to Implement These Ideas?

If you walk around a school whilst lessons are in progress, stand in corridors and listen at the change of lesson time or visit the canteen during the lunch hour, it is easy to get an impression of the pervading ethos. It is a good idea to take stock of your school occasionally to assess how calm, respectful and productive the atmosphere is. One way of doing this is to go through the following list of indicators and see if they apply in your school.

Behaviour

- How do pupils relate to teaching and non-teaching staff?
- Are lessons spoilt by a high degree of low-level disruption?
  - Is the main strategy for dealing with pupils who are often in trouble during lessons to respond reactively, such as putting them in detention or taking away their break times?

PSHE

- Do pupils complain that PSHE lessons are boring and irrelevant?
- Do teachers always dictate the subject matter for PSHE lessons?
- Do staff avoid delivering PSHE whenever possible?

- Have PSHE staff been given sound training?
- Are staff often late for tutorial lessons?
- Do staff rely heavily on work sheets, PowerPoints or videos for delivering PSHE?
- have PSHE staff been given sound training?
- Have you surveyed your Year 7 pupils to find out how well they are settling in at the school? Do they feel safe and have they made friends?

Support for Staff

- Are there regular meetings for staff where they can discuss their personal worries about their classroom practices or their personal worries about how they're handling situations or worries about individual children rather than curriculum issues?
- Is there any system for early identification of pupils at risk of disaffection?
- Is there any system of early intervention for pupils who show signs of problematic dysregulated behaviour?
- Are pupils and their peers involved in devising strategies and/or setting realistic targets for behaviour?
- Is there a system for monitoring and rewarding the achievements of pupils who have behavioural or learning contracts?

The Circle Time model addresses many of these issues by promoting self-discipline, more effective learning, team building and an ability to manage emotions, as explained in the following pages. Circle meetings provide a way of ensuring that all members of the school community are involved, listened to and motivated, thus helping to address some of the sense of isolation experienced by young people and staff. Above all else, however, the issues we have discussed in this chapter have a direct influence on young people's capacity to learn.

> Circle time creates an emotionally "safe" place for pupils to explore what they think and feel.
>
> (Glazzard, 2016, p. 2)

A Personal Open Letter from a Headteacher on Her View of Circle Time

First, I need to tell you that I have decided to end my time as Principal of Ralph Allen School at the end of this academic year. I guess what I say will be tinged with this. I have decided to work at a meta level with the education system rather than as a school leader which is what I have been doing for the last 12 years. These are my thoughts:

- I have always admired Quality Circle Time and the changes that Circle Time can bring.
- I am deeply committed to both whole person education and to securing a good primary – secondary transition and Ralph Allen School uses Circle Time in transition, in PSHE and as a methodology within a range of other methodologies such as the Peer Mentor project to support wellbeing and better community.

Everyone can bring their own contribution to this.

- The circle goes back to native Americans and their way of working – I have met some of the Ehama people and I am very interested in their way of being.
- So it's all very exciting and connected. I am very grateful for the work of Circle Time. In a big system you can sometimes only plant a seed, but the seed of Circle Time has grown, and it is now part of our way of working.

(Libby Lee, Headteacher, Ralph Allen School, Bath, 2013)

References

Department for Education and Science, 1989. *Discipline in Schools: Report of the Committee of Enquiry Chaired by Lord Elton*. London: HMSO. Available at: https://education-uk.org/documents/elton/elton1989.html.

Education Endowment Foundation, 2024. *Build a Culture of Community and Belonging for Pupils*. Available at: https://educationendowmentfoundation.org.uk/education-evidence/leadership-and-planning/supporting-attendance/build-a-culture-of-community-and-belonging-for-pupils [Accessed 4 July 2025].

Glazzard, J., 2016. The value of circle time in promoting social and emotional development in primary schools. *Journal of Social and Emotional Education*, 2(1). Available at: https://eprints.leedsbeckett.ac.uk/id/eprint/3997/1/ValueCircleTimeAM_GLAZZARD.pdf [Accessed 4 July 2025].

Gregory, A., Cornell, D. and Fan, X., 2011. The relationship of school structure and support to suspension rates for Black and White high school students. *American Educational Research Journal*, 48, pp. 904–934.

Ofsted, 2023. Education inspection framework for September 2023. [pdf] Available at: https://www.gov.uk/government/publications/education-inspection-framework/education-inspection-framework-for-september-2023 [Accessed 4 July 2025].

Rotter, J.B., 1966. Generalized expectancies for internal versus external control of reinforcement. *Psychological Monographs*, 80, pp. 1–28.

Chapter 5

The Whole-School Quality Circle Time Approach
Introducing an Ecosystemic Model

Up until now we have talked about "the circle." Hopefully you now have a picture in your mind of young people and adults sitting in circles interacting, relating and learning together. We would like to ask you to expand these ideas further by taking concepts embodied by the circle such as democracy, equality, respect, citizenship and kindness and apply them to all the systems in the school. We call this a Whole-School Quality Circle Time (QCT) Approach to Wellbeing, and it is summarised at a glance in Figure 5.1. It is an ecosystemic model and so these two titles are interchangeable. Each aspect of the model is unravelled one at a time in Chapters 3–10. It represents a personal view developed directly as a result of wanting the philosophy of respect in the circle approach to be consistent with the way other systems in the school are working.

Why a "Whole-School Approach"?

Research has, time and again, indicated that effective schools are those that have created a positive atmosphere based on school values, healthy relationships (teacher–student and student–student) and a sense of safety (Allen et al., 2021; Burley, 2025).

The Quality Circle Time model, Figure 5.1, represents a whole-school approach to positive relationships, behaviour and personal and social development. You will see from the diagram that the ideal school for us is one in which there is first a commitment to the self-esteem and morale of staff. It is vital that every child and adult has regular opportunities to speak and to be heard. Each should belong to a programme of timetabled Circle Time meetings. Teachers need at the very least to have one staff meeting per half-term where they don't have to discuss "business" or curriculum issues but can instead focus on their feelings. They talk through the various dilemmas, take time to understand certain challenging pupils and to ask for help with discipline or personal concerns without being judged or labelled as a "failing teacher." Some secondary schools may use year team meetings for this discussion, others departmental

36 A Circle Approach to Boosting Emotional Wellbeing

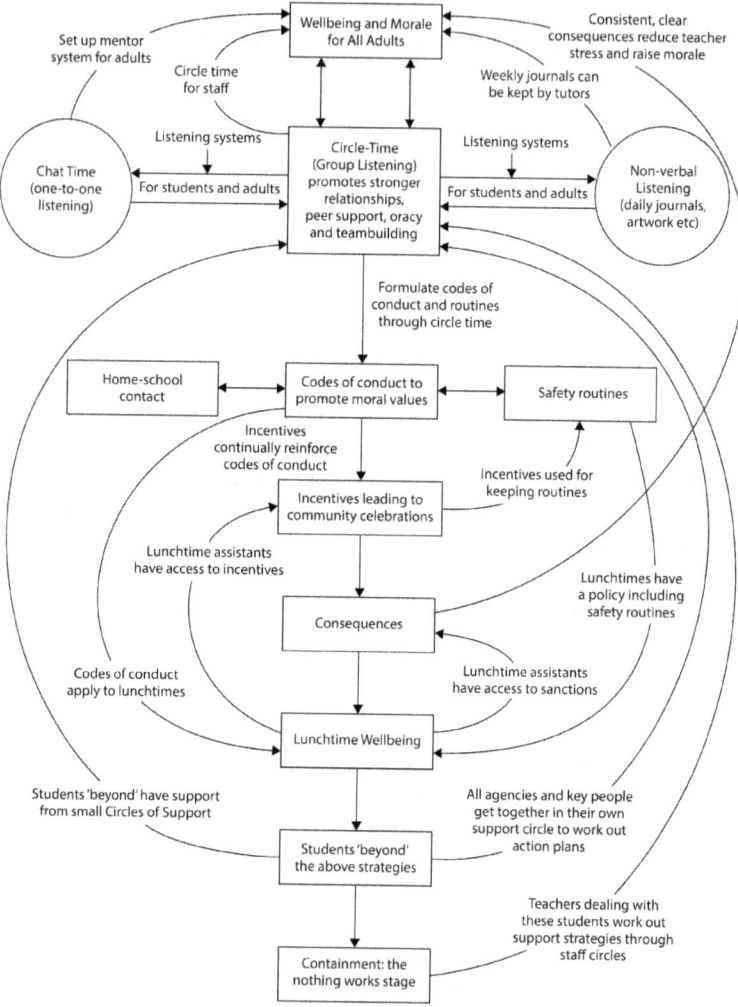

Figure 5.1 The Jenny Mosley Whole-School Quality Circle Time Model for Wellbeing – an ecosystemic model.

meetings, or house meetings. From the discussion comes a structured action plan that helps everyone to move forward.

From the beginning, one of my early books for primary schools *Turn Your School Round* (Mosley, 1998) involved not only teaching staff, but every adult that works in the school. Lunchtime supervisors, learning support assistants, office staff and site staff are all invited to circle meetings. Some schools negotiate a programme of meetings, which, even if they are only once or twice a half-term and half an hour at a time, can be very effective.

As staff and pupils become involved in their separate circle meetings, it is vital they link together by means of "bridges." The concept is that there should be a pivotal management circle, which receives the news, ideas and concerns from the other circles so that they can make informed management decisions based on a democratic consultation of all the members of the organisation. Therefore, a person is selected from every circle to create a "bridge" to the inner management circle by simply taking from their circle meeting, with the agreement of the other circle members, all the points of change or information that need to be noted by the pivotal circle.

At some stage, they have to return across the bridge with some feedback or response to the concerns or ideas. Schools that operate a school council have gone some way towards this model, and a representative from the school council circle could take pupil issues to the inner management circle.

Alongside the group listening system or circle meetings, there are opportunities for one-to-one listening in the form of appraisal meetings, mentoring, personal development planning and tutor chat time, plus non-verbal listening in the form of journals.

These listening systems can only be a safe place for meaningful discussion, however, if there is a measure of emotional "safety" in the school. The school community needs to agree, make explicit and constantly reinforce a code of moral values and a set of procedural routines so that it can function with common aims. The moral values and procedures are then shared with parents in the home-school agreement so that there is a common understanding of school expectations. Once the codes of conduct are made explicit, they can be held in place and reinforced using systems of incentives and consequences. Clearly communicated expectations and well-defined boundaries make it much easier for young people to develop positive behaviours.

Why an Ecosystemic Approach?

We maintain that the Whole-School Quality Circle Time Model represents an ecosystemic approach.

Central to the concept of an ecosystemic approach to human behaviour is the premise that humans are essentially social beings. They are dependent on their social environment for their mental wellbeing in the same way as they depend on the physical environment for their physical survival. They are not wholly free to behave as they choose, but are constrained by, and have an influence on, the social network in which they operate. It is similar to the biological notion of an ecosystem where the life-cycles of plants, animals and other organisms are linked to each other and to the non-living constituents of the environment to form a set of natural systems which interrelate. A change in any one part of a system has a "knock-on" effect throughout the whole system and may lead to reverberations in allied systems.

Two essential human needs, first for a recognised personal identity and second for a sense of belonging to a social group, cause people to operate largely in a group context or "system." Individuals depend on the group to supply particular needs, i.e. recognition of their individuality and the sense of belonging, so the group becomes the central focus of activity. The foundational social unit in secondary school is the tutorial group. A systems approach offers new ways of thinking about the interactional processes in a tutor group which has the potential to promote, sustain or redefine the behaviour of individuals.

Historically, there has been a tendency in the teaching profession to see some pupils as "having" behaviour problems. If the cause of the problem behaviour is perceived to reside in the pupil, the "cure" will be in dealing with the individual and the school need not question its structures, relationships and systems. Systemic approaches see behaviour as a product of interaction. Tong and An (2024) also advocate using ecosystemic theory to explore the connection between individual learners and their contexts. Consequently, if teachers wish to change the behaviour of pupils, they need to consider whether the behaviour is in any way a product of the environment which exists in the classroom, the school, or in the teacher–pupil interaction (Hanko, 1999) or lack of clarity of vision, or poor communication of that vision to staff or students (Bennett, 2017) This view produces a shift away from thinking about individual behaviour and towards collaborative approaches.

Pupil behaviour, which is defined as problematic, always needs to be directed. This means that from the pupil's viewpoint, it is understandable, rational and, above all, necessary. What appears problematic for the teacher may well be a solution for the pupil or for a subsystem in the classroom or the school. In a systemic approach, it becomes important then to hear how each individual perceives a situation in order to understand the interactions and explore alternative, more effective means of achieving the goals which the behaviour is perceived to serve. The circle meeting in this model provides a place for listening to individual perceptions and exploring alternative solutions. It permits pupils and teachers to view one another differently and so to reframe both "problems" and "solutions" whilst providing an image of the individual as a worthy and valuable human being.

This way of thinking has real implications, not only for the tutor group, but for the whole school, where all the systems can be seen to be interconnected and interrelated. Changes in one system create intended and unintended outcomes in other parts of the organisation. For instance, creating Circle Time as a respectful forum for listening might well generate difficulties in the consequence system because young people now have a forum in which to question whether consequences are fair. Similarly, implementing ground rules for good communication in PSHE may well generate hot debate about the way pupils are spoken to in other lessons. On the other hand, if a change generates more respect, higher self-esteem and greater motivation, there is the possibility of examining all the systems in the same light of respect and thus generating a more positive working community over a period of time.

The model we propose involves all members of the school community and every part of the school day. There is increasing evidence that short-term "add-on" interventions have short-term outcomes (Elias and Arnold, 2006) and that the most effective way forward is to "Be inclusive by design" (Bennett, 2017) and embed social and emotional learning into the whole of school life (Payton et al., 2000). The ideal would be to implement the model throughout the school as whole-school policy. We are realistic enough, however, to know that the ideal rarely exists, so where tutors and teachers are unable to influence school policy, many of the strategies can be employed on a classroom basis. As we unravel the model a section at a time in Chapters 3–10, the reader is encouraged to think of individual applications that would affect his/her personal or professional practice and to look at the wider context of the whole school.

Very simply, what the QCT model believes in is that the school is a living system of relationships and interactions. By building positive relationships, we can prevent issues and provide a systemic way to build and repair them.

An Educational Psychologist's Take on Whole-School Quality Circle Time Today

With over 30 years of working as an educational psychologist, I resolutely advocate for circle time within schools and local authorities, most specifically following the Quality Circle Time model for all ages and stages of children and students. Circle Time is not just for the very young. A school that implements the Quality Circle Time model creates positive and enabling environments in which all pupils and adults flourish, develop and learn. Walking into a school which follows the approach is always an exciting experience. It shows immediately in the welcome and positive ethos. The environment is a place where everyone is valued, where their unique contribution is realised and cherished, with each person supported according to their needs. We all learn to understand each other and accept each other's weaknesses and strengths. Quality Circle Time is about respect for all and is the most effective and inclusive model that I have experienced in developing the outstanding, creative, nurturing school climate.

(Jane Mansfield, 2025)

As a Specialist Senior Educational Psychologist, Jane introduced QCT into a secondary school curriculum. She currently works as an independent Educational Psychologist in Dorset.

References

Allen, K.A., Slaten, C.D., Arslan, G., Roffey, S., Craig, H. and Vella-Brodrick, D.A., 2021. School belonging: The importance of student and teacher relationships. In: M.L. Kern and M.L. Wehmeyer (eds.) *The Palgrave Handbook of Positive Education*. Cham: Springer International Publishing, pp. 525–550.

Bennett, T., 2017. Independent review of behaviour in schools. [pdf] Available at: https://assets.publishing.service.gov.uk/media/5a7506e4ed915d3c7d529cec/Tom_Bennett_Independent_Review_of_Behaviour_in_Schools.pdf [Accessed 4 July 2025].

Burley, D., 2025. *Whole School Approach to Emotional and Mental Well-being: Unmet Evidence Needs*. Cardiff: Welsh Government. Available at: https://www.gov.wales/sites/default/files/statistics-and-research/2025-06/whole-school-approach-to-emotional-and-mental-well-being-unmet-evidence-needs-374.pdf

Elias, M. and Arnold, H., 2006. *The Educator's Guide to Emotional Intelligence and Academic Achievement*. Thousand Oaks, CA: Corwin Press.

Hanko, G., 1999. *Increasing Competence Through Collaborative Problem-Solving: Using Insight Into Social and Emotional Factors in Children's Learning* (1st ed.). David Fulton Publishers. https://doi.org/10.4324/9780203065020

Mosley, J., 1998. *Turn Your School Round: A Circle-Time Approach to the Development of Self-esteem and Positive Behaviour in the Primary Staffroom, Classroom and Playground*. Wisbech, Cambridgeshire: LDA.

Payton, J.W., Wardlaw, D.M., Graczyk, P.A., Bloodworth, M.R., Tompsett, C.J. and Weissberg, R.P., 2000. Social and emotional learning: A framework for promoting mental health and reducing risk behavior in children and youth. *Journal of School Health*, 70(5), pp. 179–185. https://doi.org/10.1111/j.1746-1561.2000.tb06468.x

Tong, P. and An, I.S., 2024. Review of studies applying Bronfenbrenner's bioecological theory in international and intercultural education research. *Frontiers in Psychology*, 14, p. 1233925. https://doi.org/10.3389/fpsyg.2023.1233925.

Chapter 6

Unlocking the Whole-School Quality Circle Time Model for Wellbeing

The Key Will Always Be Self-Esteem First to Raise the Morale and Wellbeing of Staff

Taylor et al. (2024) highlight the importance of teacher wellbeing, saying it should be one of the first factors schools consider when looking at wellbeing for the whole community (Figure 6.1).

High Self-Esteem Staff Encourage High Self-Esteem Pupils

Ideas about whole-school approaches that support strengthening relationships and behaviour management in secondary schools are great, but they cannot happen if the adults working in the school have no energy or motivation to bring them about. It is impossible to expect adults to respond positively, warmly and calmly to pupils if they themselves are emotionally and physically exhausted and/or lacking in support. This applies to all the adults, not just the teaching staff. The Whole-School Quality Circle Time model outlined in Chapter 5 therefore first focuses on the emotional wellbeing of adults.

Figure one

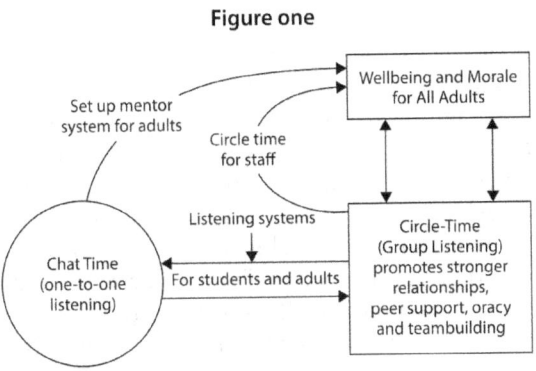

Figure 6.1 This is an excerpt from the ecosystemic model, Figure 5.1 on p 36.

DOI: 10.4324/9781003679615-8

Self-esteem is strongly linked to overall wellbeing – encompassing intellectual, physical, emotional, creative and spiritual aspects. Sound self-esteem is associated with greater resilience and positive mental health, whilst low self-esteem can drag you down to low self-confidence, exhaustion and sometimes depression.

Sound Self-Esteem

Good self-esteem brings a sense of competence and worth. An individual with good self-esteem views themself as a capable, likeable and worthwhile person. These people will welcome and enjoy new experiences and be able to relate well to others. They have confidence and optimism, which brings a positive approach to personal and professional life. Moreover, people with good self-esteem are able to learn from criticism, mistakes and failures and to view them in a calm and realistic way. They hold the different aspects of life in perspective and so maintain a sense of balance. Some of the indicators of high self-esteem would include the following people:

- who have confidence to cope with problems and surmount difficulties;
- who can cope with getting it wrong without becoming defensive;
- who can change what they think, even strongly held values, in the light of new information or experience;
- people who do not "agonise" over the past or the future can "go with the flow";
- people who think of themselves as valuable and of equal worth even when they are not good at a particular task or skill;
- people who are not threatened by other people's success but are pleased for them;
- people who notice and respond to the needs of others.

Poor Self-Esteem

Poor self-esteem brings a sense of uselessness and incompetence to the person. They can lack confidence, which results in nagging self-doubt, suffer from occasional self-pity, and have difficulty in sustaining meaningful relationships with others. On the other hand, they can be loud, opinionated and bossy, covering up their sense of inadequacy with dominating behaviour. Such people often protect themselves from hurt by being aggressive and "putting other people down," or withdrawing into a lonely "shell." Secretly, they may regard themselves as a bit of a failure or as totally misunderstood and think everyone else is more successful than they are. This negative thinking results in a pattern of behaviour that becomes a self-fulfilling prophecy. Mind you, personally, just reading that list, I definitely think you can have "low self-esteem" days due to life's ambushes – yet recover on other days.

What Can Cause Low Self-Esteem at Work?

Research carried out by the Department for Education (2023) showed that among other factors:

- 75% of teachers spent too much time on tasks other than teaching, particularly general admin;
- 44% of teachers feel high anxiety levels, with only 18% feeling very low anxiety;
- 88% of teachers experience stress in their job.

Low self-esteem can be seen in the following behaviours, i.e. when individuals:

- rarely admit they are wrong;
- see difficulties or obstacles as catastrophes;
- are hypercritical of others;
- defend their shaky self-image by pointing out other people's faults when they are challenged about their own;
- take things very personally;
- refuse to acknowledge any failure and weakness in themselves;
- "feed on" flattery and seem to need adulation;
- are wary of putting themselves forward or volunteering despite being competent to do the task.

Undoubtedly, there are individual teachers and those in management positions who recognise the importance of developing positive self-esteem in themselves and their colleagues, as well as their students. Though such efforts are valuable and worthwhile, consider how much more impact could be made if every member of the school were committed to creating an environment where everyone was regularly listened to and encouraged, given respect and support.

First Though, We Need to Take Responsibility for Looking After Ourselves

If you can view yourself as a much-needed resource for your students, colleagues and family, then you will understand that you can't keep on giving out to everyone else and not putting energy back into yourself. Like any precious resource, you need replenishing from time to time. Energy is one of the most important resources you have and in order to sustain the energy you require, you must learn how to revitalise yourself.

Golden Moments or "Time Out"

Develop a calming ritual at key times in the day and use these times to switch off from work-related problems and the nagging voices in your head. Calming rituals can be anything that might relax you – for example, a peaceful spot and the crossword, a long shower or listening to your favourite music. Some teachers like to arrive early so that they can set up the classroom, then have a calm cup of coffee before the pupils arrive. At the end of the day, it is also useful to develop a ritual that marks the end of school so that you go home in a positive frame of mind.

Visualisation Techniques

One head teacher we know drives home and as he passes a particular spot, he imagines taking his work out of the car in a bag and placing it in a big burrow, out of sight at the side of the road. He then proceeds home as a "home person." This does not mean that he never takes work home, but he does as much as he can whilst in school and once home, the focus of his attention is family. In the morning, as he passes the same spot, he visualises picking up the work again, putting it back in the car and driving to school as a "work person."

Golden Moments are based on the idea of concentrating on each of your senses, bringing them alive, whilst entering one moment of pleasure. For example, take a hot drink outside; concentrate on the taste of the drink, the heat of the cup, the touch of the breeze, the scent of plants, the sounds of the birds/traffic and the sight of the clouds and sky. By concentrating on your senses and talking yourself through them, it is possible to shut out negative thoughts associated with problems. It is disconcerting to meet teachers on courses who say they cannot find one Golden Moment in a day. Maintaining our mental health demands that we create these moments for ourselves.

Breathing Techniques

Another useful and quick way of ridding the body of tension is to learn deep breathing techniques and to use them whilst concentrating on relaxing your body. Sit on a chair, evenly distributing your weight and slowly breathe in to the count of 3 or 4, keeping your mouth closed. Imagine the oxygen going through all the pathways in your body making you feel lighter and more energetic. Then slowly expel the air through your mouth – again to the same count. It is helpful if you can learn to use breathing and relaxation techniques when standing so that the adrenaline flood, that comes under stress and triggers the fight or flight response, is brought under control. Once the adrenaline abates in your system, the blood flows once again to the thinking centres of the brain and rational decisions can be made! Consider studying mindfulness and yoga or use good apps like *Headspace.*

The Bag that Pulsates Guilt

Every school has at least one "bag person" and we are all tempted to become one. The big box or several bags are full of things to do, which we lug from classroom to home and back again. It is such a daunting burden that we can't face tackling it. It merely sits in the corner of our home ... distracting us from getting any real pleasure from our leisure time, as every time we catch sight of it, we feel guilty. The trick is to either keep the bag in the boot of your car and then go and get it, do it and put it back in the boot. Or bring it into your house, put it into a cupboard and shut the door. Later, get it out, do it and put it back. Do not leave it lying around because all that does is make you feel guilty. Many of the things in the box are good intentions; they are not strictly needed, so throw them out!

Taking Responsibility for Your Own Mood: Developing Your Personal Care Plan

Many years ago, I developed the model "Five Wells For Wellbeing." The National College of School Leadership (NCSL) advocated that it would be helpful for all teachers. It's about you looking carefully at the pattern of your days to assess whether you are creating sufficient work–life balance.

As human beings, we all have a huge capacity to be Spiritual, Physical, Intellectual, Creative and Emotional (yes, it spells SPICE – and we all need to spice up our lives!) These I call "Wells"; they are the wells we can visit to draw on their reserves to fuel our own energy (Figure 6.2).

Spiritually: if you were to learn to concentrate on just your rhythmic breathing and therefore turn the clattering voices off in your head – then something more beautiful can move through – some people will call this Prana, beauty, joy, God, etc. Every time we take time out – a golden moment alone, sitting in nature, singing together, prayer, yoga – and totally breathe it all in – this is a spirited experience – you are connecting to something bigger than yourself. Life is richer than the events or people who annoy us – connect with this belief and perspective will return.

Physically: there is nothing I can say that you don't already know! Advice on keeping fit and healthy is all around us. The problem is we can get overwhelmed by gazing at the vision, slopping back down on the sofa, having another chocolate and waving the vision away from the television. The key here is to go for a Tiny Achievable Tickable Target (TATT). Instead of saying "I'm going to get fit," say, "by the end of the day I am going to phone the leisure centre." I am actually serious here – TATTs are how we work with dysregulated children – we are sometimes dysregulated adults! Go on, plan a TATT!

Intellectually: that difficult colleague, rude student, or angry parent are not the *whole* of your life. There is a world of events, ideas, and achievements

46 A Circle Approach to Boosting Emotional Wellbeing

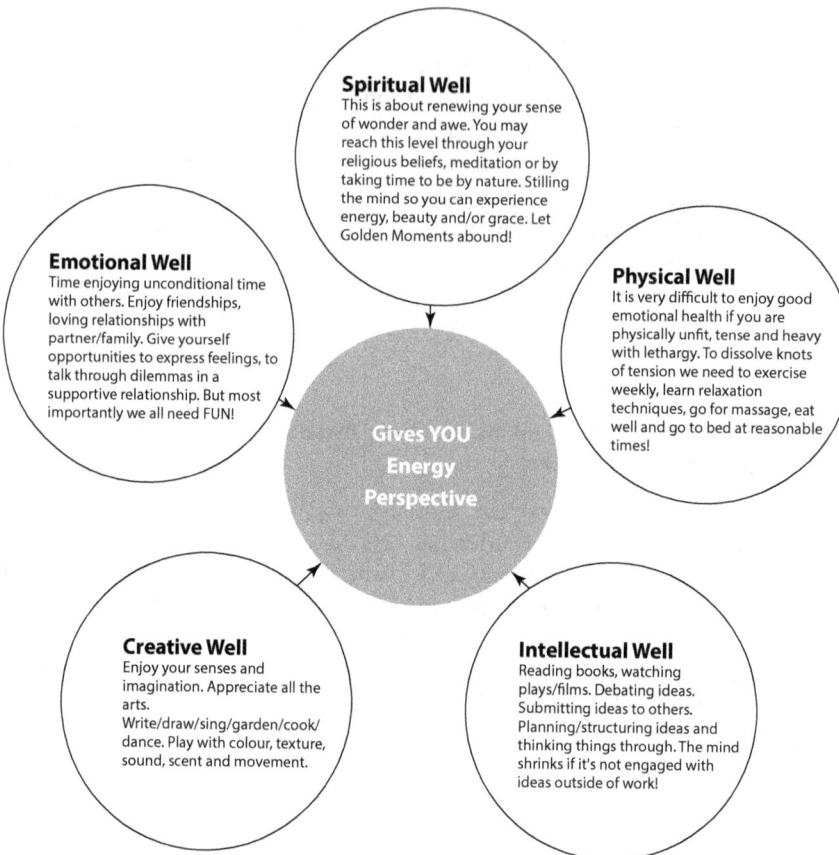

Figure 6.2 The five wells for wellbeing

out there that will stir you to see the smallness of our world. Engage in great books, searing documentaries, glorious films – we only have one life – this is not a dress rehearsal.

Creatively: look one day inside a room full of toddlers – any one of them could be an artist, sculptor, hedge layer or architect. Our capacity for creativity is what distinguishes human life. For those toddlers to reach their creative potential, they need to be in the presence of nurturing, positive adults throughout their young lives. You and I were deeply influenced by a teacher telling us that our painting was poor or our voice was off key, so we gave up art or maybe even singing … or we were so inspired by a positive teacher that we even decided to become one ourselves. Our power to influence others is magical.

Emotionally: we need friends, family and FUN. We need to enjoy our children in the moment they are in sometimes – not the way we want them to be. There is sometimes a moment to go with a spaghetti fight or join in a kitchen dance.

... Aaaah, now we're hitting the real problem – why teachers are so exhausted – perversely it's the holidays that are the "killer." What happens at the end of the term is that we dash off to binge at the Wells "swim hard, swim hard, I've got a fortnight to get fit" ... "must get all my friends over and have a big BBQ ... great ... that's over and they're all ticked off ... I still have friends left and won't need to see them for another ten weeks."

Seriously, by bingeing at the Wells during the holidays we cause ourselves post-traumatic "shock" at the beginning of the next term. In other words, we think we have refuelled ourselves ready for a new term – but we have overlooked the impact of just what one day of teaching can do to us. We stand

Figure 6.3 A blank five wells for wellbeing - to fill in yourself.

there at the beginning of term like a camel with energy all carefully stored in our hump ... "I am ready and up for anything." Within just a few hours the challenges, the clutter of demands and the clacking of endless requests – by the end of the day – your jaw has hit the floor, legs have splayed outwards with the hump flopping sideways.

What you forgot is that *you cannot store energy*. On any one day in school, your energy can evaporate with the shocks. You have to replenish energy every day, which is why you need a Daily Personal Care Plan, which you fill in and complete at the end of every week.

No word of a lie, I have a primary school where the Wells are up big on a staffroom wall. Everyone has an empty one of them to fill in and all staff have a 20-minute meetup with their co-mentor whilst the headteacher takes an assembly (yes, he also has a care plan and actually any member can access it as it's updated online).

You can choose to take responsibility for your mood or you can remain blaming your job. Life is too short not to have joy every day – why wait until the holidays?

Here is a blank Wells for you to create and use yourself weekly (Figure 6.3).

References

Taylor, L., Zhou, W., Boyle, L., Funk, S. and De Neve, J-E., 2024. *Wellbeing for Schoolteachers* (Report No. 2). Wellbeing Research Centre, University of Oxford, in Collaboration with the International Baccalaureate Organization. Available at: https://wellbeing.hmc.ox.ac.uk/wp-content/uploads/2024/04/FULL-REPORT-TWB-IB-Report-January-2024-v2.1.pdf

Part II
Putting Circle Time into Practice

Chapter 7

Setting Up Three Listening Systems – An Overview

If we accept that being listened to is the key to feeling valued and worthwhile, then we can see that young people need calm, refreshed adults who are working on their personal energy. If we are honest, we know that as teachers, we can appear harassed, busy and unapproachable to the eyes of pupils. Young people are put off trying to speak to us and the ensuing sense of frustration or even isolation can drive them to demand the much-needed attention by anti-social means such as sulking, defying or arguing. After all, negative attention is better than no attention. Perhaps the greatest challenge at this stage of the model is to ask yourself "Can I, as a teacher, role model good listening? Do I care enough to set up Listening Systems?" (Appendix B provides a helpful checklist for evaluating your ability to be a good listening role model) (Figure 7.1).

Three listening systems are suggested in the whole-school model (Chapter 2):

- Circle Time – the group listening system;
- One-to-one Chat Time – for private conversations;
- Daily Journals – for non-verbal listening or a Think Box for notes

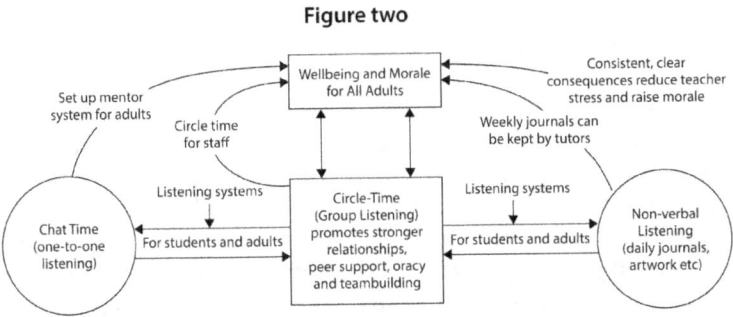

Figure 7.1 This is an excerpt from the ecosystemic model, Figure 5.1 on p. 36.

DOI: 10.4324/9781003679615-10

Your school also needs to ensure they have a School Council (SC) that meets regularly, is not cosmetic but a real forum for change. When circle requests are taken by their rep to SC, very soon after they need a response, even if it is "We can't do this because the budget won't allow it but we will try to meet your request in the future."

So How Do We Make Listening Systems Work?
Circle Time – a Group Listening System

The detail of how to establish and run a full Circle Time in the secondary school is given in Part II of this book. There you will find many ideas for lesson plans and how to structure your own. Here it is enough to point out that the circle meeting has structures and strategies that encourage the development of positive relationships, self-discipline, self-regulating behaviour, conflict resolution, assertive communication and democratic group processes, alongside the skills of speaking, listening, observing, thinking and concentrating. The meeting takes place usually once a week to consider issues relating to personal, social, health and emotional education and matters of whole-school concern.

- It involves the whole class, including the teacher, meeting in a circle so that each group member can see the faces of every speaker.
- The act of physically sitting in a circle emphasises equality and collective responsibility. As one student said, "There is no head of a circle."
- Pupils have the opportunity to speak and a commitment to listen to each other's views. The teacher is required to adopt a facilitative style rather than dominating in any way. This is an occasion when the teacher's opinions and solutions to problems are equal to anyone else's.
- It initially involves the whole class and adults agreeing to a "contract" of ground rules that facilitate open discussion.
- Honesty, cooperation and trust are encouraged in an emotionally "safe" environment where feelings can be explored and risks taken.
- In Circle Time, the teacher's ability to give pupils warmth, respect and positive regard is all-important in building pupil self-esteem and encouraging changes in thinking and behaving.

Two streams of issues emerge from the circle meeting. One is to do with personal matters relevant to the pupils in the group. Individuals or the whole group may set targets or action plans which would be followed up at subsequent circle meetings. The second stream is to do with management issues in the school. They might relate to overcrowding in certain areas of the building, bullying, queuing systems or safety in corridors and on stairs between lessons. At the end of the circle they can be summed up and then taken to the school council or communicated to the relevant member of the senior management team so that the listening system produces some action or feedback.

One-to-One Listening or Chat Time

In primary schools, this one-to-one system is called Bubble Time. In secondary schools, we can call it Chat Time or, as Carr Manor Community School calls it, "One-to-One Coaching." One of the main ground rules adopted in Circle Time is that no names may be used in a negative way. We cannot allow any shaming or blaming. However, this rule automatically means that pupils cannot tell you the names of any offenders, yet as an anti-bullying school, they do need to be able to access you when they are being bullied or emotionally hurt in any way. So the teacher will often say in the circle "if you have any personal issues or private concerns, don't forget you can come to me at Chat Time." This is not easy to organise, but some teachers have tried various ways of making themselves available.

Case Studies Regarding Chat Time

- One tutor agreed with her tutor group to take her coffee to the tutor room on one break time a week. She was always available no matter whether pupils came to talk to her or not. At first, there was little response, but over a period of time, pupils took advantage of the opportunity to speak privately. The teacher found that the key to success was to make sure that the visit was not associated with "problems" or "telling on people." She was available to talk about any issues: homework or curriculum-related; whole-school management; personal good news; personal difficulties; or private information.
- A Rota System: another group of tutors agreed to provide one-to-one listening for a whole year group. The five members of the tutor team talked with their tutor groups and agreed to take a break each in a week. When it was their turn to be on "listening duty," they took their coffee and spent the break in the designated room so that they were available to anyone in the year group who wanted to talk privately.
- Some schools put one-to-one informal tutor listening alongside a more formalised Personal Development Plan interview that takes place once or twice each year to monitor pupils' progress and personal development.
- Other schools have developed peer listening systems. They have trained volunteers from the older year groups in listening skills and set up a "drop in" listening room manned by Year 11 or by sixth-form students where they are available in the school. The school then provided clear guidelines and regular supervision for these older pupils.
- Other schools ensure that teachers have access to support teams for "inclusion (focused on developing agency), safeguarding (focused on stressed behaviours) and a SEND team (focused on the influence of conditions)" (Tom Shaw, Carr Manor Community School).

Teachers can therefore go themselves to seek what advice they need to give to individual pupils or to check if someone from the team could meet that child.

Effective schools seem to be able to combine high expectations with an empathetic ethos – it is important to strike this balance. As long ago as 1989, the groundbreaking Elton Report noted this need and made the following recommendation regarding listening:

> We are convinced that there are skills, which all teachers need, involved in listening to young people and encouraging them to talk about their hopes and concerns before coming to a judgement about their behaviour. We consider that these basic counselling skills are particularly valuable for creating a supportive school atmosphere. The skills needed to work effectively with adults, whether teachers or parents, are equally crucial. We therefore recommend that initial teacher training establishments should introduce all their students to basic counselling skills and their value. We regard such skills as particularly important for all senior pastoral staff (deputy heads, heads of houses and year).

Teacher training courses have never fully embraced the responsibility to train future teachers in counselling skills or in active group work. I suggest this training is vital to meet the huge increase in mental health problems that children are suffering (Haidt, 2024). Yes, there are sometimes foundational elements within the course but never sufficient training to give these teachers confidence.

Non-Verbal Listening

Some young people find it really hard to engage with eye contact. This has always been so, but it has been heightened by shyness or social anxiety post-COVID-19. Circle Time is still possible for them because they can offer it or receive it intermittently – but one-to-one chats can be a step too far. Some tutors offer a daily journal, which, if they put a symbol at the end of the entry – 1:1, indicates that they want a chat with you. If there is no symbol, then the teacher will just write something back.

A genuine example – a student wrote to his teacher, "you know I'm thick so what's the point of me sitting any exams?"

The teacher wrote back, "I find you very clever to talk to. You always say interesting things. Exams only test one bit of intelligence – I promise you are a very bright person."

On an anecdotal level, did any of you readers see the film *Freedom Writers* (2007). It was a true story of a teacher who inspired her at-risk students at a racially divided high school. The breakthrough came when she gave them each a journal which they would put into a locked cupboard, so it was always kept private. It is possible now to buy the book of their diary entries (*The Freedom Writers Diary*, Erin Gruwell).

Sometimes if children find it hard to speak, you can do something called "Button Sculpture." Button sculpture therapy is a creative and expressive therapeutic technique that can be used during a one-to-one chat. First, you need to collect a huge jar of buttons. In the past, I have used this technique myself. You can lay out a pile of buttons on the table and ask them to select one that represents themselves. Then they can select others that represent their family or carers. Once they have named the buttons mother/father/carer etc., they need to place themselves in relation to the buttons. So, if they feel close to their mother, then their buttons would be close together. Distant from their father? Then they would move their father button to the other end of the table. They can explain it if they want to whilst they're doing it, or not. You can ask them to represent friendship groups or anything in school. NB. keep an eye on the time; I always used to have a ten-minute sand timer ... because it is important to remember to de-role the child. "Let's put these buttons away now and as you hold the button before dropping it into the jar, just say, 'this is not me, my best friend or whoever, this is just a button' and put it in the jar." Thank them at the end for joining in with you in this exercise and helping you understand. Any activity like this or painting/drawing allows children to communicate non-verbally, fostering self-expression and emotional exploration. It can be particularly helpful in addressing social, emotional and mental health challenges.

How a Teacher Set Up a Circle Time Listening System for Her Students

Bethan Sioned Rogers-Jones, Head of Art and Design, Ysgol Brynhyfryd

Background and Summary

This piece of informal but very real and interesting research was carried out by a class teacher who wanted to get more out of the Year 9 tutorial periods. As the graphs show clearly, the students wanted active group work. The results showed a distinct preference for discussion activities compared to written work and a very strong preference for Circle Time as opposed to other possible classroom activities.

The group went on to discuss:

- Which issues they would like to talk about.
- What they would choose to call the group sessions.
- How important they think tutor periods are.
- What are tutor periods (extended reg.) for?

56 A Circle Approach to Boosting Emotional Wellbeing

- How can we improve tutor periods?
- What are your rules?
- Basic moral values.
- Our rules for Circle Time.
- What if rules are kept?
- What if rules are not kept?
- What do you think?
- General requests.
- Circle Time plan.
- Using the five skills.

The students' preferences are shown in the following four graphs (Figures 7.2–7.5).

The class was also asked if there were any other activities they would like to do and the only answer was "Circle Time."

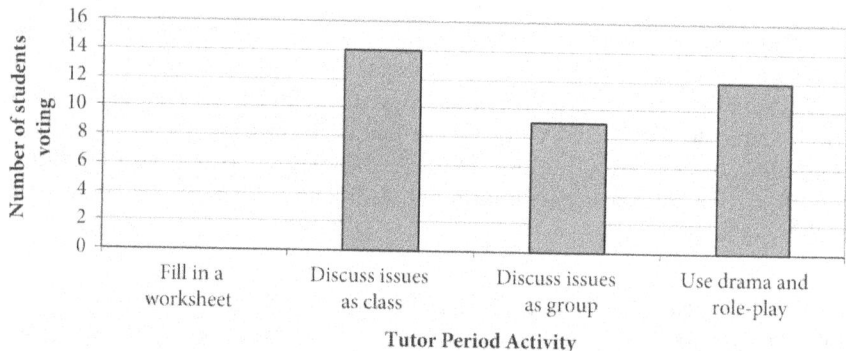

Figure 7.2 Class preferences for tutor period activities.

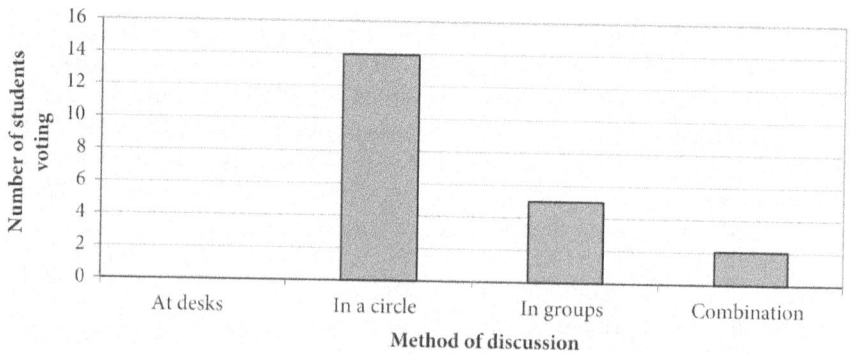

Figure 7.3 Class preferences for "Circle Time" activities.

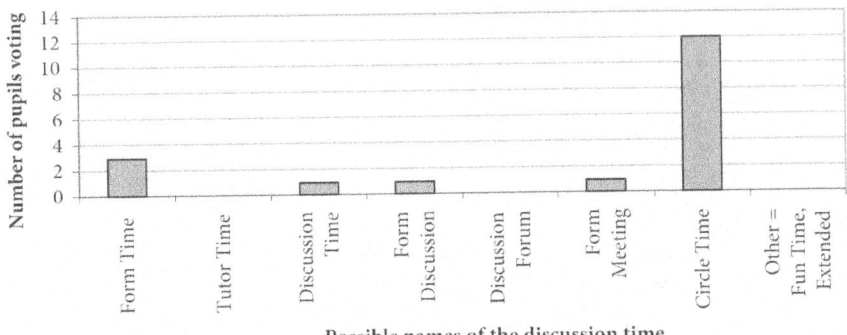

Figure 7.4 Class preferences for naming their discussion time.

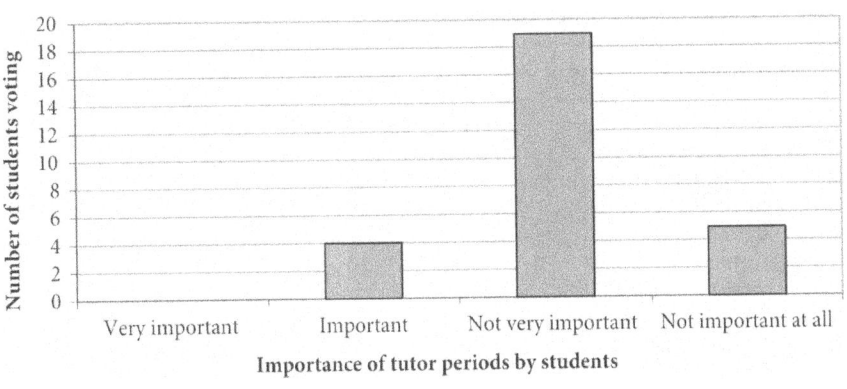

Figure 7.5 Pupil feelings about how important tutor periods are.

Observations About the Graphs

The graphs show clearly that the vast majority of students would prefer to:

- discuss issues as a class or group and do drama and role-play rather than complete workbooks or worksheets;
- use Circle Time as their method of holding discussions during the tutorial period;
- call this class discussion time "Circle Time."

In addition, the majority of pupils (who had been accustomed to completing workbooks and sheets during tutor periods) did not think the tutor periods were very important. The class was asked more open questions about the tutorial period and some of their answers are given in Table 7.1.

58 A Circle Approach to Boosting Emotional Wellbeing

Table 7.1 Class response to how tutor periods could be improved

Q:	How can we improve tutor periods?
A:	Make it more interesting, like real life situations we could think about.
A:	Be able to work in your friend groups not being told where to go.
A:	I like the idea of finding out what you would do and should do.
A:	I like the agree/disagree line.
A:	Teach us things we actually need to know.
A:	It's better to work in a group than behind desks.
A:	I think it would be much better if we did role-play.
A:	Make it interesting.
A:	Be more fun, like more games and talk instead of paperwork.
A:	I think extended reg. should be fun.
A:	Circle Time

Table 7.2 Class response to what they would like to discuss in the tutor period

Q:	What do you want to discuss?
A:	What is in the news at that time and day.
A:	Real life situations.
A:	Considering other people's feelings.
A:	Rules
A:	Bullying
A:	Communication
A:	Health and Safety
A:	Global Warming
A:	Credit crunch
A:	Poverty
A:	Underage drinking, smoking and sex
A:	Paedophilia
A:	Racism
A:	The end of the world

Answers to this question showed that students thought tutor periods could be improved by a variety of means, with answers leaning towards discussions and activities that were about real life issues, exploratory activities and games. Below, in Table 7.2 students suggest ideas for their discussions.

Pupils gave a variety of answers to this question, mostly citing several key current news topics.

Basic moral values were then discussed arising from a discussion about the students' own rules.

Rules for Circle Time were discussed to keep everyone safe during these sessions.

Our Rules for Circle Time

- Respect each other and respect the room;
- Stay safe – don't run, push, or hit anyone;
- Listen to everyone – don't interrupt each other;
- Signal to speak – don't shout out;
- One person speaks at a time;
- No laughing at each other;
- No put downs (verbal/non-verbal);
- Don't name anyone in a negative way;
- It's ok to "pass" – everyone gets a second chance to speak;
- No gossiping about anything afterwards.

The consequences of keeping or breaking rules were then discussed.

Q: *What if rules are kept?*
A: REWARDS!

Everyone was made aware through discussion of the incentives and consequences of keeping and breaking the Circle Time rules.

The students were reminded of general practical considerations for Circle Time sessions.

General practical considerations regarding Circle Time:

- stack tables neatly at the back quietly;
- bags neatly under the tables.

Reference

Haidt, J., 2024. *The Anxious Generation: How the Great Rewiring of Childhood Is Causing an Epidemic of Mental Illness.* New York: Penguin Press. ISBN 978-0-593-65503

Chapter 8

Establishing Codes of Conduct – Are They Clear, Kind and Consistent?

Whenever we have used a Circle Time to listen to young people's views about school rules and routines, there is still confusion. Despite schools' best intentions and lists of rules in the front of academic year planners or homework diaries, etc., some pupils still seem unclear about their school's expectations. The confusion can stem from the fact that some teachers show some real inconsistencies in what rules they prioritise. Every rule needs to be explicit from the start. Years ago I read an excellent ethnographic study looking at how children suss out different teachers' boundaries and flexibilities very quickly and how they behave differently for different teachers. Their acuity and energy in pressing teachers' Crumple-Buttons and then adjusting to what they can and can't do makes you smile. It was called "Initial Encounters in the Secondary School" (1985) by John Beynon. Students even give us funny names to identify our style! (Figure 8.1)

We recommend, for clarity's sake, that schools try to have two sets of rules.

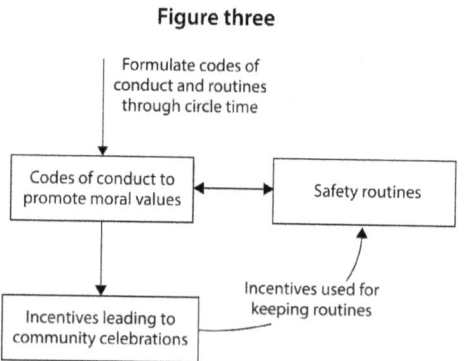

Figure 8.1 This is an excerpt from the ecosystemic model, Figure 5.1 on p. 36.

Routine Rules

Routines are negotiated. Each teacher cares more about some routines than others. Some teachers care about students lining up outside the classroom, some want them in the class, some want hands up – some don't mind too much, some insist homework is on time – some don't. Some routines depend on the room itself – the science lab has very strict routines. Each teacher needs to establish routines with their pupils to go up on the walls or in their planners.

Paul Dix, a well-respected education consultant, proposes a subtle fusion of rules and values with three clear headings – his (2021) book properly explores the following three points …

- Be Ready – emphasising a preparedness for learning and being able to focus on the current task.
- Be Respectful – emphasises positive interactions and courtesy towards others.
- Be Safe – focuses on physical and emotional wellbeing, emphasising that children need to follow routines and instructions carefully and create a safe learning environment.

Rules Based on Moral Values

Moral values are the key absolutes of the school. They are not negotiable; they underpin the ethos of the school, and they apply throughout it.

This model proposes that schools agree on a set of values which everyone in the school upholds. This would include office staff, support staff, ancillary staff, site staff and teaching staff. Some schools approach values through the notion of rights and responsibilities. Others emphasise that certain behaviours are prohibited by the law of the land. The school prepares young people for their place as adult citizens by adopting a similar set of moral "laws." Other schools prefer to have values that are explicitly stated, displayed in every area of the school and taught through the PSHE or pastoral programme.

Whatever the philosophy, Circle Time in Year 7 is the ideal forum for introducing the school's codes of conduct. Schools at the "cutting edge" of developing the Circle Time model spend some time in the Christmas term of Year 7 exploring the concept of rules and why they are necessary in a school. These can be learned and reinforced through activities and games, and they reflect the values that underpin a democratic society. In the original edition of this book, I proposed for clarity's sake four simple Respect Rules:

- respect for self;
- respect for others;
- respect for work;
- respect for property.

Schools may wish, as many primary schools do, to set them out as simpler "Golden Rules" with a positive balanced by a negative. For example:

- We listen; we don't interrupt; or
- We work hard; we don't waste ours or other people's time.

To support SEND children, we need to use pictures and photographs of either themselves or "cartoon children" demonstrating the good behaviours that we would all like to see. Whichever way the codes of conduct are displayed, a copy needs to go home in the home–school agreement so that parents are also in no doubt as to the moral expectations of the school.

Just a Suggestion

Some Restorative Practice schools use the tutorial period at the beginning of the year to engage the students in listing what behaviours and routines they want. They then put them up in the tutor classroom. I see many of them as I go in and out of schools.

My suggestion is that we ask children what behaviours they do want or don't want from each other – they can come up with quite a few don'ts, e.g. don't bully, don't push in, be kind, let people in your games …

They are a wonderful list, but we need to have consistency of language, so if we use the Four Respects, each of those pupils' suggestions could be put underneath the relevant Respect Rule. Here are some examples of what we would expect …

So, a member of staff would ask "Was that respectful to others?," "What was it you did just now that was disrespectful?" Teachers using the Paul Dix model would have similar language, e.g. "Was that safe when you did that?," "What safe choice could you have made instead?"

By putting up the school's big headings and then the student's own words underneath them, they can see that their values are mirrored by the school's rules and therefore they have more allegiance.

References

Beynon, J., 1985. *Initial Encounters in the Secondary School: Sussing, Typing and Coping* (Issues in Education & Training Series). London: Routledge Falmer

Dix, P., 2021. *After the Adults Change: Achievable Behaviour Nirvana*. Carmarthen: Crown House Publishing. Available at: https://www.crownhouse.co.uk/assets/look-inside/9781781353776.pdf

Chapter 9

Creating and Embedding Incentives – Are They Kind, Considerate and Community-Based?

What's the Point of Incentives? Shouldn't Young People Be Intrinsically Motivated?

Incentives, recognition or praise is the good news that we give to pupils, their peers and their parents about pupils' personal, social and academic development. Initially, they are needed to celebrate the positive side of the codes of conduct or rules. Often, as we have already known, a set of different "values" from those of the school is practised within the pupil's cultural background. When the rules are stated as a list of behaviours e.g. "Don't smoke on the school premises or on the buses or outside the school in the immediate vicinity," it tends to become a challenge to see if "I" can do it and not get caught! (Figure 9.1)

We have hit a problem, however. As soon as incentives are mentioned, it becomes clear that secondary colleagues cannot agree on the "currency" of a house point, dojos, praise stamps, postcards home, extra playtime vouchers

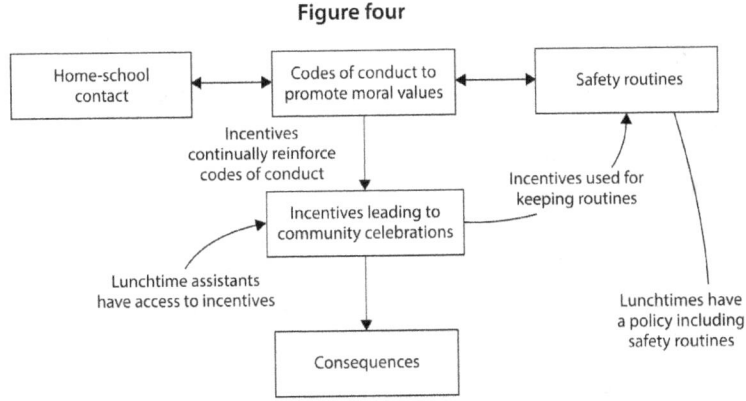

Figure 9.1 This is an excerpt from the ecosystemic model, Figure 5.1 on p. 36.

DOI: 10.4324/9781003679615-12

etc. What constitutes achievement good enough to receive a reward? For example, some members of staff give many merits/house points and some give virtually none. Such a system becomes very unfair in the eyes of the pupil.

If you are a high achieving pupil, one of those fortunate souls who happens to fit the system and are neat, organised, good at your work and respectful, of course you will receive rewards. On the other hand, if you are completely disorganised, untidy and difficult to motivate, everyone is falling over themselves to reward the tiniest hint of progress. The middle of the road pupil, or what we tend to call the "always" child, rarely gets recognised – to them your incentive system feels very unjust! Perhaps the most difficult task facing the secondary teacher is to ensure that these pupils receive regular good news about their work and behaviour. They are so easily overlooked that they can go through the entire five years of Key Stages 3 and 4 feeling that they are invisible!

Celebrating the "Always" Pupil – a Case Study

One school decided to take this whole issue of noticing and rewarding the "always" pupil very seriously. They devised a chart. The class sheet (Figure 9.2) is taken from one lesson to the next by selected pupils. It is placed on the teacher's desk and she/he notes any outstanding behaviour in the "excellent" column and any unacceptable behaviour in the "disappointing" column. The rest are automatically good. In reality, this is very little effort since the majority of pupils are "good" i.e. they arrive on time, remain mostly on task without interfering with or disrupting anyone else's learning, and have done their homework.

The list goes to the form tutor at the end of each day and pupils who have not received any "disappointing" or "excellent" comments (i.e. the "good" column is unticked) are automatically rewarded with one merit or house point. The "excellent" are given two house points and these add up to a graded certificate or privilege at the end of each half-term. The "disappointing" are highlighted for some kind of consequence.

This system works particularly well in Year 7 when pupils are generally taught in tutor groups. It becomes slightly more difficult to administer in higher years when a teaching set may be made up of pupils from several different tutor groups.

Names	Excellent	Good	Disappointing
Mark Adams	✓		
Shakira Begum			
Shane Carter			✓ calling out

Figure 9.2 An idea for acknowledging good behaviour and diligent work.

So How Can We Make Incentives Work?

Unless you consult with the students themselves, you can be deeply disappointed that your incentives are not working. One school set up a Celebration Assembly for Year 10s with merit certificates being awarded and everyone clapping. They were disappointed as time went on as behaviour went backwards. In a circle time, one of the tutors discovered that the students were highly embarrassed about going up in front of other students – it was a nightmare for them. They much preferred a certificate being sent home.

The following principles are some that we have found to be useful in planning an incentive system:

- The pupils know best what motivates them so carry out a survey among the pupils to find out the best incentives for your school.
- Be aware that the incentives that work well with Key Stage 3 are different from those that motivate Key Stage 4 pupils, so make sure both groups are surveyed.
- Incentives need to reward the quiet, hardworking, "always" pupils who neither exhibit academic excellence nor disruptive behaviour and are therefore often overlooked. Effort and perseverance are equally important and need to feature in your policy.
- Every pupil is entitled to some good news about themself. On my training courses I have occasionally heard members of staff say there is "nothing 'good' about some pupils, so I can't celebrate them ever." It is tempting to ask "What makes a person valuable?" "Are the targets you set too high?" Good teaching is surely about creating small achievable targets then noticing the pupil's success. If a teacher cannot find good news to give back to a pupil, it tells us more about that teacher than about the progress of the pupil. "Encouragers" are small incentives which are given quite frequently, such as house points or merits, for abiding by the codes of conduct of the school.

A Case Study on the Rewards and Consequences Completed by a Head of Year at John of Gaunt School

The following research on rewards and consequences was completed by John of Gaunt School, Head of Year. Many thanks for giving permission to reproduce it. Figure 9.3 provides the questionnaire used with students and Figure 9.4 gives the ranked responses from students.

"Specials" are rewards that are given less frequently, such as certificates, positions of responsibility, letters of commendation, etc. They can be given for an accumulation of "encouragers" or for special events.

- When adolescents are reluctant to receive incentives publicly, research has nevertheless shown that they like to have good news sent home to their parents where it can have a ripple effect in positivity.

The following research on rewards and consequences was completed by John of Gaunt School, Head of Year.

Rewards and consequences

Our emotions are influenced by the rewards and consequences we receive. Read the following list of preferred rewards of pupils in years 7–9, then answer the questions below.

- Letter of praise to parents
- Rewarded by a teacher commendation
- Praised by Head of Year
- Name appearing on the year board
- Mentioned in assembly
- Praised by subject teacher
- Having work on display
- Praised by form tutor
- Praised by other pupils
- Whole class praised
- Non-verbal praise, like a smile

Questions

1. Number the above points in your order preference.
2. Write out the reward you preferred most and say why you chose it.

_____

Now read the list of consequences disliked by year 7 and year 9 pupils, then answer the questions listed below.

- Removed from group
- Put on report — parents informed
- Told off in front of class/assembly
- After school detention
- Being kept in at lunchtime
- Sent to Year Head/Deputy Head
- Removal of privilege
- Told off privately
- Sent out of class
- Being moved to another set

Questions

1. Number the above points in the order you dislike them most.
2. Write out the consequence you dislike most and say why this is so.

_____

Figure 9.3 Survey on rewards and consequences, John of Gaunt School.

	Rank
Boys	
Letter of praise to parents	1
Reward by commendation	2
Praised by Year Head	3
Name on notice board	4
Mentioned in assembly	5
Praised by subject staff	6
Having work on display	7
Praised by Tutor	8
Praised by other pupils	9
Whole class praised	10
Non-verbal praise, e.g. smile	11
Girls	
Letter of praise to parents	1
Reward by commendation	2
Praised by Year Head	3
Name on notice board	4
Mentioned in assembly	5
Praised by subject staff	6
Having work on display	7
Praised by Tutor	8
Praised by other pupils	9
Whole class praised	10
Non-verbal praise, e.g. smile	11

Figure 9.4 Survey of preferred incentives at John of Gaunt School, Wiltshire (Ranked from most popular to least popular).

- Community Rewards – One of the strongest influences in the life of adolescents is the peer group. Circle Time encourages a culture of positive feedback from peers. Sometimes a tutor group will make "Class Team Certificates," which are suggested to be signed by members of the tutor group and presented within the group.
- Encourage pupils to value their own opinion of themselves as much as they value others' by providing opportunities to reflect and comment on their own performance. Carol Dweck's (2012) work on growth mindset taught us to praise the process and not the pupil. I like seeing up in classrooms the adage: Mistakes Are Great; They Help You To Learn.

	Rank
Boys	
Letter of praise to parents	1
Reward by commendation	2
Praised by Year Head	3
Name on notice board	4
Mentioned in assembly	5
Praised by subject staff	6
Having work on display	7
Praised by Tutor	8
Praised by other pupils	9
Whole class praised	10
Non-verbal praise, e.g. smile	11
Girls	
Letter of praise to parents	1
Reward by commendation	2
Praised by Year Head	3
Name on notice board	4
Mentioned in assembly	5
Praised by subject staff	6
Having work on display	7
Praised by Tutor	8
Praised by other pupils	9
Whole class praised	10
Non-verbal praise, e.g. smile	11

Individual Rewards Leading to Community Rewards

I am going to make a strong argument that the fairest and most motivating incentive system leads to a community celebration.

It's good for secondary schools sometimes to learn from and build on good primary practice …

Many of my primary schools have taken on a community award called "Jar of Good Choices." Teachers display the choice they want that particular class to make that day during a particular lesson (I always say to teachers choose the behaviour that if it were eliminated you would be a much calmer person!) Children shouting out drives teachers mad, so a common choice up in the classroom is:

- "Today the choice I would like you to make is to put your hand up and wait patiently."
- Or "To listen to me when I give an instruction."
- Or "To line up calmly."

These tend to be based on what the teacher needs most so they can get on with their lesson. On spotting the choice, the teacher will say to that child, "good choice," and quickly put a square cube or marble into the jar.

Some SEND children need a lot more practice, so they are given a sand timer between them – anything from one to five minutes and maybe have a photograph of the child keeping the behaviour that they have agreed on with the teacher. As soon as the sand timer is up, in goes the reward (marble or cube).

Primary pupils often have children who are "Star of the Day," and they like to be the ones who spot the good behaviour and put their hands up and say, "Miss, Jo has just made a good choice." In secondary, we could nominate "Prefect for the Lesson," who then becomes the person who notices the good behaviours. Ensure it is on a rota basis and every student gets a turn.

If you are in a school that has house points or Dojos, you can still keep the same system, but an individual reward would earn a cube in the community jar.

Community Reward

Once the jar is full (be kind, just have a small jar) the whole class receives a reward they have previously voted on. These can range from one whole lesson to be offered for games they like, to going outside to play a game, to being the first class out to lunch, a joke-telling session, a certificate that goes home saying "I am part of an award-winning class which is able to achieve its set targets" ... or some classes voted that so many jars full went towards a cinema trip or a bowling trip – this last suggestion may be one step too far for you so forget you read it!

This system ensures that other children don't ever resent the extra rewards SEND children receive because the whole class benefits from the good choices each person makes.

Yes, house systems can really energise and excite some children. Not all, though. Some students find it hard to practise delayed gratification – the end reward is just too far away to matter. If it works for your class – that's great. However, there is no reason why you couldn't include my suggestion for a tutor group/class treat as well. It is more immediate and creates a stronger bond between the group and yourself – just saying!!

References

Dweck, C.S., 2012. *Mindset: How You Can Fulfil Your Potential* (1st ed.). London: Robinson Publishing.

Chapter 10

Creating and Implementing Consequences – Are They Fair and Feasible?

Chapter 10 examines the role of consequences in promoting positive behaviour in schools, questioning whether current disciplinary practices are fair, consistent and effective. It argues that consequences must be clearly communicated, calmly enforced and underpinned by strong teacher–pupil relationships and predictable routines. Over-reliance on punishments can lead to escalations, resentment and compliance without genuine behavioural change. The chapter explores the need for consistency across staff, visible warning systems (such as yellow cards) and pupil voice in determining what consequences are most meaningful. Special attention is given to ensuring that consequences are inclusive and supportive of SEND students. It warns against public tellings-off, which may reinforce negative self-esteem, and instead promotes restorative, private and reflective approaches. Case studies, including practice from John of Gaunt School, provide real-world examples of how consequences can be both deterrents and learning tools. Ultimately, the chapter promotes a shift from punishments towards relational, fair and preventative strategies that push young people to make better choices (Figure 10.1).

Clearly negotiated and communicated consequences are essential for positive school and classroom management by addressing immediate behaviour and asserting the school's allegiance to the rules they have created. Perhaps

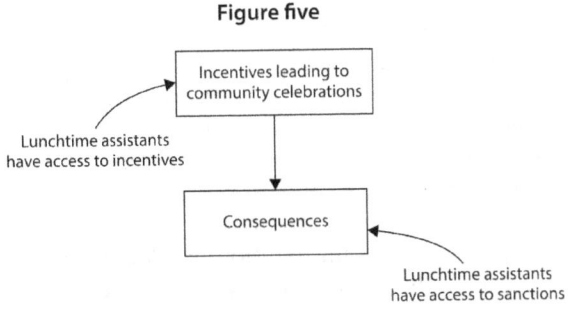

Figure 10.1 This is an excerpt from the ecosystemic model, Figure 5.1 on p. 36.

DOI: 10.4324/9781003679615-13

here is a good place, however, to draw attention to some of the worrying aspects of current practices. If we try to diminish a behaviour by mild consequences and it does not prove effective, the logical step is to try a more severe one. In other words, you can be led into an ineffective escalation of punishments rather like the postcard notice "Beatings will continue until morale improves" and as Watkins (1997) concludes "punishment leads some people to believe there are only two possible responses in our repertoire: punitive action or inaction." This is very disempowering. Consequences should support behaviour management, but strong relationships and established learning routines should be the basis of it (Dix, 2017). It is also key that we get to know our students and remain flexible, especially when supporting pupils with SEND (Cowley, 2021).

If classroom control is focused mainly on consequences, it demands a high degree of "policing" and teachers turn into monitors rather than managers of learning. Research has demonstrated that strongly authoritative or disciplinarian teachers create an atmosphere that is counterproductive to learning. Similarly for pupils, a focus on consequences may serve to generate compliance rather than self-regulated behaviour. So, the challenge is to develop an ethos where disruption is less likely to happen and for staff to focus on understanding why certain dysregulated behaviours are occurring in order to prevent them in the future.

If codes of conduct are made explicit and displayed, then broken by pupils without any consequences, the message is that rules are useless. Some pupils live chaotic lives and unconsciously yearn for firm, unshakeable boundaries. (The "No Excuses" headteacher Katherine Birbalsingh has created a school that is fascinating, thought-provoking and inspiring in its own unique, controversial way). Consequences offer clear boundaries and a safe framework. Teenagers test their power and they have learnt, particularly through the COVID-19 period, that if they nag for long enough, parents will give in. They need to know that school boundaries are secure, especially as for some young people, the only place they feel "safe" is at school. Consequences can allow a pupil to work off a "debt," which can then be forgotten about; the slate is wiped clean.

Consequences also help to create safer teachers. By this we mean that if a teacher does not have a declared set of consequences, pupils are never quite sure what consequence they will use. This leaves the system vulnerable to a teacher's inconsistency, which can be influenced by events and personal moods. The teacher is vulnerable to resorting to frequent, loud verbal "telling off." This public spectacle can result in humiliation and angry resentment, which may later produce retaliatory behaviour.

Perhaps one of the most relevant questions is "Are the consequences really deterrents to undesirable behaviour, or have they become rewards?" In one school we visited, during a Circle Time discussion about consequences, pupils were asked what happened if they misbehaved. They said that they were put out into the corridor. When asked if they minded this punishment they replied, "nah, you don't have to work and sometimes you meet your mate who's also been put out." Obviously, there is a great Corridor Club going on.

How Do I Make Consequences Work?

Young people are used to the concept of a yellow card in football, and there is psychology behind its use. When individuals are hot and angry, they are only using the amygdala part of their brain and have moved into fight or flight. Any words spoken to them will not be heard. The referee shows a yellow card, which hits a different part of the brain.

In my good primary schools, all the adults, including midday supervisors, have a yellow card. They will put it beside the child or show it to the child (if it's a midday supervisor, they will put a post-it note on with the child's name on and carry it with them). If the child repeats the same offence, it will trigger a consequence, but the adult must go through this process first. This system can only be bypassed if it is physical or verbal abuse – then no warning is needed. So, in a calm classroom, you will see a teacher or TA putting a laminated yellow warning card next to the child, pointing to the rule on the wall that they're breaking and whispering quietly, "try and make a good choice now." If they stop the behaviour, the adult must nip back and take the laminate away, saying, "good choice, carry on." However, if they break any other rule whilst the yellow card is beside them, then the consequence will be triggered. It works. For midday supervisors, they check first with other supervisors to see if they too have got the child's name on a post-it; if not, they find the child and say, "well done" and screw it up in front of them.

One of the most effective ways of checking that consequences will work is to ask the pupils which ones they dislike the most. A survey among different year groups or key stages would reveal the most unpopular and arguably, therefore, the most effective consequence for the group. Figure 10.2 shows the results of the piece of research into sanctions carried out in John of Gaunt School, using the survey sheet shown in Figure 9.3.

One of the recurrent problems teachers encounter when administering consequences is the argument over what is and is not fair or whether the pupil was the only one doing it or the first! One way round this is to use a clear, irrefutable, visible warning system so that the pupil is given the choice of changing their behaviour and so avoiding the consequence.

A Personal Note About Public Tellings-Off

This school included "being told off in front of class" as one of the consequences they used. I often hear children being told off, more loudly and more often in secondary than primary schools, although it happens they're too often outside at break time. The problems with it are several. Some young

	Rank
Boys	
Put on report — parents informed	1
Sent to Head of Year or Department Head	2
After school detention	3
Told off in front of class	4
Removed from group	5
Lunchtime detention	6
Sent out of class	7
Removal of privilege	8
Told off privately	9
Moved seats	10
Girls	
Put on report — parents informed	1
Removed from group	2
Told off in front of class	3
Sent to Head of Year or Department Head	4
After school detention	5
Sent out of class	6
Lunchtime detention	7
Removal of privilege	8
Told off privately	9
Moved seats	10

Figure 10.2 Survey showing what students thought was the most effective consequence.

people need a lot of attention, they don't get it at home and they have been constantly told off by their parents or teachers on many occasions. They have become addicted to negativity – they would rather be told off than not noticed at all. It's false self-esteem, but it gives them, temporarily, a feeling of notoriety amongst their peers. Adults telling off young people spreads the negative reputation of that young person – almost like a stain on their character. It also spreads the news that you find that child irritating... which means they will often wind that person up just to wind you up, so it becomes a self-fulfilling prophecy.

I much prefer either to use the Ignore and Distract strategy, which is to get close to the situation which is worrying you and then create a diversion, set up a game with some of the children nearby or change the conversation, so they are distracted ... Later you can talk quietly to that child on their own. You may even have a laminated warning with you and put a post-it on to show it is a warning – but not publicly.

A Personal Note from an English Teacher About the Use of Praise

In my English lessons I've found a lot of the techniques I use in Circle Time to be very effective in the more traditional lesson setup. Middle and low sets frequently resort to insult in dealing with each other. By putting down a warning card, there is a chance that you can deal with poor listening or behaviour immediately and crucially, calls for immediate improvement in behaviour in order to have the warning card removed with a quick "good choice." Although strict rules are continually applied, they are used in a very non-confrontational way. I very rarely raise my voice or give detentions for behaviour now. Another Circle Time strategy is to use pupils as models of good listening, reflection or concentration and praise it publicly and immediately. Saying "Thank you for listening to me" to the children either side of the offending child works as they get the message. Similarly, pupils reward each other by listening or picking an aspect of behaviour or work to praise. Many classes even burst into spontaneous applause now!

(Dominic Salles, English teacher)

The seminal Elton Report (1989) highlighted that: "The most effective sanction is the withdrawal of a privilege." In primary school, it is relatively easy to give children privilege time and then withdraw it a bit at a time if they fail to keep the golden rules. The challenge is to find ways of achieving the same effect at secondary school.

Here Are Some Ideas that Have Been Tried Out by Kind Teachers in Busy Secondary Schools

- Pupils can finish a few minutes early so that they leave exactly on time in order to be first in line for the lunch queue, or break. Everyone who has kept the rules during the lesson automatically has the privilege. Those who have broken a rule have been warned, then lose the privilege time in minute slots. They have to sit watching a sand timer (for Years 7 and 8) whilst their class leaves.

- If everyone keeps the rules, the class can play a five-minute game at the end of the lesson.
- In Francis Coombe School, the then Head of Year 7 used to allow all Year 7 pupils who had kept the rules all week to go home half an hour early on a Friday. The others had to stay behind until the official bell went.
- With special needs children, it is better to negotiate shorter, more achievable, specific targets with agreed rewards. Thus, minimising the need for consequences. As said earlier, a visual warning can be used with a picture of a loss of a privilege that would normally be enjoyed by that child.

References

Cowley, S., 2021. Marshmallows and traffic cops: beyond behaviourism – motivation and self-regulation in the classroom. *Impact*, 12 February. Available at: https://my.chartered.college/impact_article/marshmallows-and-traffic-cops-beyond-behaviourism-motivation-and-self-regulation-in-the-classroom/.

Dix, P., 2017. *When the Adults Change, Everything Changes.* Carmarthen: Crown House Publishing. Available at: https://www.crownhouse.co.uk/assets/look-inside/9781781352731a.pdf.

Elton, R.C., 1989. *Discipline in Schools: Report of the Committee of Enquiry Chaired by Lord Elton.* London: Her Majesty's Stationery Office. Available at: https://www.education-uk.org/documents/elton/elton1989.html.

Watkins, C.E., Jr. (ed.), 1997. *Handbook of Psychotherapy Supervision.* John Wiley & Sons, Inc.

Chapter 11
Setting Up Lunchtimes that Enhance Wellbeing

Research shows that the length and management of lunchtime breaks in secondary schools significantly impact students' wellbeing, social development and even food choices. Analysing three National Surveys over 25 years (Baines and Blatchford, 2023), the research provides insight into, among other health issues, the shortening of lunch breaks, the impact on children's social lives and the withdrawal of breaks as a response to pupils' behaviour (Figure 11.1).

Blatchford previously established that most young people enjoyed break times more than any other social activity. Baines and Blatchford (2023) sum up what our commonsense has been trying to tell us – "schools need to do more to consider how break times can be utilised to help children develop skills and explore their self-chosen interests." Schools also need to review the idea that taking away break times may indeed be harmful.

When young people are asked about the part of the school day that causes them the most anxiety, it is lunchtimes that feature most highly. They often talk in circle times about:

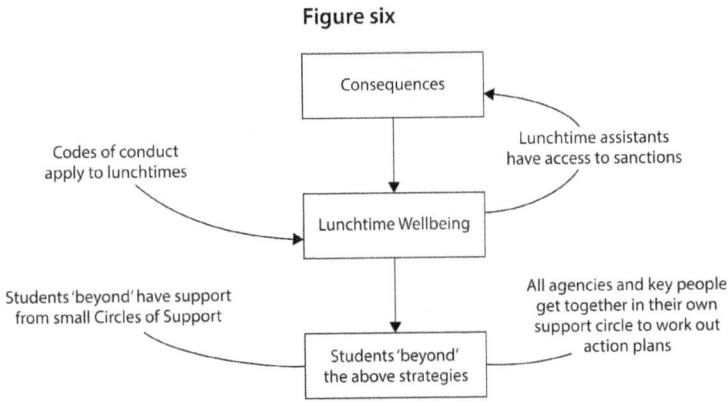

Figure 11.1 This is an excerpt from the ecosystemic model, Figure 5.1 on p. 36.

DOI: 10.4324/9781003679615-14

- Bullying and being left out, e.g. name-calling, cyberbullying and excluding others
- Bad behaviours, e.g. fighting, pushing, throwing food or other objects
- Rudeness from and to lunchtime staff, vandalism, ignoring rules
- Students breaking the rules, such as leaving the school grounds, using banned items like phones, vapes, energy drinks
- Problems with the toilets
- Problems in the canteen, e.g. too much noise, pushing in, not enough access to water or fountains don't work.

Yet how much time is spent on INSET, policy development or even inspection of lunchtimes? Schools cannot claim they have policies based on respect if they commit the disrespect of "abandoning" pupils to their fate at lunchtime without sufficient structure or support based on what the pupils want. What are the messages of the hidden curriculum in relation to lunchtime? Similarly, what happens to pupils with SEND at lunchtime?

The informal curriculum of the playground should demonstrate opportunities for the use of interpersonal skills, creativity, conflict resolution, negotiation, leadership, teamwork, empathy and self-organisation. This is the place where skills learnt throughout the day are put into practice and new skills are developed. If in the classroom, behaviour is too tightly controlled, e.g. by shouting and using sarcasm, young people feel disempowered. The danger is that they may then seize power back by bullying. For other pupils, stress is caused, not by being part of the incident, but by observing other people being hurt or misbehaving. When the experiences of lunchtime are frightening or hurtful, learning is impaired in the afternoon and it is not possible for pupils to achieve their potential.

Secondary schools need to address the importance of an enriching lunchtime policy. What are they doing to make lunchtimes emotionally and physically safe for all pupils? So many pupils are "running scared." This, in turn, could lead to pupils carrying weapons, such as knives, for their own protection, further increasing the risk of a serious incident occurring. Shortening the lunch break to the minimum just seems cowardly to me. These young people will soon be released from school and out onto the streets – they need to be given skills to cope. Worse than that, the shorter break affects their health (Seith and Speck, 2019).

Pupils are not the only ones at risk, however. Lunchtime policies also need to look at the staff. Are teachers too exhausted and stressed to teach well in the afternoon? Research highlights the vital role of taking breaks at work in enhancing both productivity and overall wellbeing. Breaks allow the adult's brain to enter a more relaxed state, which promotes creativity and the emergence of new ideas (CIPHR Ltd, 2024). Nevertheless, despite these benefits, studies reveal that one in ten adults do not take any breaks throughout their working week (Compass Group PLC, 2023). Guidance for teachers from the

NEU is that lunch breaks are not part of a teacher's directed time (National Education Union, 2025). The NEU considers any lunch break shorter than 40 minutes to be unreasonable!

Adults and young people who manage their stress levels well by looking after their bodies, including eating well and taking a break in the middle of the day, have healthier immune systems, are less likely to take time off and have greater productivity.

Calmer lunchtimes will lead to calmer, more productive afternoons.

So How Do We Go About Creating a Healthy, Positive, Calm Lunchtime Policy that Works?

- Have you offered training to your canteen and lunchtime supervisors? For me personally, it is one of the most sought-after training courses – and often involves me observing outside at lunchtime – but I don't know how typical this is across the country.
- Is there a regular review of the dining hall or canteen system and supervision? How orderly and efficient is the canteen system? Are the staff who supervise the canteen given respect by pupils? Are these staff supported by teaching staff?
- Could your outdoor spaces be divided into zoned areas for different activities? Are there clearly marked areas for ball games as well as areas for people to sit and quietly chat? I set up football policies with students in schools where the pupils often vote for and agree that there will be Football Free Fridays, and on that day, there will be rounders or cricket instead. If you're not careful, football can easily dominate the whole playground, particularly when the grass areas are out of action in winter. The hidden curriculum being – we encourage fast, active sports – you quieter, shyer, young people are not our priority.
- Can you set up lunchtime clubs run by older year groups for younger groups?
- Are there any resources or equipment available for activities? So often when I go out into playgrounds, I find that there is not enough to do and quite honestly, it's not really bad behaviour; it's bored behaviour.
- Do you need indoor supervised clubs? Some children need calm at lunchtimes. Chess clubs can be very popular; rooms of board games can be very popular, as can art, sports, music and debating – it's important not to use computers at this time. Young people need tactile, sensory activities – young people spend far too much of their time on digital devices with "brain rot" causing a whole host of negative behaviours (Yousef et al., 2025).
- Are the rules/values that the school has up inside also put up outside on durable materials? Do the lunchtime supervisors know these codes of conduct, and have they received training in dealing with pupils who present challenging behaviour?

- Do we communicate well enough with the midday supervisors? On my training courses they often complain that they are not given enough information. They understand that teachers cannot tell them personal things, but they need alerting to the fact that "this child is very fragile today," "watch out for so and so he could flare up at any minute."
- Incentives are power – we need to make sure that midday supervisors also have the power to endorse good behaviours when they see it, but this needs to be part of their training programme.
- They also need to carry warning cards as described on page 109.
- Do you have a concept of prefects or peer mediators for conflict resolution? Is there a clear policy around access to the buildings with older students on duty? Is there a clear policy about toilets? Research has shown that if these are not supervised properly, children ruin their health by training themselves not to go to the toilet during the school day due to anxieties. Many said they were scared to use the school toilets (Health Innovation Network West of England, 2025).
- Is there proactive work done to raise the status and power of midday supervisory staff? For example, they need to be invited to assemblies, and we need to share our incentive system with them so they too can contribute to house points, etc.
- Do midday staff have access to photographs in order to identify pupils who have broken the outside safety rules?
- Is there a clear policy on access to the buildings?
- Is there a policy to build a sense of community through circle approaches in tutoring or PSHE with volunteers from each small circle prepared to take the issues to senior management or the school council?

Does Your School Need to Do a Lunchtime Audit?

One way forward is to conduct an "audit" of the school, dining hall and playgrounds. Some schools get their students to colour in a map of the school buildings and grounds using green for "feels safe" and red for "I don't like it here." With this clearer picture in mind, it is then possible through your Circle Times to find out what ideas students have to make lunchtimes more engaging and rewarding. Similarly, questionnaires can be used to find out what is going on. It is, however, important to include all members of the school community so that you get a picture from many different perspectives. Everyone needs to be consulted:

- senior managers;
- teaching staff;
- non-teaching staff;
- newly qualified teachers;
- student teachers;

- lunchtime supervisory assistants;
- pupils;
- parents.

Play at lunchtime is a fundamental human right.

(Rosen, 2020)

Rosen has been working with the British Psychological Society (BPS) to highlight the importance of break times and play.

References

Baines, E. and Blatchford, P., 2023. The decline in breaktimes and lunchtimes in primary and secondary schools in England: results from three national surveys spanning 25 years. *British Educational Research Journal*, 49(5), pp. 925–946. https://doi.org/10.1002/berj.3874.

CIPHR Ltd, 2024. The importance of regular breaks at work. *CIPHR Blog*, 16 September. Available at: https://www.ciphr.com/blog/regular-breaks-at-work.

Compass Group PLC, 2023. UK lunch break now averages 33 minutes, with nearly half of workers eating lunch alone. *Compass Group*, 19 June. Available at: https://www.compass-group.co.uk/media/news/uk-lunch-break-now-averages-33-minutes-with-nearly-half-of-workers-eating-lunch-alone/.

Health Innovation Network West of England, 2025. Desperate to go: young people struggling to access toilets at school. *Health Innovation West of England*, 4 February. Available at: https://www.healthinnowest.net/news/desperate-to-go-young-people-struggling-to-access-toilets-at-school/.

National Education Union, 2025. *Teachers' Working Time, Workload Bargaining Toolkit*. National Education Union, 8 May. Available at: https://neu.org.uk/advice/your-rights-work/teachers-workload-and-working-hours/workload-bargaining-toolkit/teachers-working-time.

Rosen, M., 2020. Play is a fundamental human right – Michael Rosen. *ITV News*, 10 January. Available at: https://www.itv.com/news/2020-01-10/play-is-a-fundamental-human-right-michael-rosen.

Seith, E. and Speck, D., 2019. How do shorter lunchtimes affect student wellbeing? *Tes Magazine*, 14 June. Available at: https://www.tes.com/magazine/news/general/how-do-shorter-lunchtimes-affect-student-wellbeing.

Yousef, A.M.F., Alshamy, A., Tlili, A., Metwally, A.H.S. and Krok, D., 2025. Demystifying the new dilemma of brain rot in the digital era: a review. *Brain Sciences*, 15(3), p. 283. https://doi.org/10.3390/brainsci15030283.

Chapter 12

Supporting Dysregulated Pupils

Dahal (2017) found that disaffected students were more likely to re-engage when they felt supported and genuinely listened to. The circle approach promotes active listening by creating a structured, respectful space where every voice is heard (Figure 12.1).

If you have ever had the opportunity to shadow a pupil in a secondary school, you will have discovered that pupils behave in different ways with different teachers. Simply labelling behaviour as "disruptive" is a value judgement that overlooks the relational and often unmet needs driving it.

Research into Social, Emotional and Mental Health needs (SEMH) emphasises the importance of understanding behaviour as a form of communication (Children and Young People's Mental Health Coalition, 2023; Education Endowment Foundation, 2019). There is a critical distinction between low-level disruption and behaviours linked to trauma, neurodiversity or mental health struggles. Without a clear understanding of these causes, pupils risk being misunderstood, mislabelled or unfairly punished, exacerbating their disengagement from school.

Positive relationships between teachers and students can significantly impact classroom behaviour. When teachers understand their students well, they are better positioned to identify the underlying causes of disruptive behaviour. In secondary schools, where students interact with multiple staff members, effective communication and collaboration amongst colleagues is crucial for

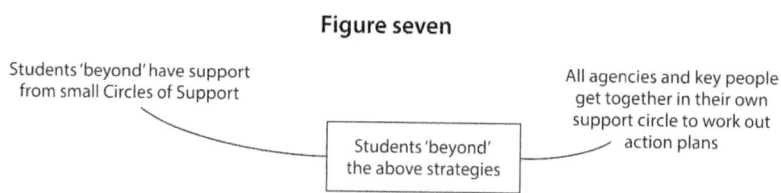

Figure 12.1 This is an excerpt from the ecosystemic model, Figure 5.1 on p. 36.

sharing insights and maintaining a consistent approach to behaviour support (Education Endowment Foundation, 2019).

Trauma-informed and relational approaches now dominate guidance on supporting dysregulated behaviour. Consistently, evidence shows that around 50% of the population have experienced at least one traumatic or stressful event in childhood (National Education Union, 2024). These adverse childhood experiences (ACEs) can lead to emotional dysregulation, disrupted nervous, hormonal and immune development, learning difficulties and even illness if support is lacking (National Education Union, 2024). Trauma-informed approaches help combat these issues by allowing young people to feel safe, seen and soothed in school environments, which is the crucial first step before they can be expected to regulate emotions or engage in learning (Bomber, 2020; Treisman, 2021).

Digital pressures and social media now also contribute significantly to emotional dysregulation. Research links "problematic internet use" with social anxiety, depression, attention deficit and hyperactivity disorders, sleep disturbances, dysfunctional parent–adolescent relationships and other challenges (Gioia, Rega and Boursier, 2021). Moreover, social media provides a new space for bullying, unkind behaviour and inappropriate content. It is therefore vital that schools adopt a whole-school approach to behaviour that is communication-based and inclusive.

In fact, without a whole-school approach that promotes a positive school environment, it becomes extremely difficult to identify pupils with social, emotional and mental health needs. It is by devising and implementing systems that cater for the physical, emotional, social and learning needs of the majority that the minority who have more specific needs can be identified. A school's culture and values are manifested through the behaviour of all its members.

We define dysregulated pupils as those requiring more support than the strategies outlined so far in the Quality Circle Time model. They are the ones who have been offered yet failed to respond to regular empathic listening opportunities and/or participation in regular class or tutor circle approaches. So, before we can identify them, we must be sure first that they:

- have a clear understanding of the codes of conduct expected by the school
- have received regular incentives for efforts and perseverance;
- have achieved moments of success acknowledged by their peers
- know the safe boundaries of a consequence system that uses the visual warning system;
- are aware of the negotiation taking place between the school and their parents.

Yet, despite all these measures, the pupil continues to adhere to dysregulated, unhappy or withdrawn behaviour.

The One Who Most Needs Us Is the One Who Most Repels Us

Pupils who have become trapped in patterns of negative interaction with teachers and peers exhibit behaviour consistent with their worldview. The behaviour we, as teachers, find so challenging serves the purpose of keeping the pupil's inner world "safe." Often life has disempowered these young people, adults have let them down and many have been subjected to various arbitrary, confusing or outright abusive experiences. They become locked into a circle of negative self-esteem (Figure 12.2) and develop behaviours designed

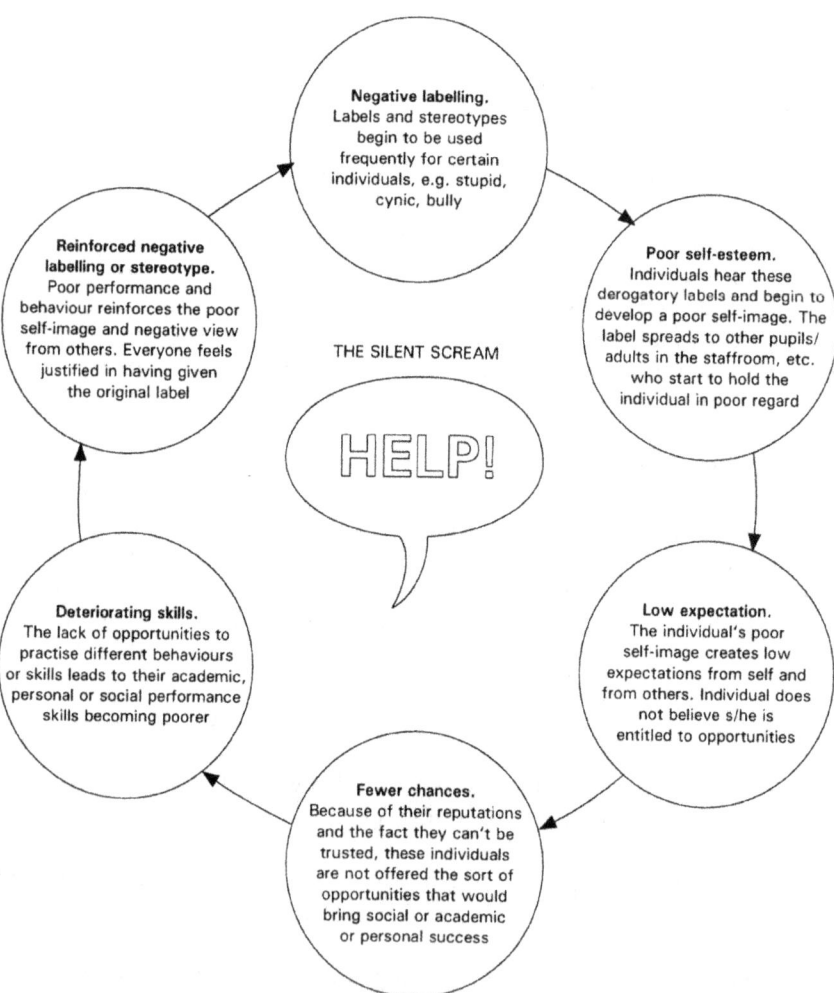

Figure 12.2 The vicious circle of lower self-esteem.

to protect and release their feelings in order to draw attention to their level of distress or anxiety. If other people fail to see beyond the behaviour and do not offer them unconditional warmth and acceptance of the unique and good person they are meant to be (Rogers, 1959) then they resort to negative behaviours as a way of receiving much-craved-for attention. Hostile attention is better than no attention.

The range of behaviours these young people exhibit is designed to hurt, anger or confuse people who come near them, thereby precluding any chance of their entering into a warm, reciprocal relationship with that person. Their behaviour keeps people at bay so, from their point of view, getting told off regularly means that at least they are the centre of someone's existence without being vulnerable to the hurt which may be incurred if they become involved in a positive relationship with them. Repetition of these behaviours then unconsciously and perversely means that they can regain a level of control over their lives and reduce levels of "unsafety."

To put it simply, if a young person with very low self-esteem is responded to in a warm and positive way, it can be a frightening experience.

It challenges the person to take on a more positive view of themselves and consider the possibility of involving themself in a relationship with another person. They then have to trust that this other person will sustain and nurture the positive experience. Trust is a risk-laden response. It is much safer to remain in control over your own world by not allowing yourself to enter into relationships. By refusing to change, the person refuses to hope and in this way remains in control. They may have a lot invested in staying negative.

Identifying and Supporting Dysregulated Pupils – Can Be Hurtful for You Too

I am sure that all teachers have at some time experienced aggressive and dismissive behaviours from pupils when they tried so hard to praise or appreciate them. The young person's work that you have just praised may well be immediately screwed up or defaced, the certificate of praise torn or thrown away. We have known the work to hit one wall and the pencil another as the chair hits the floor! When pupils give aggressive, abusive and sometimes physically dangerous responses in the teacher–pupil relationship, the temptation is to give up on the whole notion of self-esteem. The truth is that people with low self-esteem are desperately difficult to reach. Success is hugely threatening to them so the pupils who most need us are most likely to repel us. (Under these circumstances, even the kindest and most positive adults find it extremely difficult to carry on offering a warm, empathic relationship. Think about it.) How many times have I walked into the staffroom as a teacher and said, "He's driving me mad," and someone looks up and says, "He was lovely for me last week." A case of a low self-esteem teacher grabbing a quick bit of self-esteem and putting it in their own emotional purse!

Support for Adults

Figure 5.1 has an arrow from dysregulated pupils back up to the listening systems because any member of staff who is dealing with these pupils needs the support of colleagues. They need a staff Circle Time to discuss issues and strategies for coping with challenging behaviour. They might also benefit from one-to-one peer support from a peer mentor who will listen effectively and provide a debrief session from time to time. In other contexts where adults deal with dysregulated behaviour such as mental aftercare, adults with learning disabilities or disadvantaged groups needing counselling, supervision is provided. Yet schools expect staff to cope with difficult and even abusive situations with no form of formalised support. The mental health of the staff has never been a priority in education. Some schools, like Carr Manor (pages 18–19) have in place a safeguarding, inclusion and SEND team, whose remit is either to support and mentor the teacher seeking help or to become involved themselves in an intervention with the child.

Go Deeper – You Superhero – Tiny, Achievable, Tickable Targets (TATTs) May Help

The child who has embarrassed and hurt you often comes from a hugely unhappy situation. Let's stop and think about it? This is where you kind teachers are "superheroes." They need you not to give up on them. They need you to carry on creating moments of success and noticing them loudly. They need to trust they can't destroy you and that your love (it is a form of love) is bigger than negativity. What do you need ... apart from a hip flask and some Valium? You need to remember there is a life outside teaching and you need your own Personal Care Plan (page ...).

How can we guarantee daily success if the pupil with low self-esteem is frightened to face its implications? Individually agreed contracts can be drawn up that enable pupils to set realistic goals and be rewarded for small successes. The tutor, SEND coordinator and/or behavioural support staff meet with the pupil to negotiate and agree targets, which are within the pupil's capability. A motivational reward system is also negotiated with the pupil, whilst the key staff devise a method of keeping track of success throughout the school day. These systems require considerable liaison and agreement across curriculum areas in a secondary school, but where they are successfully implemented as part of a whole-school approach, they are effective in creating and maintaining a positive school environment (Mana Education, 2024).

One very valuable intervention is to create a Circle of Support (Newton and Wilson, 2005; Mosley, 2026). This is a body of knowledge in its own right and deserves exploring properly. Very briefly, in my version of the model as opposed to the Circle of Friends model, it's a group for all ages, maybe might have four dysregulated pupils and then you might have six or seven students who volunteered to be supportive and helpful. Sometimes their peers volunteer, which is great – it's always good too if two sixth formers offer to attend (because they want to study psychology in the future) as they can be my co-workers and we can debrief together. At the end of each session, they will receive positive feedback from their peers and my "co-workers" for the social and emotional skills they have been using within the group. Specific, clear praise can lead to a self-fulfilling prophecy, thus allowing for a more positive experience of higher self-esteem (Figure 12.3).

I worked with a Head of Year, Kath Shaw, at St Laurence School to document a case study of setting up and running a peer support group for helping dysregulated pupils (then described as disruptive and withdrawn) to improve their self-concept by developing more agency and responsibility for themselves (Shaw, 1991).

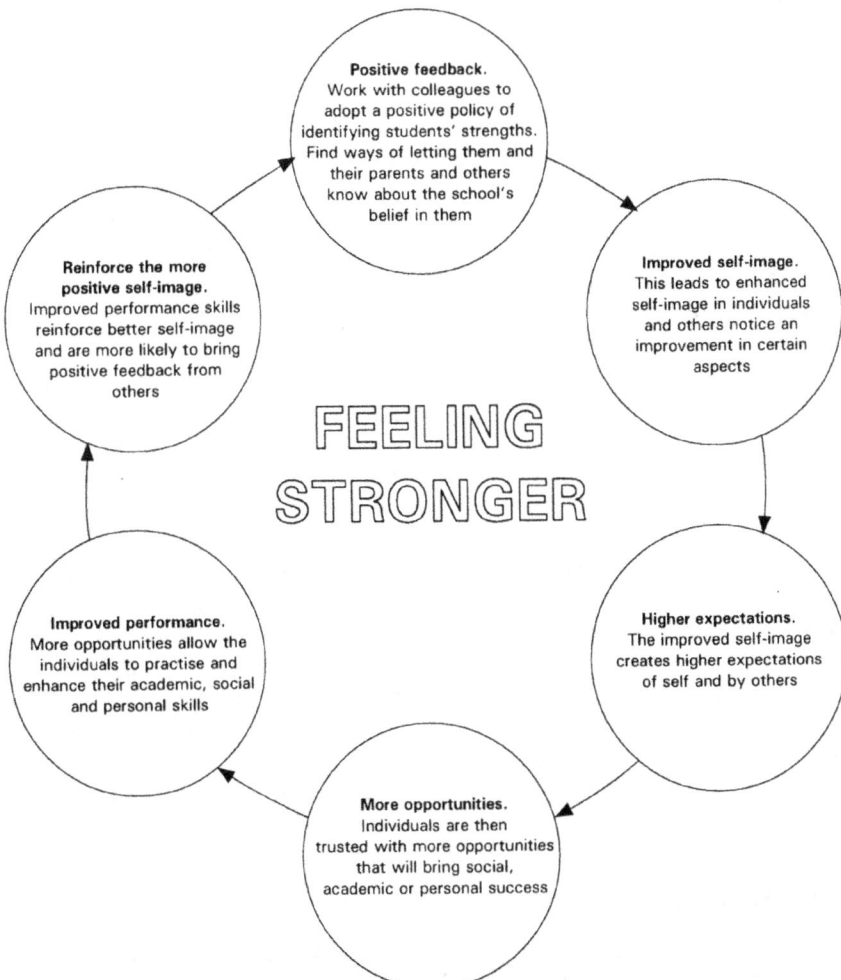

Figure 12.3 Positive circle of higher self-esteem.

Before the group could be set up, it was necessary to identify the behaviours that caused teachers the greatest anxiety. A wide range of teachers from the school were asked to provide a brief written statement describing, as accurately as possible, the pupil behaviours they found most disturbing. This resulted in a list of behaviours that naturally fell under three headings:

- Behaviour characterised by lack of self-control: These behaviours were the most usual cause of anxiety. They involved activities such as shouting out, talking whilst the teacher is talking and stopping other pupils from working.
- Hostile behaviour: These behaviours were not as frequently mentioned but tended to be more pronounced in the upper school.
- Withdrawn behaviour: These behaviours tended to be overlooked and the teacher's attention had to be deliberately drawn to these pupils in order to produce a relevant list.

(Appendix D shows a full list of the behaviours identified by the staff and could be used in your school – although you might want to first survey your teachers' opinions to check the headings I use accurately reflect their experiences.)

The next task was to identify pupils in Years 7 and 8 who were most frequently and similarly assessed by all their teachers as experiencing these behaviours and to interview them individually to find out if they found some of their school situations difficult and would like the opportunity to change their behaviour. The offer of the peer support group was taken up by 11 out of 13 pupils.

The group met weekly for one hour. Each circle meeting followed the same four-part structure of discussion, warm-up, action and reflection. The content for discussion arose from the pupils' situations and current experiences and many of the issues were explored using a variety of role-play techniques. Each student was offered ten minutes' individual time (Chat Time) after the circle to negotiate a contract of tiny achievable targets which they would take to their other subject lessons. Written and verbal evaluations from all the pupils, teachers and parents who took part in this educational programme testify to the improvements in these pupils' behaviour and relationships. They were helped to break out of the stereotyped image of the troublemaker and see themselves as individuals capable of exploring and making changes in their lives. The circle was always run by two "co-workers," so they support each other. One experienced circle facilitator and one Head of Year, key teacher or teaching assistant can make a good team and in this way you can help build teachers' group work skills.

Reflection Circles for Staff

This recommendation keeps cropping up in this book. It is just not possible to run circles for dysregulated pupils and not have your own Circle of Support at some stage for yourself (Shohet and Shohet, 2020).

References

Bomber, L.M., 2020. *Know Me to Teach Me: Differentiated Discipline for Those Recovering from Adverse Childhood Experiences.* London: Worth Publishing Ltd.

Children and Young People's Mental Health Coalition, 2023. *Behaviour and Mental Health in Schools: Full Report.* London: Children and Young People's Mental Health Coalition. Available at: https://cypmhc.org.uk/wp-content/uploads/2023/06/Behaviour-and-Mental-Health-in-Schools-Full-Report.pdf.

Dahal, H.R., 2017. Re-engaging disaffected KS4 students within the United Kingdom. Presented at the International Conference on Literature, History, Humanities and Interdisciplinary Studies (LHHISS-17), Bangkok, Thailand, 11–12 July. Available at: https://www.eares.org/siteadmin/upload/ED0717030.pdf.

Department for Education, 2024. *Behaviour in Schools: Advice for Headteachers and School Staff,* 19 February. Available at: https://assets.publishing.service.gov.uk/media/65ce3721e1bdec001a3221fe/Behaviour_in_schools_-_advice_for_headteachers_and_school_staff_Feb_2024.pdf.

Education Endowment Foundation, 2019. *Improving Behaviour in Schools: Guidance Report.* London: Education Endowment Foundation. Available at: https://d2tic4wvo1iusb.cloudfront.net/production/eef-guidance-reports/behaviour/EEF_Improving_behaviour_in_schools_Report.pdf.

Gioia, F., Rega, V. and Boursier, V., 2021. Problematic internet use and emotional dysregulation among young people: a literature review. *Clinical Neuropsychiatry,* 18(1), pp. 41–54.

Mana Education, 2024. The role of positive reinforcement. Available at: https://www.manaeducation.co.uk/blog/teaching-resources/blog-series--mastering-classroom-behaviour---behavioural-management/the-role-of-positive-reinforcement.

Mosley, J., 2026. *Early Intervention Through Circles of Support.* London: Routledge.

National Education Union, 2024. *What Is a Trauma-informed Approach and Practice?* [pdf]. London: National Education Union. Available at: https://neu.org.uk/sites/default/files/2024-08/NEU3553%20What%20is%20trauma-informed%20approach%20and%20practice%20v2.pdf.

Newton, C. and Wilson, D., 2005. *Creating Circles of Friends: A Peer Support and Inclusion Workbook* (Repr. A4 ed.). Nottingham: Inclusive Solutions.

Rogers, C.R., 1959. A theory of therapy, personality, and interpersonal relationships as developed in the client-centered framework. In: S. Koch (ed.) *Psychology: A Study of a Science, Vol. 3. Formulations of the Person and the Social Context.* New York: McGraw-Hill, pp. 184–256.

Shaw, K., 1991. Setting up peer support groups: One school's INSET response to the Elton report. *Pastoral Care in Education,* 9(4), pp. 13–17. https://doi.org/10.1080/02643949109470763.

Shohet, R. and Shohet, J., 2020. *In Love with Supervision: Creating Transformative Conversations.* Monmouth: PCCS Books.

Treisman, K., 2021. *Trauma-Informed Organizations: A Ready-to-Use Resource for Trauma, Adversity, and Culturally Informed, Infused and Responsive Systems.* London: Jessica Kingsley Publishers.

Chapter 13

The Containment Stage or How Do We Cope When Nothing Works?

"Containment" is implemented when nothing else works. At this stage, we may be dealing with pupils who may have deep psychological, social and emotional problems. There can be within them a well of violence or self-destructive behaviour that only needs the smallest trigger or even a misplaced look. They are often at the very end of the road in mainstream education, and alternative provision is being considered for this pupil as the school has provided everything it can to help. You would need to be sure that you, as a school, could genuinely agree that this pupil:

- has been offered at least one designated, respectful, valuing relationship;
- knew one specific person was his/her advocate working on his/her behalf;
- had a clearly explained understanding of the codes of conduct and received lots of positive feedback through tiny targets linked to incentives;
- had been invited to support circles but rejected the help that was offered.

We would also need to know that the school liaison staff have visited his/her home (social worker, education welfare officer or health visitor) and there have been case conferences with the specialised agencies. Only then can you say you've reached the last stage in our model.

The reality of teaching is that it is not possible for all mainstream schools to meet the needs of every pupil, and by this stage it is no longer acceptable to keep teachers and other pupils vulnerable to this level of disruption. It has become more important to consider how to "contain" the dysregulated pupil so that the class is not endangered by the threat of eruption.

Some schools have a sanctuary or "time-out" zone, monitored by key people where the pupil is kept "off timetable" until a place can be obtained at the Pupil Referral Unit or equivalent. If this is not possible, a "help" system can be used. This involves "training" a few pupils in each class to take a prearranged signal, such as a coloured card, to the office or staffroom. The timetable is arranged so that one senior member of staff is always available and on "help duty" so that he or she can be contacted in the event of an emergency. This member of staff would be informed of the need for help in a particular room

DOI: 10.4324/9781003679615-16

with a particular member of staff and would go to remove the pupil from the situation. The teacher's sanity is now of more importance than this pupil's education and it is imperative that we keep the situation in perspective.

Perhaps the most important thing when dealing with extremely challenging pupils is to support the staff with staff circle meetings to discuss feelings and strategies. Often teachers become isolated, feeling that they are the only ones who cannot handle this particular pupil. A "safe" forum for discussing what does and does not help in the situation can be very therapeutic for the teacher, and "pooled" ideas or strategies help everyone who has to face difficult and highly disruptive behaviour on a daily basis.

In Summary

This model suggests a range of proactive strategies including regular circle times, behavioural incentives and consequences, negotiated contracts and TATTs, and access to specialised support teams.

If these systems are put in place as a long-term strategic policy starting with Year 7, the number of pupils needing specialist SEMH support would be greatly reduced. It is also likely that, as a result, there would be a happier school ethos, less absence and far fewer fixed-term exclusions in the later years (Shaw, 2019).

A Personal Note

When I was teaching full time from 1972 onwards, there were far more therapeutic community schools (day and boarding) and alternative provision for excluded SEMH pupils. Despite the dramatic rise and recording of adolescent mental health problems, many of these schools have closed. If teachers had the energy and the time, we would all be rising up and lobbying the government for more provision. A school society is only as successful as its weakest member.

Reference

Shaw, T., 2019. You want to cut exclusions AND maintain staff morale? *Tes Magazine*, 8 November. Available at: https://www.tes.com/magazine/archive/you-want-cut-exclusions-and-maintain-staff-morale.

Chapter 14

Achieving the Biggest Impact with Circle Time

Common Arguments as to Why Teachers Can't Set It Up

- "We haven't got the time."
- Unless senior management takes on this whole approach, it's very hard for individual teachers to try out the circle approach. However, it's only by being brave and showing people that you are very keen to support it that eventually these small movements lead to larger revolutions. When I first started teaching, nobody was using circles in secondary schools, making sure that I always survey the children's responses after half term or a term was one way of collecting evidence, which I then distributed to the Heads of Year (Mosley, 1988). Encouraging those participants to go to School Council or to senior managers is another.

  The research evidence throughout the book points to the fact that the circle approaches create a much calmer, positive ethos. Wouldn't it be better, given the fact that 80% of teacher time can be lost through disruption, if we could use that time instead to work on circles?
- Involve others with your new determination. Sometimes your students have a one-to-one support helper, or the SENCO would like to work as a co-worker. In the past, I have gone to the sixth form and invited any students who were intending to study to become a teacher, social worker or psychologist, and asked for them to be released to work as co-workers. All they ask for is that you find them ten minutes sometime after to debrief and listen to their observations.

Having now unravelled the whole model, we need to move on to look at the role of Circle Time itself and how to run successful circles.

PSHE initiatives in secondary schools have regularly arrived, enjoyed a season of popularity and disappeared. Often this is because of new curriculum pressures, or because teachers lose sight of the reasons for doing it. Circle Time requires a degree of classroom re-organisation, which can prove daunting in the stresses of school life. One way of ensuring that it continues to happen is to involve the pupils in the physical organisation of the room. If it

DOI: 10.4324/9781003679615-17

is treated like a military exercise with numbers under the desks and a master plan on the wall, pupils will join in the work involved in order to get the Circle Time that they enjoy. You, the classroom practitioner, may well feel that this five minutes at the beginning and end of each lesson is wasted time. We would encourage you to run a series of six or seven weeks, review how much time is redeemed by pupils being involved in the lesson, "on task" and not disrupting, then decide whether it is worth the time investment.

What are the Ground Rules That Make Circle Time Safe?

The key to Circle Time working is to establish ground rules in a fun, easy way throughout the first few sessions – rather than running through a list of them – which won't engage their attention.

1. We do not name anyone in a negative way.

Young people can say positive things to each other, but when they have something negative they want to say, they cannot use the name of that child or teacher.
   They have to learn to say:

"Some people call me and my family names ..."
"Somebody takes my lunch ..."
"Some people never let me join in the lunchtime football ..."
"Some person shouts at me in the classroom ..."

It is important to remind them that anything too personal, such as about their family or anything else that they don't want to bring up in the circle, can be discussed in your second listening system, Chat Time (see pages 93–94)

2. Everyone has the right to be heard.

Everyone has the right not to be interrupted when it is their turn to speak, usually in a round (Step 2). We hand around a speaking object like a wooden egg. They only use this when they are completing a sentence stem e.g. "I get angry when ..." However, some children hold the egg and natter on for ages, which turns everyone else off! The teacher has the right to go across the circle, touch the egg and say, "I'm very sorry to interrupt you, it was very interesting, but I did explain that we only had a short sentence each."

3. Everyone has a right to pass.

There can be a problem with this ground rule. Some children are "power brokers." If they say "Pass", then other children copy them and then suddenly most of the circle have said pass. This can happen in the initial circles. I used to get round this by giving every child a card the week before with the sentence stem on which they then completed and put their name to it, and then I gave them out at the next circle so no one could say pass. When children do say pass, they must always be given another opportunity at the end to speak.

4. You are in a relentlessly positive mood.

It's vital that you are in a positive mood because you need to highlight the good behaviours that you have seen in the circle. I set up a praise agenda with Year 7s; as the circle continues, I will be saying "Thank you for the way you are looking at me when I am talking"; "I like the way you listen without interrupting"; "That was a very thoughtful thing to say"; "What a really calm speaking voice you're using"; "I can see you are really concentrating." In other words, I have identified the Five Skills. In the younger classes, you can actually name the skills and after every game that you introduce at the Step 1 stage, you can ask them "What skills were you using just now?" Having this skills agenda in my head enables me to look out for positive examples. If a child is rocking on their chair, don't look directly at that child but praise either side of that child: "I like your stillness when you are listening"; "Your body looks as though it's really concentrating" – it's called proximity praise and it really works!

Also, being positive means that you use the "Ignore and Distract" strategy. If your praise is not working then do another Step 1, which is a game, as games are young people's favourite activity, and you can go into the game with gusto without having told any child off.

When teachers are upbeat, enthusiastic and positive in their approach, there is a different atmosphere in the room.

5. Evaluate your Circle Times regularly with the group.

Perhaps use an ending round of "The most boring/interesting activity in this group for me was …" Check with the group if there are any school systems that are going wrong that have cropped up in the circle and they need to go to school council with it.

The Student "Beyond" CircleTime

There are some students who may just not be able to be part of a group yet. They may be making progress in other areas but not in a group. You might play games brilliantly, you might have been incredibly positive as above, but there is still this unhappy child who is disrupting your circle. Do not talk about their behaviour within the group, just ask the child for a quiet Chat Time. When you and the child have ten minutes together, then explain that it is not acceptable that they ruin the fun for everyone else. They can have a choice – you can keep an empty chair in the circle for them and they can sit outside the circle doing some self-chosen work as long as they don't disrupt and then come back into the circle when they are ready. The other option is that they can choose to be part of a Circle of Support and then be with a different teacher when their own class has Circle Time. Whatever they choose needs to be written up as an agreement between the two of you.

Join In and Have Fun

I have said this elsewhere – but honestly, a good laugh together in a fun game is emotionally and physiologically great for you all. The research is overwhelming (Lyle, 2023).

References

Lyle, L., 2023. Impact of laughter on health, happiness and wellbeing. In: S. Chetri, T. Dutta, M.K. Mandal and P. Patnaik (eds.) *Understanding Happiness*. Singapore: Springer. https://doi.org/10.1007/978-981-99-3493-5_8.

Mosley, J., 1988. Some Implications arising from a small scale study of a circle-based programmeinitiated for the tutorial period. *Pastoral Care in Education*, 6(2), pp. 10–16.

Part III
Activities, Games and Resources

Chapter 15

The Five Step Structure of Quality Circle Time

Sometimes it is hard to read something on a page and actually envisage it in action. I often have to demonstrate Circle Time with classes of students and a circle of adult observers on the outside. Seeing is believing. The following quote came from a headteacher sitting with her staff observing the Five Step Circle Time with a Year 8 group in February 2025, who had not done Circle Time since primary school.

> Everyone felt it was something special and the pupils ability to share, listen, express and share was a joy to watch. What really struck me was how speaking and communicating collaboratively was not an age-related experience. People think it is something for the realm of younger pupils … The most impactful thing I observed was how older pupils quickly felt safe, maturely and sensitively approached topics that interested them and listened to each other. Their realisation that they could resolve matters that otherwise have proven challenging was quite moving. Most of all, to feel safe to be they actual age they are and not the age that society and unintentionally we as educators expect them to be.
> (Cecile Halliday, Head Northwood College for Girls London)

Northwood College for Girls has been named Independent School of the Year for Diversity, Equality, Inclusion and Justice by the Independent School of the Year Awards 2024 and is now consequently setting up a Listening Project in the school (Figure 15.1).

Step 1 – Meeting Up for Team Fun

This first step aims to bring everyone together and always involves the leader in introducing an opening game which provides a sense of fun and enjoyment. The idea is they see that meeting up with other people creates a good atmosphere. It allows the group to get rid of any tension and often, because they are

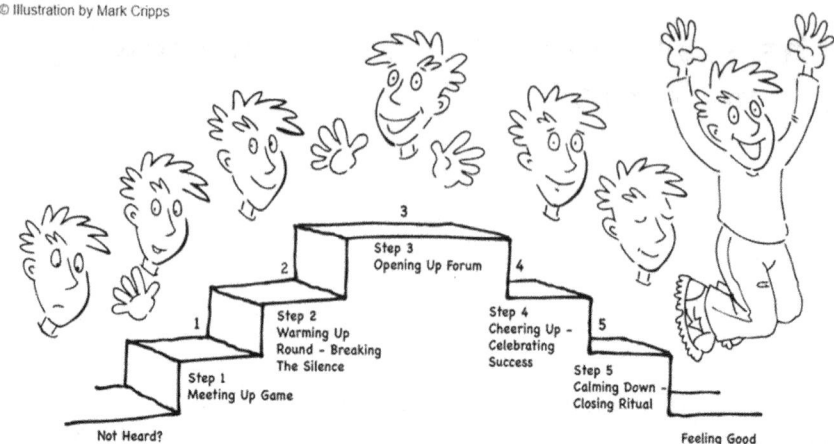

Jenny Mosley's 5 Steps to Quality Circle Time

Figure 15.1 Jenny Mosley's five steps to quality circle time.

very motivated, it reinforces learning skills, values and codes of conduct due to cooperative participation.

Step 2 – Warming Up to Speaking

This step involves a round which helps everyone warm up to the idea of speaking aloud. Choose a stem sentence and then the wooden egg is passed around and each person finishes the sentence "I …" Everyone has the right to pass. If there were any passes the teacher at the end says "Would anyone like a second chance now to speak?" They can then thumbs up if they would like the egg. Often students get ideas from their peers so now want to contribute.

In the Circle Time Sessions further in the book, some teachers use an activity called "Silent Statements" where a teacher reads out a statement and if the student agrees they have to cross the circle and swap seats. I have called this a Step 2 because the statements can often get them to reflect on issues that matter to them, thus warming them up to Step 3.

Step 3 – Opening Up Issues that Matter to Us

The idea of this step is to open up some of the issues or emotions that may have been touched on in the previous round. The round would have been helpful in enabling people to realise what they have in common with others; but this step is for those people who are feeling they need some help to face an emotion or issue. So, once the speaking round has finished, the facilitator then addresses everyone.

One way forward a facilitator can choose is to ask the class:

"Is there anyone here who would like some help from us with a feeling, challenge or worry?"

"If you would like some help with something, this is how I would like you to say it 'I need help because I …'"

Several young people will thumbs up at this point to give an idea. For example, someone might say:

"I need help because I lose my temper too quickly."

Facilitator to the rest of the class:

"If you would like to offer some helpful suggestion, this is how I would like you to frame it. Put your thumb up and wait to be chosen and say 'Would it help if …'"

The circle can then thumbs up if they have an idea to help. When the student who is asking for help chooses someone, the rest of the class puts their thumbs down to create a calmer atmosphere.
Student to focus student:

"Would it help if you counted to 10 before you flip out?"

Focus student:

"I can't get past three but thank you!!" (encourage thank yous)

Student to focus student:

"Would it help if you walked away from those who are annoying you?"

Focus student:

"No, they keep following me around."

Student to focus student:

"Would it help if you told the adult on duty?"

Focus student:

"No, they keep telling me to ignore it and I can't."

In this situation it's clear that our suggestions aren't going to help. Therefore, the facilitator might say:

"Can anyone here suggest a 'Would it help if I'?"

Student to focus student:

"Would it help if I stopped calling you names?"

Focus student:

"Thank you, that would help a lot."

The above is a situation that is genuinely true and has played out in lots of classrooms. Sometimes the example is not as complex as this. I have heard sixth formers say:

"I get nervous with my exams."

Student to focus student:

"Would it help if you took some deep, calm breaths before you started the exam?"
"Would it help if you had a good breakfast before you went into the exam room?"
"Would it help if you made revision cards and then got us to test you on them?"
"Would it help if I told you how my strategy works for me?"

Nobody forces their advice on anyone. The person asking for help can give their response, e.g.

"I have never thought of that, it's a great idea" or "That wouldn't work for me because …"

The facilitator needs to occasionally say to the focus child, "Would you like to stop now?" or "Tell me when you want to stop?"

At the end of Step 3, the focus student needs to be encouraged to say

"I would like to thank everyone for their ideas. The idea I am most drawn to is …"

A Personal Note

If you are using this circle approach for an exploration of a PSHE topic, then Step 3 would involve you directing them to the topic that they have just learnt about to see if any of them have worries or issues about that topic. So, the I need helps might go along the lines of …

"I need help to understand why ..."
"I need help to know how to get out of a situation when my friends are pressuring me."
"I need to know what to do when something inappropriate comes up online."

It might be that there was some information that they didn't understand and they want further explanation.

Step 4 – Celebrating Positivity, Success and Fun

The only proviso of this is that students cannot pick their best friend to praise.
Often the facilitator can instigate this by saying something along the lines of ...

"Please remember we can only chose a person who is not in your close friendship group."
"Who in this class team are you pleased with because they have contributed much more than they normally do ..."
"Who have you noticed is much calmer now than they used to be?"

As Step 4 is about celebrating each other and enjoying each other's company, you could choose to bring in a Step 1 Fun Game. We will call it Step 4 because it is near the end of Circle Time, and you need that sense of togetherness that comes with fun. I love a parachute, and it doesn't matter what age students are from Year 7 to sixth-form; they all love it.

Step 5 – Calming Down, Moving into Mindfulness

Whilst it's wonderful to have the support, warmth and positivity that come from being part of a team – in life it is important to be developing our own inner peace. The simplicity of breathing calmly is always welcomed by circles of young people. You are returning the students to themselves, their own imagination and resilience.

Visualisation techniques help us to understand the power of our own imaginations to create a feeling of happiness and wellbeing. Below is a typical visualisation which I often use in secondary schools. However, some children have never practised mindfulness before: their life has been turbulent and noisy, and they can be afraid to shut their eyes in case the world has changed when they open them. I often give them the choice of an eye mask if they would prefer.

Regarding Step 5, often there is not enough time – it's fine if you have an hour's PSHE – it's not fine if you just have a 30-minute tutorial. Mindfulness, however, is so important. I would encourage you to look at the curriculum closely to see where you can teach the children how to enjoy it. I have written some calming visualisations on pages 237 onwards.

Find your most comfortable position on your chair, with feet slightly apart so that you are balanced. Put your right hand down on the base of your tummy and your left hand on top of it.

The first image you have is that there is a gentle sun on your shoulders which is helping them to slope down, so all your worries slide off. Now close your mouth, close your eyes and keep your ears open; gently breathe in through your nose ... 1 ... 2 ... 3 ... you can feel your hands going forward with your breath.

Slowly let the air go out of your mouth ... 1... 2 ... 3 ... you can feel your hands come back in – and give your stomach a little press to get rid of the last little bit of old air.

The secret to staying calm is to breathe in and out to the same beat; as you breathe in, imagine you are breathing in oxygen and pure energy to the count of 3.

As you breathe out, let go of the old hot carbon dioxide and toxins –

Imagine you are sitting on a beautiful beach in a very comfortable chair; the sun is warm but there is a little salty tangy breeze. You look down at your bare feet and realize that they are not in white sand, they are not in pebbles – They are in the most amazing beach of tiny diamonds. It is the only diamond beach in the whole world. They glitter and sparkle and radiate energy.

Then (leader slowly inclines the rain-stick), you can hear the wave come up onto the diamond beach and as the sea moves forward, you can hear the diamonds shift and shuffle. The wave returns and as it does, the sun's rays hit the white frilly waves of the sea and it creates millions of tiny rainbows all over the beach. Now the beach looks alive. It is dancing with colour and shapes and it is the most beautiful, magical place you have ever seen.

However, you know that you need to come back into the class; so, to come back in safely, here comes your own special Memory Bubble – it stops in front of your face. Put the picture of yourself sitting on the chair with your feet in diamonds and a huge smile on your face inside the Memory Bubble. Quietly blow the bubble so that it floats over the top of your head and pops into your memory bank at the back of your head. You know that you need to come back into your class now and you are really pleased to see the other children so when I count to three, 1 ... 2 ... 3 ... I want you to open your eyes and when I count to 4 ... 5 ... and 6 ... I want you to see how many children's eyes you can smile into within 3 seconds.

A Personal Note

If there is another adult joining in with you or observing, make time to have a quick chat with them. Note what worried you or what you found interesting and decide if you need to approach a couple of the children and offer them

Chat Time because they seemed a bit low, upset or withdrawn. Often they will say "no" to you because they are not emotionally ready to chat to you. Sometimes offering a Think Book may help.

Top Tips!

☆ As a teacher/circle facilitator, join in the games and join in the rounds.
☆ In Step 3 you can also put your thumb up to suggest an idea to help the pupil. Sometimes the pupil won't choose you – don't get grumpy!
☆ In Step 3, choose one child to focus on and solve their issue. If you try to solve everyone's issue, it will take too long. At the end of the round, the focus child must thank everyone for listening and speaking and say what their favourite idea was.
☆ To avoid children skipping their go in the round, it is good to start by asking who wants to go first. Usually, at least five or six children will put their hands up. Now, put those children next to each other by asking people to swap places. This group will now warm up the rest of the circle, and hopefully, this will reduce the number of passes.

Chapter 16

Glimpses of Circle Time Practice, Followed by a Case Study

This chapter presents a collection of wide-ranging practitioner reflections, case studies and research-based examples, which illustrate the diverse impact of Quality Circle Time across primary, secondary and alternative education contexts. Through authentic teacher voices and school-based narratives, it highlights how Circle Time boosts self-confidence, empathy, positive discipline and problem-solving skills in pupils of all ages. Teachers describe transformative moments when structured praise, cooperative games and emotional safety reshape group dynamics, even among resistant or students with challenging needs.

This is followed by an in-depth case study of how Fallibroome Academy implemented Quality Circle Time (QCT) across nursery, primary and secondary phases to enhance pupil voice, emotional wellbeing and transition to secondary school. Teachers and teaching assistants underwent Train the Trainers sessions, observing and delivering Circle Time, whilst Year 10 students supported Year 6 pupils, promoting empathy between different year groups. Evaluations indicated improved staff collaboration, pupil confidence and stronger relationships. Circle Time facilitated problem-solving, respect and teamwork, particularly aiding the primary-to-secondary transition. Though suspended during COVID-19, its principles continue in PSHE lessons. The project demonstrates the value of structured dialogue, emotional intelligence and continuity in developing resilient, engaged learners.

We asked a number of teachers who have been involved in using Circle Time in a variety of contexts to talk about their experiences.

Tutor's Comments

Caroline Atherton, Cranford Community School

I began using Circle Time in registration with Year 7 groups. I ran six 20-minute sessions and included themes of friendship, cooperation, the community, feelings and self-awareness. Even in these short sessions, the tutors and I have noticed an increase in the self-confidence of some students ... It is intended that tutors will continue to use Circle Time with their tutor groups throughout their school lives, thus providing them with a forum for problem-solving and building self-confidence.

Esther de Burgh Thomas, Islington Comprehensive

Esther watched a demonstration I ran of Circle Time and attended a debrief training session before trying out the strategies herself. She wrote:

What I noticed was the huge difference that can be made by positive discipline.

For example: "And you're putting your hand up, which really helps me … That was good listening … At least you know what you do (to a boy who said he deliberately annoys his teachers) – a lot of people don't know it … You owned up to a lot of things – your honesty is one of your strong qualities."

During Circle Time demonstrations, as an observer, I watched as this ongoing positive script transformed a very average class into a hardworking, considerate and sensitive self-help group. Even a notoriously boisterous Year 7 class in an Islington comprehensive became eager to please and extraordinarily sensitive to each other's needs.

I have had to work very hard at remembering to be positive with my own form. It's not easy to break the pattern of a lifetime, especially when one's form knows (or thinks they know) what to expect from one and is suspicious of any newly adopted style. As if this isn't enough to contend with, there is the tiredness factor, peculiar to all the state schools I have worked in. The word "don't" can trip all too easily from the lips in these moments of exhausted weakness. The best way to avoid the tiredness trap is to make a conscious effort to counteract it. In order to be as positive as possible (which should be done before any Circle Time session (even if it means 30 seconds standing in the corridor telling yourself you are happy and relaxed)). I recommend five minutes sitting on your own.

Tiredness aside, it is more effective to praise those who are being good than to focus on those that are less cooperative. Positive discipline will, in the long run, not only save you energy but also give you energy as your pupils go out of their way to get you to give them yet more positive feedback.

The second secret is the games. As to which games are played during Circle Time, it doesn't matter as long as they are short (between three and five minutes). If in doubt as to what game to play, ask your pupils – they will have vivid memories of organised games from primary school days and will be happy to share their expertise with you. After a quick game a pupil is so alert and ready for action that they cannot help but be tuned in to the whole-class conversation that follows. Games are an experiential way of teaching pupils rules such as gentleness, kindness, hard work, turn-taking, honesty and skills such as looking, listening, thinking, speaking and concentrating.

When I began to use games within Circle Time, I allowed the games to go on for too long – the focus has to be the Circle Time discussions because these can make such a huge difference to children's emotional lives. So five minutes is an absolute maximum for games. The reason I treasure the above two "secrets" is that the principles they are based on are universally applicable. They have wrought a transformation over the way I work and the way I feel about children.

Jennie Burley, Head of DT and a Tutor, Dorset

Circle Time was used with a Year 10 tutor group where there was evidence of a group pressuring an individual. The class used the drama studio for the circle and it gave tutees an opportunity to speak and be listened to. They shared their feelings without embarrassment and allowed those who did not want to speak to pass. The group felt secure, confidentiality was maintained and it helped in clarifying and setting about resolving the problem.

Sue Chudley, Head of Girls' PE and a Tutor, Dorset

I used Circle Time with a new PSE group. We moved the tables and made a large circle of chairs. The topic was talking to new people and ways of making people feel good by our comments. A soft ball was used to ensure that everyone had the opportunity to speak. (It also gave the nervous something to fiddle with and squeeze!) The pupils said how nice it was to have something good said about them, especially first thing in the morning. The attributes others acknowledged in them were often ones they had never thought of, e.g. hair looked nice, always smiling, never put others down, etc. Despite it being a new concept, everyone enjoyed it.

Isobel McFarlane, Inverkeithing High School

I became interested in Circle Time initially through my involvement in the Area Group (the high school and its six feeder primaries) and a long-term interest I have always had in primary/secondary transfer. I have certainly been concerned that, in spite of making great strides forward in primary–secondary liaison, we still have a huge gulf between the ethos of a primary and that of a secondary. Given the sheer size of our school (1400 pupils), things are bound to be different. But I have long felt that we should be doing more to provide continuity and progression in the hidden curriculum and in approaches to discipline as well as across all the modes. It seemed to me that our primary schools, to a greater or lesser degree, were committed to Circle Time, but it all stopped when the pupils crossed the high-school threshold.

So far, I have used Circle Time with my first year Personal and Social Education class. I have also, as an experiment, used Circle Time with a difficult Year 9 group whom the teacher had to come to me for help with. This was a learning experience for me, and whilst the class and the teacher were enthusiastic about the session, I had my reservations. However, I learned a lot from it. I have used the warning cards with various classes to great effect.

Quality Circle Time is a great means of delivering the PSE programme where above all we are trying to create a climate of mutual trust and raise self-esteem with golden rules to encourage self-respect. A dream of mine would be to have a suitable room designated for Circle Time – look out for low-flying pigs!!! I loathe having to talk to children about personal issues with them stuck behind desks. Unfortunately, many classrooms in secondary do not lend themselves to arranging a circle (fixed benches in Science, for example).

PSE tends to be timetabled after the academic subjects, so it's whatever rooms are left that are designated for PSE. Added to that, some of the teachers who deliver the PSE programme are "conscripts" and not volunteers. However, I am hopeful that through myself giving in-service training I can introduce Circle Time in PSE and encourage staff to overcome the difficulties in less than suitable classrooms.

It is difficult to envisage how the Whole-School Quality Circle Time model could be introduced into secondary. Certainly, golden rules displayed throughout the school would be great, but it would be difficult, for example, to introduce a privilege on a regular basis given the pressure on staff to complete a course when they only see the class for perhaps 2–4 periods per week. It would be particularly difficult given the time pressures of the Standard Grade and Higher curriculum. Here we have introduced in the past year "Recognised Achievement" certificates for Years 1 and 2 pupils. These certificates are awarded annually with a trip in the summer term for those who are awarded two certificates.

Although recognising that rewarding good behaviour is a major step forward, from my point of view, the difficulty with this is, as you know, asking some pupils to behave for a whole term is almost impossible. They need much more achievable targets with regular rewards (like weekly Golden Time provides in primary).

Edith Forrest, Behaviour Support, Perth and Kinross – Using Circle Time for Transition

I am working with a primary seven class of children with social/emotional difficulties at Northern District School, Perth. It was felt that the children would benefit from small support circles prior to coming together for Circle Time.

Currently, there are three groups of children following the same Circle Time cooperative skills programmes, which have been pre-planned by the members of staff leading the groups (Building Bridges Project). The programmes are focused on identifying feelings in themselves and others and incorporating this into a problem-solving model.

The groups will continue until Easter, then amalgamate for Circle Time in the summer term. At this point, Circle Time will be used specifically as a forum to address the children's concerns about moving to secondary school.

Members of the secondary staff (Guidance and Support for Learning) will attend Circle Times to answer the children's questions and respond to their concerns. They also wish to become experienced in the structure and language of Circle Time, in order to continue it in secondary and support other colleagues in doing so.

Pupils from the secondary school will join us to give peer support through Circle Time.

Finally, we hope to be able to run a Circle Time for the children in their secondary school before the summer holiday so that they know there is a listening system for them in their new school.

Mandy Robinson, Head of RE and a Tutor, Dorset – Year 10

I used Circle Time with a Year 10 PSE group that was new to me. I felt that I usually talked too much during these lessons and I wanted a way of getting them all to have a say, not just the vociferous. We moved the tables to the edge of the room and sat in a fairly cramped circle in the middle. I found that the group was not as chatty as I would have liked. Some were patently dumbstruck with this new technique. After all, they had already experienced three years of letting the noisy answer all the questions. Some found it hard to think of any positive aspects of themselves. They were much better at finding other people's good points. It "broke the ice" and some seemed to appreciate the chance to speak. I'll need to work at this in order to get a freer exchange of opinions.

I also used Circle Time for a Year 7 PSE lesson on loss and change at the beginning of the spring term. We were looking back at changes, especially in friendship groups since starting at secondary school and would move on from loss of friends to bereavement. We passed a purple egg and any pupils who wanted to speak held the egg and finished the sentence "My friends have changed because …" Virtually every child spoke and the couple of boys who chose not to say anything passed the egg with an embarrassed laugh. Two main themes emerged, firstly the loss of junior school friends and secondly, making new friends. I shared the loss of my former tutor group that I had had for five years. It did not seem like a PSE lesson, more an exchange of shared experiences. Children who do not normally volunteer to speak felt "safe" to do so and the sharing helped us to become a more cohesive group.

Case Study

Ann Boardman, South Essex Health Authority and Norma Cox, Tameside Community Care Trust, South Essex

Whilst working as health promotion specialists in South Essex, we became aware that primary schools in our area were increasingly using Circle Time as an approach to school management, behaviour management and delivery of many areas of the National Curriculum, including PSHE. Many schools were recognising the potential of this approach for the development of the competencies associated with mental wellbeing and the crucial links between mental wellbeing and effective learning.

The National Health Service Advisory Service suggest competencies should include:

> the ability to develop psychologically, emotionally, intellectually and spiritually;
> the ability to initiate, develop and sustain mutually satisfying relationships;
> the ability to become aware of others and to empathise with them;
> the ability to use psychological distress as a development process so that it does not impair further development.
>
> (HMSO, 1995)

A number of Circle Time models have been developed over the past years. In South Essex, we found considerable support amongst local advisors, headteachers and special educational needs coordinators for the Quality Circle Time model. This model was considered to provide a psychologically and philosophically well-structured practical strategy which can be embraced by a whole-school community so that the mental wellbeing of every child, every member of staff and every member of the school community is enhanced.

Similar approaches have also been developed in the United States for the development of emotional literacy (Goleman, 1996). The programmes featured in many such models are strikingly similar to the UK models as are the outcomes, including widespread benefits for children's emotional and social competence, for their behaviour in and out of the classroom and for their ability to learn. Goleman also advocates the use of such approaches during periods of transition, for example for pupils moving from one phase to another.

As Circle Time becomes more widely used in primary schools in South Essex, we realised that young people entering secondary schools will increasingly expect such a forum to be available to them. Consequently, we have started to explore the potential for introducing quality Circle Time to secondary schools in South Essex.

To advance our exploration of the potential use of Circle Time in secondary schools, teachers from health-promoting schools in south-east Essex were invited to participate in an INSET day. Before the INSET, senior secondary staff thought Circle Time was essentially a primary strategy with no relevance to the secondary context. After participating in the training day, some teachers took the ideas away to use in their secondary schools. They have started to use Circle Time with a variety of groups:

- pupils on an Alternative Education Programme;
- to investigate barriers to revision with a GCSE group;
- for Year 7 pupils to foster a sense of community as they enter the secondary school.

Case Study

Possible ways forward for using Circle Time.

Sam Butler, Acting Head of Year 8, Shoeburyness County High School

Shoeburyness County High School has been looking at ways of implementing the Whole-School Quality Circle Time model and adapting it to their situation. Their thinking was summarised in the following bullet points:

- Pupils identified as manifesting behavioural problems should meet regularly for Circle Time. However, if this strategy were to be adopted solely for pupils with behavioural difficulties, there would be a danger of it being regarded as having limited value elsewhere. It could be argued that other pupils would not appreciate its value for them and see it as something the pupils with "special needs" do, making it difficult to implement across the entire school at a later stage. It is considered better to adopt Circle Time right across the school so that all pupils have access to it.
- During form period, time could be allocated for Circle Time to take place once a week and a skeleton agenda or selection of relevant pastoral tasks could be provided. There is also the scope for any issues that have arisen that week to be addressed.
- During form period, some time could be allocated for the form to have a circular discussion of School Council issues.
- During the allocated PSHE lesson, the School Council representatives could use a circle discussion to explore the issues raised by their year groups.
- One-to-one tutor time – perhaps Years 7 and 8 could have a big ear on the board and they could put a small mouth on it when they want to speak to their form tutor privately. Older pupils could have an appointment system where they put their names – similar to a business diary.
- The one-to-one tutor time would give pupils an appropriate time to speak with their form tutor and thus would hopefully prevent sensitive personal issues from being divulged to the class inappropriately during Circle Time.
- Teachers could be made aware, if not already, of using the circle as another teaching strategy. The more teaching strategies we have, the better.
- Each term a department could be responsible for arranging a staff event, e.g. a meal, go-kart racing, bowling, etc. The whole school's staff would be invited. The activities should suit all members of staff, especially those

with significant home commitments. Friday night down the pub, important though this activity is, unfortunately doesn't include everyone.
- Each member of staff throughout the school is to have a "buddy."
- Each member of staff is to have a "peer support system" to turn to in moments of need and for this to be non-judgemental.
- Perhaps during INSET to have more time specifically spent on the staff's mental health, e.g. sessions on dealing with stress and managing difficult pupils.
- The model is built upon "Personal Mental Health Plans" for all staff, which is good for all concerned. It invests in the staff and tries to raise self-esteem among the staff. This investment has the potential to help increase staff morale and thus the standard of teaching, not only during Circle Time but for the majority of their teaching as well.
- A pilot system could be introduced to assess the scheme's potential.

Using Circle Time in an Alternative Education Programme

Mary Bright, Alternative Education Programme, Shoeburyness County High School

The primary aim of alternative education is to raise the self-esteem of pupils who see themselves as failures and thus reject school. Building relationships is our first task. Many of the pupils we work with have a high level of frustration and show little understanding or tolerance for others in the group. Their comments can be vitriolic and damaging. Physical assaults and threats are not unusual.

In tutor period, we work very hard to reverse the ingrained negative responses. Developing social skills underpins all aspects of the course, and Circle Time has been an excellent vehicle for this. We began by discussing positive aspects about ourselves, i.e. "One thing I'm pleased about ..." In the group this year, the girls have enjoyed the opportunities to explore ideas, but for several weeks, the boys would simply opt out. This went on until one of the girls suddenly said, "They're out of order. They never say anything." The rest of the girls joined in at this point and passed the card to John. Faced with this female solidarity, eyes down, John said, "I've been here for 100% this term and I'm proud of myself." A round of applause from the girls! Since then, we seem to have broken the ice and it is OK for the boys to join in, although they are still not as voluble as the girls.

I use Circle Time every two or three weeks to discuss relationships within the group, problems and difficulties, and to celebrate success. It has been very useful to raise issues that would otherwise probably lead to a one-to-one confrontation. We have been able to deal with things by mutual agreement rather than teacher directives, which anyway don't work with pupils like these. Their response to difficult situations is to walk out of school and not come back.

Circle Time has enabled us all to work things through together and develop bonds in the group.

We still have our moments, like every day, but the difference in attendance, attitudes and goodwill is palpable. A number of tutors in Year 7 have also started to use Circle Time.

> In our group we have used Circle Time for us to be able to talk to each other as a group one at a time when we get the card. We do this mainly because half of us have no confidence in ourselves and it helps us out of our shells. I felt that it helped me to get my opinion across to other people.
> (Female, 16 years)

> In our group we sometimes use Circle Time. It's been interesting and helpful because boys find talking and discussing things very hard.
> (Male, 16 years)

A Cross-Phase Teaching School Project Based in Fallibroome Academy

An Exploratory Case Study

This project was an exploratory action research project – no tests were standardised and none of the results are "research-valid." As a small-scale piece of work, its purpose was to ask questions, prompt discussion, involve young people, reveal inconsistencies and discover shared values.

Heads of Year 7 in several secondary schools took a quick "heads up" survey with their pupils and asked "How many of you regularly experienced weekly or fortnightly Circle Time in your primary school?" – they found it to be around 75%. Pupils said they appreciated:

- whole class circle discussion;
- their teacher being interested in what they all have to say;
- being relied on, as a group, to identify and solve problems;
- being a team that is responsible for each other, no matter what their ability level
- knowing that engaging in the group will lead directly to action.

Background to the Project

Learning Brain Europe holds regular conferences for primary and secondary schools together. At one of their conferences in Manchester, Jenny Mosley was presenting, running workshops and she delivered a keynote speech. As a result of opening up the workshops to primary and secondary teachers together, practitioners discovered they had similar hopes and enthusiasms regarding Pupil Voice and a willingness to explore ways of working together across the

Table 16.1 Table showing staff delegates participating in the project

Staff member	Role	School or setting
Claire Burstow	Assistant Principal: Teaching and Learning	Fallibroome Academy
Hayley Wightman	Teacher of English/Community Manager	Fallibroome Academy
Jayne Ruscoe	HLTA and Inclusion Resource Coordinator	Fallibroome Academy
Jacki Pepper	Teacher (SEN)	Fallibroome Academy
Nic Curran	Learning Manager	Fallibroome Academy
Lisa Hurst	Pastoral Supervisor	Fallibroome Academy
Dawn Tristram	Foundation Stage Teacher	Broken Cross Community School and Nursery
Elaine Pearson	HLTA	Upton Priory School

phases so that young people could experience education as a continuum of provision.

Therefore, when Fallibroome High School was offered Teaching School status, staff were trained in the Quality Circle Time model. The time commitment was five days over three months and involved teaching time alongside observation of good practice in each of the participating schools (Table 16.1).

The Hosting High School and the Teaching School Concept

Fallibroome Academy in Macclesfield is a high-achieving school of 1500 students, with a distinguished sixth form of 350 pupils. As a Specialist Performing Arts College, Leading Edge and a National Support School, the Academy is proud of its success, which the Principal emphasises is based on a commitment to personal growth of the adults and a desire to meet the needs of individual students and teachers. The Academy has achieved Teaching School status. The Teaching Schools national network is modelled on the Teaching Hospital idea and works on the assumption that practitioners who are excellent in their field should drive the agenda for change within the school development programme and support local schools to reach the same excellence.

As a Teaching School, staff need to be confident in training other adults, as well as teaching children. A Train the Trainers project was chosen.

a. to support teachers in gaining further skills and boosting confidence to train other adults;
b. as a way of introducing the Quality Circle Time model into a secondary setting;
c. to support pupils of all ages seeing primary and secondary school as part of the same continuum of provision.

A small band of teachers and teaching assistants from secondary, primary and nursery schools volunteered to become a network of accredited local schools trainers. A key feature of the Train the Trainers programme is that trainers go to classrooms and nurseries to observe the trainer working with children and young people of all ages. Consequently, secondary school teachers, for example, were able to see the use of puppets with 3-year-olds, and nursery teachers were able to observe Year 8 students working on how to rebuild bridges back to each other after some bullying issues. Teachers then commit themselves to running a programme of Circle Times back in their schools.

Year 10 students were also invited to be part of the training programme and on the last day worked in a circle with the incoming Year 6 from a local primary school. The final session involved a huge circle of teaching assistants, teachers, Year 6 and Year 10 pupils – all learning new games, songs and clapping activities together. The emphasis was on the large circle being a learning community who all have something to offer each other as part of a larger vision of education.

Most importantly, for transition, the Year 6 pupils were learning that the very grown-up looking Year 10s were interested in them. They were learning that secondary pupils still shared the same values of caring, teamwork and fun. The fact that teachers and pupils introduced themselves meant that they now had a familiar face in secondary school to whom they could go if they needed help.

Methods

The key method of working involved using a combination of experiential, active learning for the participants; observation of master classes across all age groups; and then embedding the observed learning into a theoretical context with a supporting knowledge base. This combination of teaching approaches enables participants to experience the power of circle work for themselves, including an exploration of their own hopes and fears in teaching; see how it can be managed and used with a range of children and young people, including some challenging members of a group; and reflect on the links between theory and practice.

Evaluation of the work was carried out through a combination of reflective description, daily journals, written observations and questionnaires.

Results and Evaluations

A. Teachers' and teaching assistants' pre- and post-questionnaires enquiring about Circle Time methods

Staff were presented with a pre- and post-questionnaire about their current use of Circle Time and Circle Time initiatives. The number of staff surveyed in the

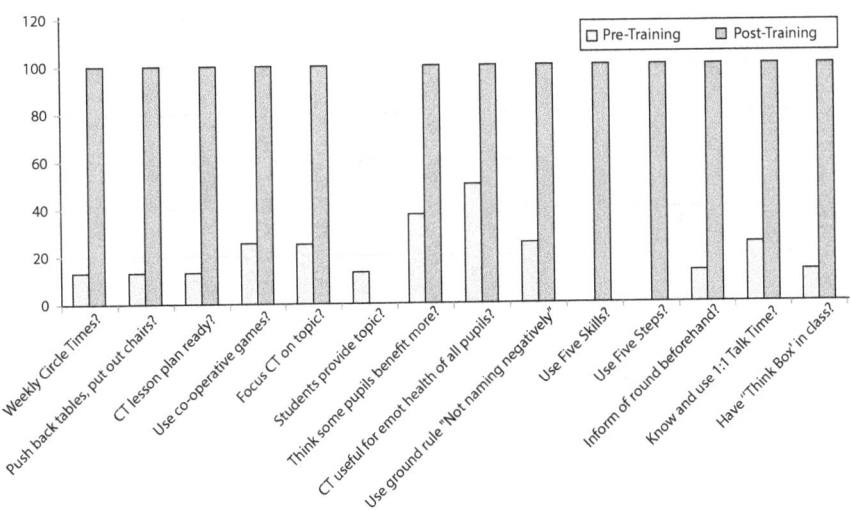

Figure 16.1 Graph showing the pre- and post-training results of a Circle Time procedures survey given to staff.

first instance was greater than in the second instance, with Train the Trainers delegates featuring strongly in the post-questionnaire request for information.

Pre-training, only 12.5% of staff surveyed ran weekly Circle Time or used other supporting features of the Circle Time approach (see Figure 16.1). It is interesting to note that, despite not regularly carrying out Circle Time, 50% still believed that Circle Time was useful for the emotional health of all pupils.

Post-training all the delegates surveyed used most aspects of Circle Time, such as planning sessions, using cooperative games, focusing on a topic, using ground rules, five steps and five skills, and other initiatives. This means that the training programme had embedded well and the delegates had taken on board all the key programme features to ensure the best chances of success.

B. Teachers and teaching assistants pre-questionnaires enquiring about schools and how supported staff feel in their respective schools

Staff were asked, in a questionnaire, to agree or disagree with statements as to how they felt about school life in the run-up to the training programme, how supported they felt, how caring the community was, and whether they were proud to be members of the school.

It was very encouraging and a great testament to the school's achievements that nearly 90% of staff agreed or strongly agreed that the school enhanced their self-esteem, and also that they were valued and recognised at school. Additionally, nearly 90% thought that the school activities and curriculum enhanced the self-esteem of staff and pupils alike. One hundred per cent of

118 A Circle Approach to Boosting Emotional Wellbeing

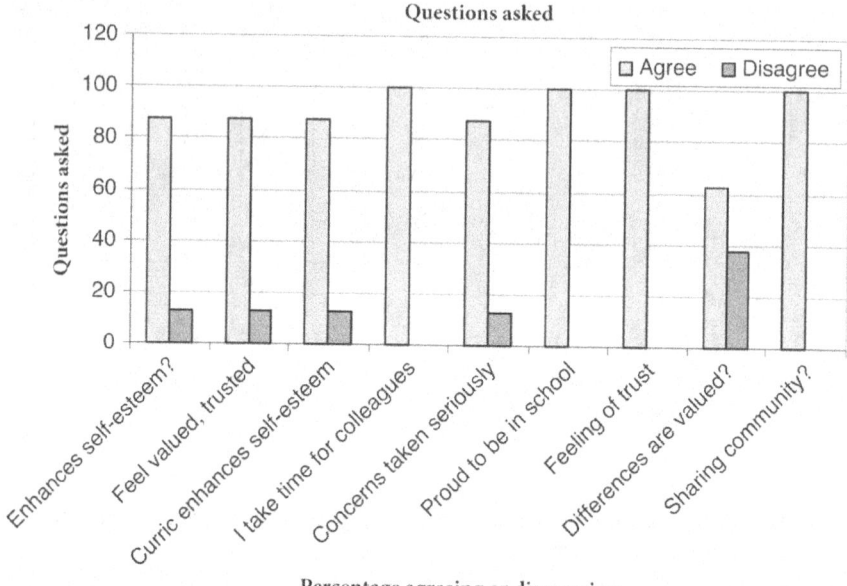

Figure 16.2 Graph showing the results of a questionnaire given to staff delegates concerning their feelings about school.

people thought that the community was a sharing one and that there was a feeling of trust between staff and students. Sixty-three per cent of staff felt individual differences were valued and appreciated (see Figure 16.2). These were felt to be strong indicators of the success of the school and the staff. Zeros in the above table represent Circle Time initiatives not yet put into practice as staff completed the questionnaire not long after training (Tables 16.2 and 16.3).

C. Pupil questionnaire results

Year 7 students were asked to complete questionnaires before the Circle Time training and project implementation in May 2012 and then post-implementation in January 2013. The questionnaires were designed to find out what pupils felt about their own presence in the school, for instance how much they were listened to, whether the school valued them and whether they knew how to give feedback (Table 16.4).

It was encouraging to note that, in the pre-questionnaires, most pupils (62%) felt that their school listened to them; 77% knew how to give feedback on lessons; 78% were proud to be a member of the school; 90% agreed that

Glimpses of Circle Time Practice 119

Table 16.2 Results of Circle Time procedures pre and post-training questionnaires given to staff delegates

	Pre-training teachers plus TTT delegates grouped responses	Post-training just TTT delegates responses
Weekly Circle Times?	12.5	100
Push back tables, put out chairs?	12.5	100
CT lesson plan ready?	12.5	100
Use cooperative games?	25	100
Focus CT on topic?	25	100
Students provide topic?	12.5	0
Think some pupils benefit more?	37.5	100
CT useful for emotional health of all pupils?	50	100
Use ground rule "Not naming negatively"	25	100
Use Five Skills?	0	100
Use Five Steps?	0	100
Inform of round beforehand?	12.5	0
Know and use 1:1 Talk Time?	25	83
Have "Think Box"	12.5	100

Table 16.3 Results from a questionnaire given to staff delegates concerning their feelings about school.

Abbreviated question	% Agree or strongly disagree	% disagree or strongly agree
Our school is a place which enhances my self-esteem	87.5	12.5
At our school I am valued, recognised and trusted as acontributing member of the school	87.5	12.5
Activities and a curriculum which enhance self-esteem are encountered daily by staff and students alike	87.5	12.5
I am willing to spend time and effort to enhance and improve my colleagues' self-esteem	100	0
Others listen to concerns that I have and take them seriously	87.5	12.5
I am proud to be a member of this school	100	0
There is a feeling of trust between staff and students	100	0
Individual differences are valued and appreciated	62.5	37.5
This is a sharing community	100	0

Table 16.4 Summary of Year 7 results

Survey question	Year 7 May 2012 Overall agree %	Year 7 May 2013 Overall agree %	% change from pre to post
I feel that my school "listens" to me	62.5	84.5	+22
Any ideas that I raise are "listened to," valued and really taken up by the school.	68	71.5	+3.5
I know how I can give feedback on my lessons	77.5	83.5	+6
I am proud to be a member of this school.	78.5	98	+19.5
This school, and the things we do here, helps me to feel happy and confident in myself.	90	93.5	+3.5
I know who I can talk to if I need to speak to a member of staff	89	94	+5
There is a feeling of trust between staff and pupils here.	86.5		+17
Our school is a sharing school	88	93.5	+5.5

the school helps them to feel happy and confident; 89% knew who to speak to if they needed someone; and 88% thought that the school was sharing one.

However good these figures sound, there is always room for improvement, and the questionnaire results from a few months post-training showed an improved score in all areas, some as much as nearly 20% in those feeling that the school listened to them and that they were proud to be a member of their school.

At Fallibroome, Circle Time was extended into a circle of support, set up to address an ongoing problem of isolation and depression a particular student was having within her form. This gave the student the support she needed at the time. Following this and other steps that the Academy took to support the student, s/he developed better relationships with other members of the form and was in a much better place personally.

One member of staff delivered Circle Time to the Year 7 school rugby team as there were some bullying issues taking place both on and off the pitch.

Pupil Comments

> We can interact with each other – its important because it's a time when you can talk freely about something
>
> (Pupil comment)

We sometimes talk about how we feel and if we think someone in the class needs help we try to help them it is sometimes hard to help them but I try my best.
(Pupil comment)

I liked passing the egg around and voicing our opinions. I thought it was cool how people had different opinions about different things.
(Pupil comment)

This will help the student – teacher relationship become stronger and closer ... this 30-minute period can have an effect on our entire lives.
(Pupil comment)

Circle Time Progress Report from One Train the Trainer Delegate Claire Burstow, Director of Teaching and Learning, Fallibroome Academy 2013

After the Circle Time training, the Academy felt it needed to answer two key questions:

Are we a listening school?
Can we do anything else to support our staff?

The pre-Circle Time questionnaires showed that with Years 7 and 8:

67% said they felt the school listened to them;
60% said they felt their ideas are valued and taken up by the school;
69% said they know how to give feedback on lessons;
81% knew who to talk to if they had an issue.

The percentages were based on the numbers of students who agreed or strongly agreed with each statement, and questionnaires were completed by approximately 100 students. Using this information, the school has responded positively and decisively by:

1. Encouraging the Year 7 pastoral team to use Circle Time to develop students' skills and to ensure every student had a chance to get their voice heard. It was also used to help build relationships within the form and encourage students to support and help each other.
2. One tutor time per term is devoted to Circle Time, the focus of the first was allowing students to discuss any issues they were having settling in, with members of the student council in these sessions acting as role models/offering advice and reassurance. The second session coincided with the launch of the voice boxes, aimed at giving students the opportunity to

suggest ways the school can be improved. The topic for the third session was on respect and relationships.
3. Training sessions were scheduled to train Year 7 form tutors in delivering Circle Time as there weren't enough trained staff to expand the initiative. This training has been opened up to all primary schools and secondary schools in our learning community.
4. Voice boxes were set up around the school and launched by students from the Leadership Community Council in student assemblies. These students are responsible for looking at all ideas and going to the school Leadership team to present these suggestions on behalf of all students. The Council informs the rest of the school about action taken by the Leadership Team. There is also a forum on the school website for students to post their ideas.
5. A display has been put up to help ensure students know who they can talk to if they have any issues. A video has also been produced to reinforce this.
6. A voice box and display were set up in the staffroom and a staff wellbeing committee was set up to organise staff social events.
7. The school continues to pay for mentoring sessions for staff on an annual basis.

Following the success of the small-scale Circle Time pilot, we have decided to:

1. Re-write the Year 7 pastoral curriculum to include Circle Time on a more regular basis (once a half-term).
2. Train the school counsellor and Pastoral Support Centre staff so they can use Circle Time as part of their anger management and raising self-awareness sessions.
3. Roll Circle Time into Year 8 – once a term to start with.
4. Explore the possibility of going into primary school and delivering Circle Time with Year 6 students at the end of the summer term, which may be initially trialled on a small scale and evaluated before rolling out to all feeder primary schools.
5. Deliver a Circle Time session to the secondary Teaching Assistant Network.

What Participants Wrote

Circle Time is a great project to be involved with, the pilot that I was with involved early years, primary and secondary schools. We went to each school and experienced Circle Time. This was a great opportunity to see how effective Circle Time can be with different ages and different environments. It was fascinating to see the children become very involved and engaged. At times it was humbling to witness the care and honesty of young people. I think it was very important that all the schools worked together. We were able to take older students to primary schools and this helped to calm a great many fears of the Year 6 children coming to us in September. It also let us have greater communication with partnership schools which will now continue in the future. I think this would be a great model to use in the future across the country as it not only benefits children but adults as well as keeping lines of communication open can only be a good thing.

(Lisa Hurst, Pastoral Supervisor, Fallibroome Academy)

I feel that this pilot was a great success and benefitted from the joint venture between early years, primary and secondary. I have never worked in a primary school so for me it provided an insight into that aspect of education. It was interesting to witness Circle Time with such young pupils and to observe the wisdom of their responses in peer counselling. It highlighted the importance of the transition from primary to secondary and the benefits to be gained in terms of building self-esteem and peer relations by continuing with Circle Time in Year 7 as a natural progression from one world to another, rather than something you do at primary that suddenly stops at secondary. Expressing ourselves and relating to others is a skill that often gets lost somewhere between Years 6 and 7 and can lead to behavioural issues in Year 8 and I think Circle Time at the beginning of Year 7 is crucial in bridging this gap and making these skills part of the process and development of our pupils.

(Fayne Ruscoe, HLTA and Inclusion Resource Coordinator)

One thing that struck me was that Circle Time is a very accessible system to hear pupil voice. The format makes it possible for all children to have a forum for their issues, this then targets all pupils. The year group models were an excellent learning opportunity for me to see Quality Circle Time. Embedded and sustained Circle Time throughout school life will enable pupils to become comfortable at sharing opinions and thoughts. I feel this is profound teaching of the lifelong skills needed for emotional intelligence. Pupils who then develop these skills from the early years will surely be proactive in addressing the issues they are faced with as they grow into adults. This in turn will lead to positive experiences and relationships.

(Elaine Pearson, HLTA, Upton Priory School)

I just wanted to say "thank you" for the Circle Time training. I have certainly been inspired by how empowering it can be. The techniques you have shared with us to encourage pupils to take ownership of themselves and the importance of respect for each other and our values, I have started to embed in my everyday teaching. I'm looking forward to September when I can use Circle Time with my new form. Working with some of our primary partnership schools during the training has really been valuable. It's been a real learning curve to see how it can be delivered across the different key stages and the benefits it can bring to all pupils. It can only be beneficial to pupils if each KS has Circle Time within its curriculum, as pupils move from KS to KS they are able to develop their skills through a structure that they are familiar with and they understand. There are many benefits for staff and pupils to work with pupils from different KS's this is one structure which allows for that where everyone's voice is valued.

(Facki Pepper, Specialist Teacher, Fallibroome Academy)

The purpose of education is to prepare young people to become active citizens in a complex world. They will need a combination of qualifications and skills but the pressure on school leaders to focus on the former, at the expense of the latter, is immense. This would be a serious mistake. Qualifications matter but emotional intelligence and empathy will be more significant factors in defining a successful life when formal education is completed.

This belief led us to explore Quality Circle Time with our Primary Partners. Our aim was twofold: to smooth the transition from Primary to Secondary school and to create an effective vehicle for student voice to influence school policy.

The skilful training enabled us to achieve both aims. The Teachers' and Students' reflections confirm the power of the model. The success of the pilot will lead to a policy that will embed the opportunity for all students to develop the emotional resilience required to secure future success.

(P. W. Rubery, Pincipal, Fallibroome Academy, 2013)

The reasons why the nursery/primary/secondary model worked include:

Allowing us to observe Circle Time across all key stages including nursery highlighting its potential especially if used in a consistent manner across all key stages. Currently all our feeder primary schools engage in cooperative learning which means when students arrive in Year 7 we are using the same structures/language they are used to which helps them deal with the transition more easily. The introduction of Circle Time could be another vehicle to help ease the transition between primary and secondary school allowing us to see how Circle Time could be used with Year 6 students across all our feeder primary schools to allow students to express any concerns they may have about coming to secondary school in a safe environment. Built into this could be a chance for the students to meet their Learning Manager. It was a great opportunity for staff to observe different key stages which is a very rare but valuable experience. As a result of this training the primary school staff have actually helped deliver Circle Time in the secondary school which is great professional development for them

The reason it is important to work with children in these sessions is that you can see how the students respond to this type of activity and observe what to do if students do not respond as expected. It also allows you to discuss how to deal with individual students who might find this type of activity hard as we had a student who had to leave the session.

(Claire Burstow, Director of Teaching and Learning, Fallibroome Academy)

As a pastoral head, I am always looking for ways in which to improve Student Voice and also for opportunities to improve social cohesion within a form or a year group. The QCT that I have seen Jenny do in both primary and secondary settings has convinced me that it is a really useful tool. The training that I received has made me feel confident in leading Circle Time and I have been able to discuss issues with classes such as transition from Years 6 to 7 and also to collect their views on how the school is run. I feel that Quality Circle Time enables pupils to express their feelings in a safe and structured environment and it gives the teacher the opportunity to see the pupils thinking and communicating in a different way and vice versa. As Learning Manager for Year 7, I have made the decision to incorporate Circle Time in the pastoral curriculum and will be using it regularly in the future.

(Nie Curran, Learning Manager and Pastoral Head, Fallibroome Academy)

The pioneering pilot Circle Time project I was involved in was a fabulous success! It provided colleagues from various key stages the opportunity to learn and to observe how valuable and powerful Circle Time is in giving pupils from the ages of 3 to 12 a voice and a "platform" to discuss their thoughts, anxieties and problems in a neutral and safe environment. The structure of the training not only highlighted the importance of supporting transition from Primary school to Secondary school, but gave colleagues the opportunity to compare, view and understand education and children's emotional intelligence at each key stage. Watching Jenny work with early years, primary and secondary children was both fascinating and at some points emotional. Observing the structures we had been learning, discussing and practising being modelled, taught us the skills to introduce this positive experience into our own settings as well as providing us the confidence and inspiration to deliver Circle Time effectively! The training model used has supported communication between partnership schools but most importantly been extremely valuable in providing our pupils a consistent structure that will encourage them to have positive relationships and enhance their life skills!

(Dawn Tristram, Foundation Stage Manager, Broken Cross Community School and Nursery)

We learn from this constructive feedback that delegates in general felt:

- The training provided a crucial opportunity to see Circle Time throughout the different stages of education – early years, primary, secondary;
- Delegates were often humbled to witness the caring, honesty and wisdom of young people;
- Communication between partnership schools was promoted by the model, as are positive relationships and the enhancement of life skills;
- Many felt that Circle Time at the beginning of Year 7 is crucial to bridging the gap between primary and secondary education.
- Circle Time is an accessible system for listening to pupils' voices and enabling pupils to share opinions and thoughts;
- Circle Time could offer profound teaching of lifelong skills for emotional intelligence that are necessary for adult life;
- During Circle Time, pupils are encouraged to take ownership of themselves and to respect each other and the values;
- Circle Time enables pupils to express their feelings in a safe and structured environment, giving teachers the opportunity to see pupils thinking and communicating in a different way;
- Observing, discussing and practising using the model helped give confidence and inspiration to deliver Circle Time effectively.
- The training helped the delegate feel confident in leading Circle Times and gauging feedback on issues.

The Way Forward

It was felt that this project had many strengths for staff and pupils alike and that it would be a very useful model to support other Teaching Schools in taking their own settings forward. Overall, some key strengths of this project were felt to be:

- improved empathy and understanding of all year groups;
- children perceiving transition as not so scary – some of the initiatives can be run by older pupils;
- teachers involved in ongoing Circles of Support for each other – where they can bring issues and try out ideas;
- listening is at the heart of all good schools, and a school is only a listening school if real listening systems are in place;
- If Circle Time is a recognised feature from nursery through to secondary school, then this is a support for transition in itself;
- Learning that children can be teachers – and that children have a huge interest, compassion and motivation to help others. The Year 10s have huge potential for the future. Even Circle Times with Year 4s and 5s showed that pupils were interested in teaching younger pupils games;

- Teachers need training in how to train others – in this project, a nursery teacher taught secondary staff. This is a boost for self-esteem when teachers use their skills from across the board to teach.

With the growth of technology – the role of the school to help children develop social and emotional intelligences, explore shared values, debate right and wrong, develop empathy and values will become even more important.

Sample Circle Time Session Plan – Year 6
Skills Reminder: Listening, Looking, Concentrating, Speaking, Thinking

Step	Activity	Outcome
Meeting/Game	Start with changing places game, the pupils asked for this as a warm-up	They were really careful passing over the circle so that did not touch the hoops.
Discuss Rules	Trying to get past the obstacles placed in the circle – changing places – solid liquids and gas. Rock, water, steam. Hoops placed next to each other in the circle. i suggested that they might be attached to a batter and some wires.	
Warm-Up Round	Who do you admire? Famous people, family, friends, teachers. I admire? because …	Some pupils chose family friends in the class famous athletes other family members They spoke of what they admired about them and their qualities.
	When I am … I would like to be …	Pupils in a round chose; University Like to be a sports trainer Mechanics Hairdresser Also personal goals of playing instruments. Playing in football teams
Forum	What helps us …?	Working hard at school Family Watching talented people Influences of our friends.
	What might stop us getting there? Obstacles.	Bad influences from our friends Money

Step	Activity	Outcome
	Discussed each obstacle and removed a hoop for each solution with thumbs up until all hoops gone (bullying issue to be revisited).	Bullies (pupil said that bullying in school stops you working hard and affects your home life because you feel unhappy) Negative feelings Making the right decisions Might get confused Don't know how to Might get disappointed if there are no
	The pupils agreed that they didn't believe me when I said the hoops were wired up.	
	Some people have told me why.	Pupils then discussed removing
	Pupils explained that hoops were not conductors of electricity so they knew I was not being clear.	
	Praised them for questioning something they knew was wrong and using thinking skills.	
	Praised them for being vocal and speaking out.	Understanding that they must value their own opinions even though others may not agree with them
Celebrate	Take turns to say something we admire about the person next to you.	
Calm	Enjoy success Play video clip from 2012 Olympics.	

Sample Circle Time Session Plan – Year 7

Students had a 10-minute assembly at the start of this session, so there was time to get the room arranged into a circle. The assembly was used to talk about Circle Time so that students and tutors are aware of its purpose. The Community Council was included in these sessions.

Step	Activity
Step 1: Meeting-Up Game	Get all the students to sit in a circle and ask them to think about what skills they are using. Looking, listening, speaking, thinking and concentrating. **"What skills are you demonstrating now that are making me happy?"** Explain why you count the number of hands up – one thinking skill, etc. Research says that if I wait at least five seconds before asking for a response 50% more hands go up so this is a way I use to slow myself down. When you go round each student in the circle and get students to look at you to emphasise the need for eye contact follow this up by saying: **"How do you feel if somebody does not look at you when you speak to them."** Try to also link in the following skills; Respect, Discussion and Cooperation as these are additional skills focused on through the Behaviour for Learning pastoral sessions. Praise effective skills: **"I like the way you're …"** **"Good choice, I like the way you always wait for me to stop talking before …"** **"Great listening body langauge …"** Reinforce the skills through games of your choice. For example, "Simon says." **"How do you feel if you make a mistake?" "I feel …"** **"What do other people do to make you feel even worse?"** **"If you make a mistake, what is the kindest thing somebody could do?"** **"Waves"** (p. 191). One person stands in the middle, the rest move from seat to seat – the aim is not to let the person go back into the circle. DO not leave them in the middle for too long Follow this up by **"If you can't get back in the circle – how does this make you feel …"**
Step 2: Warm-Up Round	Introduce the ground rules – In this next part you must not name any teachers/students or subjects No shouting out, we need to listen to everybody **"What have you found hard last week?/What are you worried about?"** **Students say: "I am worried about …"** Pose a thinking question. Move students so that those who are offering answers sit together. Assign the "leader" and give them the egg. Students all answer the question – option to pass. The leader is asked to offer the egg back to anybody who passed. **"Would anyone who passed, like to add something?"** Teacher summaries the issues which have been raised – form tutor records as they could pick up any issues raised in tutor time

Step	Activity
Step 3: Open-Up Forum	Introduce the next question. Be prepared to role-play if nobody volunteers. **"Who would like some help with what they are worried about?"** Teacher allows each student with their hand up to suggest why they have offered themselves: **"I need help because I ..."** Teacher chooses one student/issue. **"Who has a suggestion for ... to help them to ...?"** Asks students to offer solutions to help that student with their issue. Remind of eye contact, first name use and how to start the sentence: **"Would it help if ...?"** Clarify agreed strategies: **"I am going to try ..."** Student who asked for help thanks the other students
Step 4: Cheering-Up/ Celebrating Success	**"Who are you pleased with in your class because they have been really helpful and looked out for others since starting at Fallibroome? Who agrees with this ..."**
Step 5: Calming Down/Closing Ritual	Celebrate the use of skills in this session. Introduce two calm down games: "Zoom–Eek" (p. 227) "Wink Murder"

Circle Time Progress Report from Claire Burstow, Assistant Headteacher at Fallibroome School, 2025

Following the case study above, we continued to integrate Circle Time into the pastoral curriculum for Years 7 and 8. It served two primary purposes: to give all students a voice and promote team-building activities, and to provide a structured forum for discussing sensitive topics such as cyberbullying. Additionally, Circle Time formed a key component of our Year 6 transition programme, during which we visited primary schools to explore students' expectations and concerns about moving to secondary school. To support this, selected Year 7 students received training to help lead aspects of the sessions.

The use of Circle Time was suspended during the COVID-19 pandemic due to social distancing measures and the guidance against students sitting face to face. Although we recognise the significant benefits Circle Time offers, it was not reintroduced once restrictions were lifted. This was not due to a lack of appreciation for its value, but rather the practical limitations of delivering it meaningfully within a shorter tutorial session, particularly given the time required to rearrange classroom furniture.

Currently, students participate in PSHE sessions throughout the academic year as part of our Respect curriculum. These sessions are led by RE specialists, who, whilst experienced in facilitating discussion-based learning, have not received specific training in delivering Circle Time. The PSHE curriculum consists of a well-established set of lessons that incorporate a range of cooperative strategies designed to enable students to express their views in a respectful, safe and supportive environment.

Comment by Jenny Mosley

The above case study and Claire's 2025 comment do represent the pattern that can happen in many schools. Huge energy, wonderful vision and senior management (Peter Rubery, Headteacher, has now left) totally support the initiative – and for a while the system works well. Plan, Do and Review when operating regularly keeps the system vibrant and positive.

The impact of COVID-19 cannot be underestimated – it pulled the previous rug of stability and safety right from under everyone's feet. There was such a short time to gather people back together and get everything working again. After having two disrupted years of family life and school life, it's not possible just to return to how things were. Challenging initiatives like face-to-face contact in Circle Time after the experience everyone has just had cannot just be picked up and run with again. People have lost their confidence and resilience.

In addition, if you change the systems and timings change and PSHE assumes its right for a stronger place on the curriculum, then there will be tension between the pastoral needs of the tutor group and the curriculum needs of PSHE.

The transition aspect of Fallibroome's case study was one of its most successful components. I still believe this is one of Circle Time's most effective contributions to children transferring emotionally safely and happily to secondary school.

A huge thank you needs to go to Claire. It was 25 years ago that she came on a trainers course and I admire and celebrate how much she achieved as a result of staying faithful to so many initiatives.

References

Goleman, D., 1996. *Emotional Intelligence*. London: Bloomsbury.
NHS Health Advisory Service, 1995. *Together We Stand: The Commissioning, Role and Management of Child and Adolescent Mental Health Services*. London: HMSO. Available at: https://education-uk.org/documents/elton/elton1989.html.

Chapter 17

Introduction to Circle Plans

Pick and Mix Circle Times But Never Finish on Step 3

Once you are familiar with the Five Steps of Circle Time, depending on the needs of your circle, depending on the time you have been allotted, it's perfectly acceptable to pick and mix the steps to create your own Circle Time lesson plans. You don't need to abandon all your usual teaching strategies like paired work or introducing materials that might support your theme ... you just need to make sure that you write out your lesson plan so that you know exactly where you're going to place these – keep an eye on the time because you need to end in a positive way. A lot of teachers get so fascinated by what students are saying in Step 3 that although my explicit advice in the book was to only choose one focus child to help – the teacher draws in other children too – so the issue gets longer and more multi-layered. Then all of a sudden, the bell goes – everyone out. This can be harmful – these young people have just opened their hearts. They are being the best version of themselves and being vulnerable. If they are suddenly catapulted into the hurly-burly of the corridor – it's too much of a shock and they don't have the resilience to cope. Watch the time and either end with a quick game or a breathing exercise.

Many teachers don't feel ready to do mindfulness visualisations for their ending. They prefer to go back to Step 1 and finish on a game – this can be a good choice.

The most important aspect of Circle Time is you feeling comfortable with what you are doing. I would rather you chose Step 1 – a game, Step 2 – a round and back to Step 1 again ... because that's all you feel ready for and that's all you can present with positivity and warmth. Gradually, as you and your circle relax together you can start bringing in more complex activities from the other steps.

The following Circle Time lesson plans are for you to explore and pick and mix the ideas that you feel you can work with easily. What these lesson plans will teach you is how to choose activities that will help children explore the themes stated at the top of each lesson plan.

The more that you get used to this, the more you will be able to look at the new PSHE topics and structure your own Circle Times to help discussion after you have presented the information.

The next six lesson plans were drawn together by Anne Cowling and Penny Vine – originally working with the "I, Too" Partnership (Claire Whiteley was the "I, Too" Project Manager). In 2001 we (Positive Press) then published all these lesson plans in the book *Bridging The Circle – Transition Through Quality Circle Time*. Some lesson plans are timeless – they are the themes of humanity – anxiety, loneliness, need for connection, friendship and its issues, worry for the future. It always amazes me when I look through ranges of lesson plans as to how relevant they are here and now. As long as they have been structured into either the Five Steps or picked and mixed into different steps – or structured into introduction, middle phase and ending activity … they have pace and vibrancy.

In the "How To Use" section of the book at the beginning – we explain it is best that you create your own lesson plans depending on how comfortable you feel.

Some teachers just to get established as a facilitator of fun and firmness just do a Step 1 i.e. a games activity, followed by Step 2 which is a round and go back to Step 1 to finish.

The issue that is at stake is that it's your relationship with them and the trust they have in you to keep their discussions and interaction safe that is the key to excellence in Circle Time.

Once you have won them over to the circle with your warmth and ability to make life fun, they will trust you when you start to expand it to help them deal with their vulnerability and need for knowledge about sensitive topics.

Please note: elsewhere we have explained that as Step 4 is a Cheer-Up/ Celebration step, it is very acceptable to play a game that you may have used as a Step 1 in other sessions.

Secondary Transition First Day/Lesson 1

AIM: To enable young people to feel positive and supported by all in their move up to secondary school.

Process	Resources	Rationale	Knowledge/Skills/Attitude
Welcome and Ground Rules	On the flipchart: "Welcome" Ground rules	Students will feel safe and secure with firm boundaries and clear expectations.	I know/understand the rules. I can follow rules. I respect, value and see the need for rules.
Step 1 Game – Name Exercise Students to introduce themselves and say one food they like. The catch is that they have to introduce the person on their right first: **"This is Sarah who likes baked beans and I am David and I like chips."**	On the flipchart: "Getting to know you"	To loosen inhibitions, relax the atmosphere and allow students to introduce each other.	I can follow instructions, express myself clearly to others.
Step 2 Round – Pair Work **"One thing I have enjoyed so far about secondary school is …"**; **"One thing I am concerned/worried about is …"** (Write down the concerns in preparation for Step 5.)	Flipchart for recording things enjoyed and concerns.	To allow the students to celebrate the positive aspects of transition and to develop trust in expressing current concerns.	I can identify, express and listen to concerns about transition. I respect and value the positive thoughts and anxieties belonging to me and others about transition.
Step 2 Silent Statements Cross the circle if: you lost your way here today/the first morning (well done for getting here!); you thought you would but didn't (well done again!); you're still a little uncomfortable in your school uniform; you're starting to feel comfortable in it; you had a sneaky fashion show with it in front of the mirror during the holidays;	On the flipchart: "How does it feel to be here?"	To help the student identify the many different feelings associated with transition.	I can identify and express my feelings about transition. I respect the feelings I and others have associated with this new phase of our lives.

Introduction to Circle Plans 135

Process	Resources	Rationale	Knowledge/Skills/Attitude
you think everybody looks enormous here; you like that grown up feeling at secondary school; you're enjoying having all the different lessons to go to; you like having your own planner; you've crossed the circle because somebody else did; you stayed seated because somebody else did; you're beginning to find your way round school.			
Step 3 Open Forum Can we help each other to find solutions to our problems? Invite responses to individual concerns from Step 2 above. Individuals may field responses. Responses begin with words **"Would it help if (I, you, we, etc.) …?"** Encourage the problem-holders to thank each respondent, and at the end summarise a course of action.	On the flipchart: "How can we help each other?"	To encourage young people to help each other with and to allay anxieties around transition.	I know how to get help with my transition anxieties. I can offer help to others. I respect and value the help that people have offered to me/others.
Step 4 Game – Dinner A fun game – teacher to go round circle marking groups of four naming the individuals as sausages, beans, eggs, potatoes in turn. Then in groups of four they have two minutes to negotiate with each other and together form the image of dinner on a plate with a comment/caption if they wish. They can use the names given or they may decide to become a different dinner. Other groups could guess what they are.	On the flipchart: "Cooperation game: Sausage, beans, eggs, potatoes." It helps if you have clean floor space.	To encourage cooperation in a fun way.	I can work with others. I respect and value the thoughts and opinions of others in my group.
Step 4 Celebration Round Something positive that I have learnt in this lesson today is …		To encourage students to think positive thoughts.	I know, am aware of and can express the positive aspects of this lesson. I respect and value the thoughts of others.

Secondary Transition Lesson 2

AIM: To help the young people be aware of when they need help and how to get it.

Process	Resources	Rationale	Knowledge/Skills/Attitude
Introduction/Recap Explain the aim – do I know when I need help, and do I know how to ask for it? We don't always recognise when it is OK to ask for help, and sometimes we're too embarrassed to ask.	On the flipchart: "How do I know when I need help?"	To provide the students with a clear structure of the lesson.	I know/understand the reason for the lesson.
Step 1 Game – Silly Answers One student stands in the middle, whilst others take turns to ask questions of the person in the middle. The person in the middle gives a silly answer whilst trying not to smile. If they smile, the person who last asked a question takes her/his place.	On the flipchart: "Silly Answers"	Warming up activity which involves asking questions.	I can control my face muscles! I can also ask questions in public.
Step 2 Round – Pair Work Remind class of confidentiality rule. 1. When might you need help at secondary school? 2. What fears might stop you from asking for help? Encourage students to look at things that they find hard or upsetting. Feedback the answers to the second question. I might not ask for help because … Write up the different fears.	On the flipchart: Questions 1 and 2.	To explore the fears around asking for help, and to examine the ways sensitive others should behave at this time.	I am aware of/sensitive to situations where I and others may need help and to the fears involved. I can express my fears and listen to other people's fears. I respect and value the need for confidentiality.
Step 2 Silent Statements Cross the circle if: you feel confident to ask people for help when you know them; you feel less confident to ask people for help when you don't know them; you've ever felt embarrassed about having got something wrong; you've ever wanted help but have felt too embarrassed/stupid to ask; you feel more confident about asking for help when you're not the only one.	On the flipchart: "It's OK to make mistakes. It's OK to find things hard."	To raise awareness of the different levels of comfort associated with asking for help.	I know/am aware I may have less confidence in new situations. I can express these feelings. I respect and see the value of openness about these feelings.

Introduction to Circle Plans

Process	Resources	Rationale	Knowledge/Skills/Attitude
Step 3 Open Forum How do we need people to behave towards us when we have these fears? We can help ourselves but sometimes we need people around us and they need us. How do we help Alex? (Teacher to role-play this fictional character) *I don't like maths. The new teacher – I can't remember his name – is always being unfair to me. I did try at first but I can't do the work so I just chat or doodle. I got a detention last lesson. He doesn't explain it properly. I can't understand the questions that are written down – I'm not a very good reader. I took the homework to my Mum but she didn't have time because she had to go to work and then she said she wouldn't understand it anyway – maths has changed since she went to school. I don't like asking for help because I feel stupid. Nobody else asks for help. I know I'm going to end up being put down a set.* Ask the students to offer help using the words "*would it help if …*" Thank each offer of help and state whether this would be useful or not and why. Summarise a plan of action through the help given. It should include talking to parents and asking them to contact the school to ask for help. Further questions: How does Alex feel? What kind of comments from people (friends or family) might improve or ruin his/her confidence? What would happen if Alex did not ask for help? Does the same apply to other sorts of problems?	On the flipchart: "We can help people but they must be able to trust us" and … "You're OK, I'm not OK" and … "If I ask for help I can prevent things from getting worse."	To engage students in a problem-solving exercise that explores issues around needing help, what happens when we don't get it or people don't listen, and the importance of persistence.	I know of ways to respond to those fears around asking for help. I can help others. I understand how not asking for help can lead to more problems.

138 A Circle Approach to Boosting Emotional Wellbeing

Process	Resources	Rationale	Knowledge/Skills/Attitude
Step 2 Round – Pair Work Sometimes when we're upset or anxious, the words can come out all wrong, or they might not come at all. This can either rub people up the wrong way, or people may not even realise we need help. In pairs think of how you behave when you're anxious or upset and how you can control this. **"When I'm upset or angry I …"; "One way I can stay in control is …"**	On the flipchart: "When I'm upset or angry I …" "One way I can stay in control is …"	Raise awareness of how anxiety can sometimes prevent us from communicating effectively.	I am aware how anxiety can prevent me from being understood. I can identify solutions to this.
Step 4 Game – Electric Squeeze All hold hands and watch the electric pulse (hand squeeze) pass round the circle. Two squeezes mean change of direction. One person could be "on" and go outside the room whilst the class choose a person to be responsible for the change. The volunteer returns and has to watch and try to catch who it is.		Warming-down exercise.	I can enjoy working in a team.

Introduction to Circle Plans 139

Secondary Transition Lesson 3

AIM: To help the young people become aware of the losses and gains associated with transition.

Process	Resources	Rationale	Knowledge/Skills/Attitude
Introduction/Recap The lesson is to help people to get to know and trust one another some more, and to explore awareness of losses and gains so far.		To clarify aims and purpose of lesson.	I know/understand the reason for the lesson.
Step 1 Warm-p All members to think of an adjective that begins with the same letter as their forename, and to introduce themselves in turn, e.g. "active Angelica."	On the flipchart: "Losses and Gains"	A fun way to start the lesson, encouraging people to be positive about themselves.	I can say something positive/fun about myself.
Step 2 Round Explain to the group that transitions involve losses and gains, and that this transition will mean personal losses and gains for everybody. It helps if teacher can relate a personal experience such as moving on to a new job, or new house. "One thing I miss about my old school is …"; "One thing I have gained in my new school is …"; "One thing that I am doing more of and one thing I am doing less of since coming to secondary school is …"; "One feeling I have about my old school/new school now is …"	They can do this in pairs to get help. You need to have ideas ready to help the students if they get stuck. On the flipchart: "Transition" Have ready the losses/ gains sentence stems.	To allow the student to explore feelings around losses and gains in relation to old and new schools.	I know and am aware of my feelings around loss associated with transition. I can express those feelings. I respect and value my and others' feelings and thoughts about this.

Process	Resources	Rationale	Knowledge/Skills/Attitude
Step 2 Silent Statements Cross the circle if: you think you can find your way round school now; you feel there are good things about being at the new school; you've talked about your new school to someone at home; you've felt tired this last week; you feel there are some "not so good" things about being at the new school; you are missing your old school and teachers; you've walked past your old school since you've moved to secondary school (did it/would it feel strange?); you've been back to see your old teachers (how did that/would that feel?)		To explore feelings about the change and raise awareness of how many feelings people have in common.	I am aware that I am not alone with my feelings around transition. I respect the feelings of others if they are different from my own.
Step 3 Open Forum Students are asked to bring any particular problem to the group – it could be the way somebody is treating them, or that they are missing someone, or that they keep losing their temper, or they're finding the work too hard. Remind them of the rules, particularly the rule which does not allow names to be mentioned. Use the script, **"I need help because I…"**, **"Would it help if …?"** Students can put their thumb up to offer helpful ideas.		To provide an opportunity to share problems and help each other.	I know, respect and value mine and others' feelings around loss and gain at transition. I can express those feelings, listen to the feelings of others and offer help.
Step 4 Game – Rainbow People are labelled one of four colours. One chair is removed. Person in middle calls a colour and all of that colour cross the circle. Person left in middle calls. Rainbow = all colours cross the circle.		A warming-down activity	I can work/have fun with others whilst respecting and being sensitive to their needs.
Step 2 Round **"Something positive that I have learnt about myself today is …"**		To leave on a positive note and to sum up.	I am sensitive to, value and can express my developing inner self.

140 A Circle Approach to Boosting Emotional Wellbeing

Introduction to Circle Plans 141

Secondary Transition Lesson 4

AIM: To look at expectations around the subject of transition.

Process	Resources	Rationale	Knowledge/Skills/Attitude
Introduction/recap Explain that the aim is to raise awareness about some of the difficult issues around transition, looking at what a range of people expect from new students at school and what the students themselves feel.	On the flipchart: "Expectations"	To clarify aims and purpose of lesson.	I know/understand the reason for the lesson.
Step 1 Game – Noise Three people are chosen as callers and three as receivers, both groups to stand outside the circle opposite each other. Callers secretly decide on a message to send to the receivers. Teacher could provide the message. They have two minutes to get the message across. Remainder of class to distract with noise etc. to prevent message being sent – no physical interference though. To pass message callers can mime, shout louder etc. Allow other people to take a turn.	Have a message ready if they need it.	Fun warm-up game reducing inhibitions and involving teamwork.	I can work with others to achieve a purpose.
Step 2 Round Students to work in pairs for two minutes to help each other to come up with a response: **"Now I'm at secondary school I feel people expect me to be …"** Write the comments up on the flipchart if there is time and invite comments on any changes from the primary setting.	On the flipchart: "People expect me to be …"	To explore what people expect of us at secondary school and whether it's any different from primary school.	I can identify ways in which expectations of me have changed with transition.

142 A Circle Approach to Boosting Emotional Wellbeing

Process	Resources	Rationale	Knowledge/Skills/Attitude
Step 2 Silent Statements • Cross the circle if (you feel that): you've had an argument with an adult in the morning; • you're expected to be more responsible now you're at secondary school; • what you want and what adults want for you are sometimes different; • you're sometimes still treated too much like a child; • you sometimes behave like an adult; • you sometimes behave like a child (be honest! – remind them that adults do too); • you think you're expected to remember more now you're at secondary school; • you get more freedom now you're at secondary school; • you wish you were given more freedom; • you're expected to fit more things into your life now you're secondary; • you've found yourself running out of time a lot more than before; • you're expected to help round the house more as you get older; • you feel you're expected to know more than you do.		To explore some of the conflicting aspects of growing up, in terms of expectations.	I am aware of the positive and negative effects of expectations from different people. I value those expectations which are to improve my wellbeing.

Introduction to Circle Plans 143

Process	Resources	Rationale	Knowledge/Skills/Attitude
Step 3 Open Forum – Role-Play Alex Ask a student if they could read this script out with feeling ... *I'm really fed up. People expect me to do things all the time. I never have any time to myself now. I'm always having arguments with my Dad because I haven't done things like tidy my room or clear up after myself. I can't be bothered with it all. Last night I had three lots of homework, which teachers are expecting today, and I haven't done all of it because some of it was set last week and I forgot. I was doing other things last night and then I didn't want to miss the football on TV. Then Dad was on at me for getting up late this morning and not having my bag packed. Why don't they just all leave me alone.* Encourage responses: **"Would it help if ..."** *What does Dad expect of Alex? Is he being unfair?* *Why can't Alex be bothered with it all?* *What are they feeling about themself?* *What does Alex expect of themself?* *What does Alex need help with?* *What could happen to Alex if they do not get any help?* The teacher can draw attention to the words on the flipchart at the end to help summarise the situation.	On the flipchart: 1. It feels like people expect too much from me 2. Thinking ahead 3. What do I expect of myself? 4. I can try my best and no more	To seek solutions for a person experiencing difficulties with new expectations and routines.	I know/understand how I might not meet other people's expectations. I can find ways of dealing with this. I respect the need to communicate politely.
Step 4 Game – I Love You Honey But I Just Can't Smile Teacher turns to neighbour on left, looks into their eyes and says, **"I love you honey,"** trying to make them laugh. Neighbour responds (without smiling), **"I love you honey, but I just can't smile."** Neighbour then repeats this to person on their left.		Fun anti-inhibition game with positive communication and eye contact.	I can use positive eye contact and body language (only when appropriate and comfortable for students)
Step 4: Celebration **"Something positive that I know I can do is ..."**	On the flipchart: "I can expect good things from myself."	Recognising that we can have our own personal goals.	I value and can express positive expectations I have of myself.

Secondary Transition Lesson 5

AIM: To look at how friendships might affect me.

Process	Resources	Rationale	Knowledge/Skills/Attitude
Introduction/Recap Teacher to explain that the aim of this lesson is to explore how friendships grow and change, how natural this is, what to expect and how to cope with the changes.	On the flipchart: "Change in friendship"	Setting the scene.	I know/understand the reason for the lesson.
Step 1 Game – Elephant, Palm Tree and Aeroplane Everybody stands up. One chosen person stands in the middle and points to someone in the circle, saying elephant/palm tree/aeroplane. To make an elephant the person pointed to leans forward, swinging arms forward to make a trunk. The people on the immediate left and right makes the elephant's ears by creating a circle with their arms and leaning towards the person with the trunk. To make a palm tree the person pointed to stands with arms straight up (the trunk) whilst the people on either side use their arms to be the fronds coming out of the trunk. To make an aeroplane, the person pointed to stretches their arms out horizontally for the wings whilst the people on either side bob down to become the engines		This is a fun warm-up game which requires a lot of concentration.	I can work and cooperate with others.
Step 2 Round Teacher to explain that although friendships do sometimes go wrong, they are extremely valuable. When things do go wrong, it can be devastating. Think about a time when you have had a friendship problem. **"When friendships go wrong, I feel …"** Comment – how many of those feelings expressed are the same as those associated with loss that we covered in Lesson 3.	On the flipchart: "When friendships go wrong, I feel …"	To recognise the feelings around friendship problems.	I know/understand the many feelings associated with friendship problems. I can openly express those feelings.

Introduction to Circle Plans 145

Process	Resources	Rationale	Knowledge/Skills/Attitude
Step 2 Silent Statements Stand up and cross the circle if: you came from primary school with friends; you knew someone already at the secondary school; you have already made some new friends; you have noticed your old friends making new friends; there are friends in this class whom you would like to be able to trust; you ever had someone you have thought of as a best friend; you have ever felt let down and hurt by a friend; a friend has ever felt you had let them down; you forgive people easily; someone has ever forgiven you; you think it's better to sort arguments out rather than let them carry on; you've ever felt left out; you think it is possible to have a lot of good friends		To help students raise awareness of their present friendship situations and how their needs reflect the needs of others	I know/understand and can express feelings about my present friendship situations. I respect and value the friendship of other people in this group.
Step 3 Open Forum – Role-Play – The Teacher Becomes Alex *Scenario: I feel really down. My friend and I are from the same primary school and we moved up to secondary school together. We always used to be good mates but now somebody else has started hanging around – someone who lives near my friend. They went out together last night without me and were talking about it all day today and I feel really mad and upset that I wasn't invited. Also I don't know what this new friend thinks of me – I get the feeling I'm not wanted. I feel really hurt and let down.*	On the flipchart: "Old friends and new friends – is it possible to have both without upsetting either?"	To encourage the students to resolve a new friend–old friend difficulty using a win–win approach.	I know/understand the potential difficulties attached to making new friends and of keeping and sharing old friends. I can respond maturely to friends enjoying being with others. I respect and value my friends' needs to develop friendships with others.

Process	Resources	Rationale	Knowledge/Skills/Attitude
The teacher/facilitator stays in character as Alex and the children thumbs up if they have an idea using the script, **"Alex, would it help if …"** If no one wants to contribute, then start a discussion about how Alex may be feeling.			
Step 4 Game – Touchdown Teacher shouts out a number and in pairs, students cooperate to touch the floor with that number of body parts, e.g. three could be three feet with one person holding one leg up in the air. Each set of pairs should try to be different from the rest.		Cooperation exercise.	I can cooperate and work with a partner.
Step 4 Round – Celebration Students may need time in pairs to prepare this. **"When I'm a good friend I …"**		Students can think about their own "giving" within friendships.	I know and can express the positive friendship qualities I have.

Secondary Transition Lesson 6

AIM: How am I doing so far?

Process	Resources	Rationale	Knowledge/ Skills/ Attitude
Introduction/Recap Explain to the students that this lesson is to reflect on all that has happened since they arrived at secondary school, and to celebrate the positive gains and achievements so far. Also, the aim is to look at what they found difficult, and to try to feel more comfortable with that.	On the flipchart: "How am I doing so far?" Have ready big cut out stars.	To encourage the students to reflect positively on the transitional process they have gone through.	I know/understand that change can be difficult, but it can bring positive gains. I can reflect on the progress that I have made and can allow myself to make mistakes. I respect and value my achievements.
Step 1 Game – Our World Put several sheets of newspaper on the ground. The students walk, swim, float around the room until a given signal. At this point everyone must stand on a piece of the world. The students continue moving and the process is repeated, each time a piece of the world being taken. Eventually only one or two pieces of the world are left. No student must be left outside when the time for standing on a piece of the world comes. It can be done if everyone cooperates. Questions: What helped? What didn't help? Did any part of the game remind you of any feelings/thoughts you've had since you've started secondary school?	Newspaper.	Working together, cooperation, and working towards a common aim.	I respect and value the need to think about others in order to achieve a win–win situation.
Step 2 Round Close your eyes and think back to the very first day – think of coming through the school gates … your very first lesson … your very first meal … the first piece of homework you received … the first person you spoke to. In pairs, students to think of two things they have both found difficult. **"We found it difficult to …"**	On the flipchart: "We found it difficult to …"	Students can not only express the difficult aspects of secondary school, but discover they are not alone with some of those feelings.	I know/understand that I have not been on my own in finding certain things difficult. I can express the things I have found difficult. I respect and value my thoughts and those of others.

Process	Resources	Rationale	Knowledge/ Skills/ Attitude
Step 2 Silent Statements Stand up and cross the circle if: you have found it hard getting up earlier in the morning; you have got used to getting up earlier now; you have found it hard getting used to all the different teachers; you feel you're getting used to all the different teachers; you're used to the new routines of secondary school; you think you can remember most of your school timetable now; you are using your planner every day; you are mostly remembering to bring the things you need; you are pleased with the new friends you are making; you are enjoying most of your lessons; you feel you're a different person now than before the summer holidays; you feel to have learnt a lot about "life" since primary school. **Step 4 Open Forum – Star Students** Cut out lots of printed stars with different feelings and thoughts on, e.g. "Secondary school has felt good so far," "Glad that there were people I knew," "Felt pleased that we've made new friends," "Enjoy all the lessons," "Have shown positive behaviour," "A bit scared at first but feel OK now," "Felt people have been helpful here," "Like the teachers so far," "Been trying our best with the work," "Managed to hand in homework on time," "Spoken politely to teachers," "Let friends make new friends without jealousy," "Included people who looked left out," etc.	On the flipchart: "We have coped with change." "We have achieved!"	To help the young people to realise how much they have learnt through the process of change.	I know/understand that I have done well making adjustments to my new lifestyle. I can survive change

Introduction to Circle Plans 149

Process	Resources	Rationale	Knowledge/ Skills/ Attitude
Then display them in the middle of the circle. Ask the students in pairs to select two stars that best match their mutual feelings and thoughts. When they have chosen their stars they return to sit in the circle. When all students have chosen their stars, two by two the students read out their stars and place them on a sheet of paper in the middle of the circle. This continues until all students have had a turn. The teacher encourages all the students to reflect on the importance of the process through which they have gone. The completed sheet can be displayed as a symbol of the students' positive achievements in their form rooms.	Cut out printed stars with feelings and thoughts on.	To help the students to recognise that purely through coping with change, they have already achieved much of value since their arrival at secondary school.	I know/understand how change can be positive. I can work with someone to identify some of the positive achievements we have in common. I respect and value my thoughts and those of others.
Step 4 Game – Knots All except for two in the group, hold hands in a line. The leader leads the group by hand, twisting and weaving under arms and through people without letting go of hands until the group is tangled. The two remaining people are the untanglers who advise how to unknot the group.		A fun warming-down exercise.	I can work with others and have fun.
Step 5 Round – Celebration **"Our team has done well because …"** Teacher then gives out a celebration card to each student. Play some calming music during this step.	Make some celebration cards with either a class photo or nice images. Add a thoughtful congratulatory message.	To give the teacher a chance to personally congratulate each person	I feel respected and valued by the teacher.

Twenty Minute Tutor Sessions

The following transition circle plans are for 20-minute tutorial sessions (Mosley, 2005). They could be very useful for small vertical tutor groups or for schools that are wanting to use their tutorial activity for the whole class to help the children start developing their speaking and listening skills, sense of empathy and trust. These circle plans would be very useful for a group whom you later want to use the full Five Step Structure to discuss the more in-depth PSHE topics.

Tutor Circle Session 1

THEME: A place to learn.
RESOURCES: Speaking object.

Activity	Explanation	Rationale
Step 1 Meeting-up game	**Rocket launch** Class are seated in a circle. Any person can start by standing up and immediately calling out "one." Then anyone else can stand up and call out "two" and this continues until two people stand up and call out the same number at the same time, when everyone sits back down and they start again. The aim is to get as many people standing up as possible by keen observation, subtle communication and turn taking.	To develop observation skills by looking at body language, promoting team work and practising the ability to wait and watch.
Step 1 Opening-up	**Silent Statements** Cross the circle if ... • You lost your way to the tutor room on the first day • You thought you would but didn't • You're still a little uncomfortable in your school uniform • You like having your own planner • You've crossed the circle because somebody else did! • You've stayed seated because somebody else did!	To help students mix up and to help them to identify some of the different feelings associated with transitions and realise that they are not alone with those feelings.
Step 2 Closing round	**How to Make School Better** "One thing that would make this school better to learn in would be ..." Scribe their ideas to take to the next tutorial.	For some feedback from the pupils to help them think about the ideas for the next session.

Introduction to Circle Plans 151

Twenty-Minute Tutor Circle Session 2

THEME: A place to learn.
RESOURCES: Nothing.

Activity	Explanation	Rationale
Step 1 Meeting-up game	**Moving Changes** Ask the students to volunteer or choose someone to begin a movement, in the circle. The movement is then copied by the person on their right. In turn, without speaking, each person in the circle should perform the action until the action has come full circle. Now change the action and begin the process again. Now choose a detective who goes out of the circle. Ask this person to close their eyes. A leader to start the movement is chosen, who starts the group off and then the detective has to re-enter the circle. They have to keep turning and have three guesses to who the leader is. Tell the leader to change the movements every time the detective's back is turned.	To warm up the group and remind them of the idea of "changes."
Step 3 Opening-up Pairs agree a sentence and which person is going to say it, e.g. **"We found it difficult to find the rooms."**	**Changes Happen** Explain to the students that this session is to reflect on what has happened since they arrived at secondary school and to celebrate the gains and achievements so far. Another aim is to look at the changes they found difficult and to try to feel more comfortable with those changes now. Read the following script to the class: *Close your eyes and think back to your very first day – think of coming into the school, your first lesson, your very first meal, the first piece of homework you received, the first person you spoke to in your tutor group. Now open your eyes and in pairs think of two things you both found difficult at first.* They can then report back to the circle as a pair: **"We found it difficult to ..."**	To celebrate achievements made at secondary school and to look at what they all found challenging.

(Continued)

Activity	Explanation	Rationale
Step 4 Cheering-up	**Nominations** Explain that when changes happen there are usually positive and negative things associated with that change. Ask students to nominate other students (remind them not to choose their best friend) who they feel have really made progress in any way. List the ways – can find their way round more easily, e.g. put their hands up more often, don't shout out so much, hand in homework on time now, etc. Then ask other students if they agree. If they do, the nominated student receives a "Class Team Honours" – signed by the whole class.	To reinforce the systems/ideas that students can use to help themselves. To notice other students' achievements and to celebrate them.

Tutor Circle Session 3

THEME: A place to learn.
RESOURCES: Bag or box of different hats, paper, pencils; speaking object.

Activity	Explanation	Rationale
Step 1 Meeting-up	**Spot the Leader** A "spotter" is chosen from the circle and should leave the room until they are called back. Meanwhile, another person is chosen to be the "leader." The leader should decide on an action, e.g. a cough, a scratch of the chin or tap of the foot which they will use as a signal – to lead the rest of the group. The spotter is called back into the room and stands in the middle of the circle, turning on the spot to scan all players. The rest of the group begin the game by saying "1 … 1 … 1 … 1 … 1 … 1 …" They carry on until the leader changes the number by using the agreed signal. At the leader's signal the group continue "2 … 2 … 2 … 2 … 2 …" When the leader performs the signal again, the group changes their chant to "3 … 3 … 3 … 3 …" The game continues in this manner, and it is the spotters job to spot the signal and therefore the leader and identify the action. Can the group reach the number 10 before being spotted	To help students warm up, concentrate and feel part of a team.

(Continued)

Activity	Explanation	Rationale
Step 3 Opening-up	**Left and Right Hands** Put the pupils into pairs and each pair needs two pieces of paper and a pencil. They take it in turns to lay their hands down, side by side with fingers outstretched whilst the partner draws round them, then they swap round. Each pupil should have their own hands outlined on a piece of paper. Ask the students to write down up to five things they have found frustrating since starting secondary school on the fingers and thumb of the left hand, and up to five things they have been pleased about on the right hand. Then go round the circle and each student shares one idea from each hand. **"One thing I have found frustrating is …"; "One thing that has pleased me is …"**	Helping students to see that the changes whilst starting at a new school have plus points and negative points but that they mostly balance out.
Step 4 Cheering-up	**Remembering Round** **"One thing I find hard to remember is … And one thing I always remember is … But I am pleased about …"**	Helping pupils to find their voice and express some of their frustrations and things they are pleased about.

Tutor Circle Session 4

THEME: Learning to be together – social skills and empathy.
RESOURCES: Nothing.

Activity	Explanation	Rationale
Step 1 Meeting-up	**Foot Tapping** Begin this game with all students making the same foot movement. Once they are all doing this, walk round the outside of the circle and tap someone on the back. That person must change their foot movement and the others must be alert to spot the change. Once all the students are doing a new movement, touch another player on the back and the game continues.	For fun and to help with observation skills and all working together.

(Continued)

Activity	Explanation	Rationale
Step 3 Opening-up	**The Empty Chair** Explain that the following game will remind us of the good feelings we get from being part of a group and the bad feelings we get when we feel left out or different. Choose a popular, confident member of the group and ask them to stand in the middle of the circle. Tell the rest of the class to move clockwise, covering the seats with their bottoms as they move from chair to chair (so that there is always an empty chair, but it appears and disappears as the students move round). The volunteer has to try to sit on an empty chair and the class have to try to prevent them from doing so. When the game is over (the child may well have got a seat or we stop and we allow them to get a seat) ... ask them how might this person be feeling now and if this game had gone on for too long and all of you were having a good laugh? Ask them to put their thumbs up and address the focus child who at this stage is not going to answer. At the end they can say how they would have felt if the game had gone on for too long. Thank that child for helping us play the game – turn to the group and ask them if they can explain how it is reminiscent of playground scenarios. Can any student describe similar situations and make a list of them? Offer a choice of sentence stems like **"A time when I felt left out was ..."** or **"Some people feel left out when ..."** Use the list and ask students to share strategies that they have found useful in similar situations. You may choose to support their suggestions by offering them the sentence stem **"Would it help if I ...?"**	This reminds us of the good feelings we get as part of a group and the bad feelings we feel when left out. It teaches students about empathy and can be used in many Circle Time meetings.
Step 4 Cheering-up	**Thank You** Ask students to thank other students for any qualities that they notice – but they cannot choose to thank their best friends. Use questions such as "Who in this class have you noticed always includes people?" The pupils can put thumbs up and then follow it up with "Rick, we have noticed that you always include people – congratulations." Point out that they are learning the meaning of the word empathy. Be specific and thank some students personally whilst praising the group as a whole.	It's always very moving to see students thank other students who are not their best friend. Something simple like "Maisie we've noticed that you always let people in your games."

Tutor Circle Session 5

THEME: Learning to be together – social skills and empathy.
RESOURCES: Script for John's day and a speaking object.

Activity	Explanation	Rationale
Step 1 Meeting-up	**The Bean Game** A central person calls out the names of various types of beans. Everyone else has to act out the description: "French Bean" – everyone flicks their wrist and says "Ooh-la-la." "Runner Bean" – run up and down the room. "Jumping Bean" – jump up and down on the spot. "Has Been" – shaky jelly. "Baked Bean" – frozen. "Broad or Kidney Bean" – the others must mime this until the next bean is called out. It can be done round in a circle or moving around or standing in the middle of the circle. (Variation – create their own interpretation for these beans!)	Good for energising the group and for having fun and a laugh together.
Step 3 Opening-up	**John's Day – Boost Ups and Put Downs** (teacher/ facilitator reads the story) *One Thursday morning, John got up earlier than usual to do some exercises because he really wanted to be in the school football team. His sister, Joanne, asked him what he was doing. "I'm trying to get fit so that I am chosen for the football team." "I shouldn't bother," she replied. "They won't choose a slow twit like you." At breakfast, Joanne was mean again and told their mother that John would never be chosen. "You keep exercising, John," said his mother, "if you don't try you will never succeed. If you put your mind to it, you'll have as much chance as everyone else." At school, the first lesson was maths but John couldn't find his maths book anywhere. When he eventually got on with his sums, he couldn't remember how to do them. So he asked his teacher if she could remind him. "You'd forget your head if it wasn't attached to your body," said Miss Davies. And all the other pupils laughed.*	Helping students to see that the changes whilst starting at a new school have plus point and negative points but that they mostly balance out.

(Continued)

Activity	Explanation	Rationale
	The next lesson was English where they watched some videos and were asked questions about what they watched. John put up his hand to answer a question. "Nerd," said Sally just so that John could hear her. John got the answer right and the teacher praised him for being so observant. When John got out to the playground after lunch he was a little late and the lunchtime football game had already started. John asked the boys if someone would let him have a go. "You can have my place for a while," said Simon "I've got to get a drink of water." One of the other players, Peter, wasn't so kind. "I'm glad he's not going to be in my team!" he said. After playtime was art lesson. John was pleased with his picture. "Cor," said Sally, "my 3-year-old brother could do better than that!" John felt upset. At the end of the day, John couldn't wait to leave the school. It had been a horrible day and he felt close to tears. He felt like he couldn't do anything right and some of the comments he'd had today were so harsh. In an Open Forum, ask the pupils: • what put downs John had suffered that day • how John was feeling about everything • how other people could have made his day better • is there anything John could do to help himself have a better day tomorrow.	
Step 2 Closing	**Good Friends** Ask the students to complete the following sentence in a round: **"When I am a good friend I …"** Thank the students for their honesty and for sharing their thoughts about friendships. Thank and praise the students for their work on friendships	To help students think about how to be a better friend to others.

Tutor Circle Session 6

THEME: Learning to be together – social skills and empathy.
RESOURCES: Speaking object.

Activity	Explanation	Rationale
Step 1 Meeting-up	**Don't Say Yes or No!** One person volunteers to be questioned about anything. The trick is that they must not say "yes" or "no" or "don't know." The teacher can start off doing the questioning to set the scene. The faster the questions, the more likely they will be caught out. Then encourage the students to be the questioners. When the volunteer gets it wrong, someone else can take over.	To help concentration and confidence.
Step 2 Opening-up	**Silent Friendship Statements** Ask the students to cross the circle if: • They came from primary school with friends • They knew someone already at this school • They have already made some new friends • They have noticed their old friends making new friends • There are friends in this class who they can trust • They have ever gone round in a crowd • They have ever had someone who thought of them as a best friend.	To help raise awareness of their present friendship situations and how they have needs in common with others. Don't allow any put downs
Step 2 Closing	**Friendship Feelings** Ask the students in a round to complete the following sentence: **"When friendships go wrong I feel ... and when friendships go well I feel ..."** Anyone who wishes not to speak can say "pass" and pass the speaking object on to the next person. Praise any students who worked well in the session today	To help students feel that everyone has these feelings and that they are a normal part of relationships.

Tutor Circle Session 7

THEME: Learning to be together – social skills and empathy.
RESOURCES: Speaking object, wooden giraffe or other animal)

Activity	Explanation	Rationale
Step 2 Warming-up	**If I Was An Animal** Using the speaking object, ask each student in turn to complete the following sentence: **"My favourite animal is ..."** Those who do not wish to speak may say "pass" and give the speaking object to the next person.	To warm up the group and prepare for the next activity.
Step 3 Opening-up	**It's OK** Point out that a lot of people chose different animals but that there were no wrong answers. It was all a question of preference and everyone has their own reasons for making that particular choice and should feel happy with their choice. Hold up a wooden giraffe (or any other animal) and say that you are going to say three things about it: "This giraffe has four legs." (Fact) "This giraffe has long legs." (Fact) "Giraffes are very beautiful" (Opinion) You can then ask for a show of hands. "Who agrees this is a giraffe?" (Should be everyone) "Who agrees it has four legs?" (Should be everyone) "Who agrees it has long legs?" (Should be everyone) "Who agrees it is beautiful?" (Should be divided opinion) Repeat this with another animal if necessary to bring home the point. Now ask one or two students to think of another animal and state two facts and one opinion. If time permits, show the students how we justify opinions by telling them how we use the word "because" which means "for the reason that follows." Explain that it is a real social skill to be able to accept people's opinions even if we think something different.	To help smooth social interactions by enabling students to see that there are facts and there are opinions, and that opinions are not right or wrong, just an opinion.
Step 2 Closing	**In My Opinion** Using the speaking object, ask each student in turn to complete the following sentence, which follows on from the first exercise in this session: Choosing their favourite animal each: **"I would like to be a ... because ..."** (students complete the sentence). Those who do not wish to speak may say "pass" and give the speaking object to the next person.	To reinforce the previous opinion exercise and end on a high note.

Tutor Circle Session 8

THEME: Keep on learning – motivation
RESOURCES: Six picture postcards (one for every five students); a piece of paper and pencil for each and a box

Activity	Explanation	Rationale
Step 1 Meeting-up	**Silent Statements – Look What I Have Achieved** Cut each postcard into five pieces. Write A on the back of each piece of the first postcard, B on the back of each piece of the second, and so on. Shuffle the pieces well and give one to each student. Explain that every piece has a letter on the back. Without talking, they must find the other students with the same letter and then put the pieces together to make the postcard. The first team to finish is the winner.	Good for non-verbal communication, enjoyment and teamwork.
Step 1 Warming-up	**Silent Statements – Look What I Have Achieved** Ask the students to think of all their achievements since arriving in secondary school. Cross the circle and find a different seat if: • You think you can now find your way around this school easily; • You feel there are more good things than bad things about being in secondary school; • You are missing your old school and teachers; • You have been back to see your old school and teachers since you have been here; • You feel there are things to look forward to in your new school in the future; • You are pleased with what you have learnt already. Praise the students for being honest about what they have achieved. Point out that they have already learnt a lot since arriving in secondary school and that there is a lot more fun and learning to be gained in the years to come.	To raise awareness of how many feelings people have in common and hopefully how far they have come in their transition.
Step 4 Cheering-up	**Our Gifts To You** Ask the students to write their name on their piece of paper, collect in the papers and place them in the box. One at a time, take a name out and invite the students to put their hand up to volunteer a gift they would like to give that person. Choose three students to say what they would like to give. Encourage them to be imaginative in their choices; for example, a safari in Africa, a ride in a hot air balloon, a robot to do their homework, a diamond necklace.	Students are positive about their peers and this creates a good atmosphere and good self-esteem.

(Continued)

Activity	Explanation	Rationale
	To take this activity a step further, you could ask students to make the gift more abstract, for example, wisdom, the ability to fly or to talk to animals. Thank them and praise them for using their imaginations. Remind them to think carefully first – is this a kind gift? Would you like to receive it?	

Tutor Circle Session 9

THEME: Keep on learning – motivation
RESOURCES: Speaking object.

Activity	Explanation	Rationale
Step 2 Warming-up	**Two Things** Divide students into random pairs then get them to find out two things about what they both enjoy doing at the weekends. They can then introduce their partner and say what they share in school – or, for an extra twist, they can try miming it and have people guess.	To help students get to know each other, break down barriers and have fun.
Step 3 Opening-up	**My goals** Give the students the opportunity to talk about some of their more immediate goals, such as to improve their handwriting, avoid fights, learn to swim. Ask them to say **"My goal is to …"** At this point you have let a lot students speak. So just choose one student, check they would like to be the focus student and choose them for the fact their goal is similar to other students. Ask them to reframe it again, **"I need help because I want to … learn to walk away from fights, or to get my homework done or to swim …"** The other students can help each other to take steps towards that goal by offering help or advice using the following sentence stem: **"Would it help if you …?"** Ask the focus student to give their favourite answer and say thank you at the end. Remind the group that if they want to gave help with their goals or are stuck with them then they can ask you for Chat Time (see pages 93–94) It may help to keep a note of these goals and the assistance that was offered so that you can check on progress during subsequent sessions.	To help students to learn that they all have goals in many different areas of life and that there are steps they can take.

(Continued)

Activity	Explanation	Rationale
Step 4 Closing	**Sitting in the Long Grass** You will need an extra chair to put in the circle. Choose a place to put the empty chair in the circle. Whoever is sitting to the right of the chair moves onto it and says, **"Here I am …"** The next child moves onto the newly vacated chair and says, **"… sitting in the long grass."** The next child moves onto the vacant seat and says, **"… on a beautiful sunny day."** the next child moves onto the vacant chair and says, **"… with my friend"** and beckons to someone seated opposite to come and sit next to them on the vacant chair. This then produces a vacant chair on the other side of the circle, so the actions are repeated starting with the child to the right of the chair. Encourage children to choose people from different parts of the circle so that the activity can be enjoyed by everyone.	Reinforces the concept of friendship and the whole group is basically a circle of friends.

Tutor Circle Session 10

THEME: Learning about me – managing feelings.
RESOURCES: Speaking object; "well done" or smiley face stickers; picture of a smiling person

Activity	Explanation	Rationale
Step 2 Warming-up	**"I Like It When …"** Using the speaking object, ask each student in turn to complete the sentence: **"At school, I like it when …"** Students who do not wish to speak may say "pass" and give the speaking object to the next student.	To bring out the positive in school.
Step 4 Cheering-up **Tip:** Only do this activity when you feel the class is ready to be positive to each other.	**Smiley Faces** Do prior work on this by reading out – in a tutorial session – a list of all the good things you've noticed about each of your students. Make sure you've always got something good to say about each student. Even better, weeks before doing this exercise, make sure you publically notice good things about each student, so the others will notice too!	To help students to understand that they have the power to make people feel good.

(Continued)

Activity	Explanation	Rationale
	Give each student an unpeeled "well done" or smiley face sticker. (Don't think that Year 7 pupils are too old for these – we've done surveys, and they miss what they had in primary school.) Choose one student and ask them to unpeel the sticker and put it on someone else's jumper. As they do so, they need to say, **"I am giving you this sticker because you are ... (good at being kind, good at helping me, etc.)."** When each student has received a sticker, go round the group and ask them to repeat the reason why they were given the sticker. Did they like receiving the sticker and the kind words from their classmates? They can give other people this warm feeling at any time because all they have to do is smile and say something nice. Now see if they can think of someone who might like to receive the gift of some kind words – their mum or dad perhaps. Set them the task of remembering to say something kind to everyone at home and someone at school every day and see how much happiness they can make all by themselves.	
Step 2 Fun Closing Again – you need to trust the class before you play this game!	**Gloop** Some imaginary slime is "thrown" from one group member to another. The "slime" always lands on the person's face and as it's pulled off, the group makes sucking, slurping noises. The person who it has landed on then "throws" it at someone else.	Generates good eye contact and laughter. It can give power to people who rarely have it.

Tutor Circle Session 11

THEME: Learning about me – managing feelings.
RESOURCES: Speaking object.

Activity	Explanation	Rationale
Step 1 Meeting-up	**Sausage** The aim is to make the person in the centre laugh. They stand in the middle and ask the other students questions, e.g. **"What are your shoes made of?"**; **"What do you brush your teeth with?"** The answer every time must be "sausage." If the person laughs or smiles, they swap over. Remind them the questions must be sensible otherwise we may have to stop the game.	To warm up the group ready for discussion.

(Continued)

Activity	Explanation	Rationale
Step 1 Further Meeting-up	**My Group** In turn, people can be chosen to stand in the centre of the circle and invite members of the group to join their group by naming a category for entry into the group, e.g. **"Anyone who likes 'Eastenders' can be in my group." "Anyone who likes bikes can be in my group."** Students who fit the category stand in the middle with the group leader until a new leader is chosen. Participants keep a tally of how many groups they belonged to. Note: groups must not be joined on the basis of personalities but of categories. This game could lead into discussion of what it feels like to be included in a group, left out or different from others, and how we are influenced by whoever is the group leader. Is this a good thing?	To explore feelings around group membership in a fun way.
Step 2 Closing	**Reflection** Ask the students to complete the following sentence in a round using a speaking object. Any student not wishing to speak can say "pass" and pass on the speaking object to the next person. **"One thing I have learnt today is …"** Thank the students for helping the class to think about being included and being left out and about the feelings that we have about this.	To reflect on achievement and for a calm end to the session.

RSHE (Relationships, Sex and Health Education) Circle Times

The next four lesson plans have been structured by Maya Menon from the Teacher Foundation in India (I have talked about her work in the Acknowledgements section). Over the 25 years I've known her, she has created a range of fantastic lesson plans using our traditional Five Steps Structure.

Here Maya has written some very enriching, very thoughtful ideas for the one-hour PSHE lesson. I have put extra materials that she has suggested for follow-up development if you wish to keep going with that particular theme in the next session.

Theme 1: Teasing/Bullying (Age 13–15)

Process	Resources	Facilitator notes	Expectations
Step 1 Meeting-up The facilitator introduces the five skills (with actions) that would be used during the QCT session – Thinking, Looking, Listening, Speaking and Concentration. (**"In Circle Time we use five skills …"**) Share the ground rules with the students (especially if they are doing QCT for the first time). (**"In Circle Time we use five skills …"**)Share the ground rules with the students (especially if they are doing QCT for the first time).		**The Ground Rules** *Once the children have understood these you don't have to mention them each time. throughout all your circles thank them if they are keeping to the Ground Rules.* 1. Whoever has the speaking object uses their speaking skills and we look at them. 2. If you don't wish to speak when the speaking object comes to you, you could say "Pass" 3. In Circle Time we can discuss any problem/issue you may be facing, but we never name anyone negatively only name them when it's a positive comment 4. You can say pass if you don't want to speak and you will be offered another chance at the end of a round. 5. We signal when we want to contribute a comment.	To help the students know the Five Skills and Five Ground Rules.
Step 1 Game – Exchanging Places One student volunteers to be in the Centre to make various call outs – those who love football exchange places; those who enjoy hanging out in cafes, those born in the first half of the year; etc). Whoever is left in the centre continues the game.	Chairs in a circle, one chair turned around to indicate non-availability.		To help the participants to relax. Gives students the opportunity to connect with their peers and build a group identity. To get students to use their five skills in a fun, energetic manner.

Introduction to Circle Plans

Process	Resources	Facilitator notes	Expectations
Step 2 Warming-Up One thing I like about hanging out with my mates is … (Speaking round)	Speaking object		To give all students in the circle, the opportunity to speak and contribute to the shared experience of the circle
Step 3 Opening-Up **"One thing that worries me about hanging out with my mates is …"** This time children can put their thumb up and contribute. Once they have spoken, ask the students if one of them would be happy to be the focus person who gets real help from the class (in opening up round we only help one student at a time per session otherwise it is too long). The student listens to their peers and to every **"Would it help if …"** suggestion. They say,	Speaking object	To help children think of things that worry them, you can ask the following trigger questions … • do you need help because you get teased a lot? • Do you need help because no one ever listens to your ideas?	To invite students to explore an issue and honestly share their opinions and feelings. Anticipate "teasing"/"bullying"/body shaming as some of the issues that may get surfaced or mentioned repeatedly. It is also possible that some students may share that they don't have anyone to hang out with.

Process	Resources	Facilitator notes	Expectations
"Yes, that might help thank you"; "I haven't tried that before, thank you";"I've tried that and it doesn't work for me but thank you." Once the class have stopped coming up with ideas to help that person (don't forget teachers can also thumbs up an idea) then the teacher thank the focus student for being brave and honest and the other students for being kind and helpful. The teacher asks the focus student, **"What idea are you most drawn to?"** They can come to a Chat Time later in the year if they need more help.		The facilitator appreciates the participation of the students by saying **"Thank you, you have all shared so honestly and bravely."** OR **"You all used your five skills!"**	
Step 4 Cheering-up/Appreciation Game	Large soft ball		To give the pupils the opportunity to have fun.
Students are sitting down. The facilitator starts with a soft ball and shouts out the name of a student who stands up **"Sakira you have listened well today."** Sakira then sends it to another child and congratulates them, e.g. **"Well done Luca you listened well."** This continues until everyone has been congratulated.			

Process	Resources	Facilitator notes	Expectations
Step 5 Calming Down Teach students how to be calm "lose your eyes, put your right hand on your tummy, left hand on top. Slowly breathe in the energy and the oxygen 1 ... 2 ... 3. Now open your mouth. Slowly expel all the tension and the toxins 1 ... 2 ... 3 ... Keep breathing whilst I play a very short piece of calming music (just play one minute) – when the minute is finished say to the students, slowly now I want you to have a stretch, open your eyes and see how many children's eyes can you smile into whilst I count to 3." Finally thank them.			To help the pupils to experience a closing calm ritual that would ensure that their transition to the next part of their day is smooth and successful.

Theme 2: Emojis and Emoticons (Age 13–16)

Process	Resources	Facilitator notes	Expectations
Step 1 Meeting-Up The facilitator introduces the five skills (with actions) that would be used during the QCT session – Thinking, Looking, Listening, Speaking and Concentration. Share the ground rules with the students	Get resources ready for Step 3 and 4.		Communicate simple actions that would enable a smooth flow to the session.
Step 1 Game – The Sleeping Spell The students stand in a circle. A student is chosen to be the detective and leaves the room. Another student is chosen to be the magician, and the detective returns to stand in the centre of the circle. The detective turns on the spot to scan all the students around the circle and try and spot the magicians signal whilst, without being seen by the detective, the magician winks at any student, who then "falls asleep" big sighing deeply back onto their chair. The round ends when the detective identifies the magician, then new students take on the roles. (if it works better for the group they can be sitting and just fall asleep on their chair)	Chairs in a circle.		To help the participants to relax. Gives students the opportunity to connect with their peers and build a group identity. This game helps concentration as the students have to pay attention at all times.
Step 2 Warming Up with Thumbs Up (not a round) Today we are going to discuss emojis and emoticons. When do you use emojis online? (gather a few quick responses with thumbs up answers and thank the students who shared) Open question (speaking round): **"When did you realise that emojis can have hidden meanings?"** ("When I ...")	Speaking object		To give all students in the circle, the opportunity to speak and contribute if they want to.

Introduction to Circle Plans   169

Process	Resources	Facilitator notes	Expectations
Step 3 Opening-Up Facilitator: Today we're looking at how emojis are sometimes used not just to show feelings, but to signal group identity or beliefs – including some that are harmful or dangerous. *What are the dangers associated with emojis?* "**Emojis can be harmful because …**" At this point, students are encouraged to put their thumbs out if they wish to or are ready to speak. Some students' views are gathered. Facilitator hands out the emoji sheets based on some harmful online subcultures which misuse emojis. See further information below the lesson plan. The facilitator asks the students: "**Do you know why any of these emojis may be harmful or what they could represent?**" Once students have shared their ideas, the facilitator can read out the further information on the harmful subcultures from the handout below. The next question to ask the students, "**Is anyone worried about their friends, class members or family using these emojis?**" To this open question they can just put their hands up. The final question is "**Would it be hard for you to challenge any people using these emojis – and how could you do it in a way that is safe for you?**" Thank the students for their honesty.	Speaking object or thumbs up. Have a sheet of paper with the flexed bicep, face with sunglasses, skull emoji, black circle and red circle emoji for each student.	What are the things we heard people say? How can young people stay safe from the harmful effects of emojis? Is there anyone who feels brave enough to ask for help regarding social media? For themselves or for a friend? Anyone who is possibly experiencing cyber bullying will have the platform to share their concerns and peers could offer help. Not all students will be familiar with these examples. Tips for the facilitator: These answers could go along the lines of "**I could report it to a teacher, I could try and be nicer to the person who was using the lonely emojis, I could not react online to/ just ignore it.**"	To invite students to explore an issue and honestly share their opinions and feelings. At this point, any thumbs up answers need to be thanked and it's helpful if you comment on them being brave or thoughtful.

Process	Resources	Facilitator notes	Expectations
Step 4 Cheering-Up/ Appreciation Round The facilitator shows the students what each of the coloured heart emojis can symbolise. The facilitator asks the students to pick any of the coloured hearts and present to the person sitting to their right and state what that heart means. The facilitator appreciates the participation of the students by saying **"Thank you, you have all shared so honestly and bravely."** You can make extra so the students can give them to friends or family outside the circle.	Multiple cut outs of emoji hearts in different colours.		To give the pupils the opportunity to have fun and show their appreciation for each other.
Step 5 Calming Down Teach students how to be calm "lose your eyes, put your right hand on your tummy, left hand on top. Slowly breathe in the energy and the oxygen 1 … 2 … 3 … Now open your mouth. Slowly expel all the tension and the toxins, 1 … 2 … 3 … Keep breathing whilst I play a very short piece of calming music (just play one minute) – when the minute is finished say to the students, slowly now I want you to have a stretch, open your eyes and see how many children's eyes can you smile into whilst I count to 3." Finally thank them.			To help the pupils to experience a closing calm ritual that would ensure that their transition to the next part of their day is smooth and successful.

Notes for Teachers:

Emojis and emoticons are both tools used in digital communication to express emotions, but they are fundamentally different in form and origin:
Emoticons are made from standard keyboard characters – punctuation marks, letters, and numbers – arranged to resemble facial expressions or emotions, such as :) for a smile or :(for a frown. They originated in the early days of the internet, with one of the first uses traced to 1982 at Carnegie Mellon University. Emoticons are limited by the characters available on the keyboard and are typically read sideways.
Emojis are actual images or pictographs encoded into Unicode, allowing them to be displayed consistently across devices and platforms. They go beyond facial expressions and can represent objects, animals, symbols, activities, and more – think 😊 (smiling face), 🚗 (car), 🍔 (hamburger), or 🏀 (basketball). The word "emoji" comes from Japanese: "e" (picture) and "moji" (character). Emojis were invented in Japan in the late 1990s and have since become universally popular in digital communication.
Gender stereotypes In incel and manosphere spaces, certain emojis like flexed biceps or cool face with sunglasses are used to represent "Chads" – a derogatory slang term used to describe conventionally attractive, dominant, or sexually successful men.

These can be harmful as they reinforce toxic masculinity.

Hopelessness or Violence (Black-Pilled Ideology)

The skull emoji and black circle are often used by people in incel communities to symbolise black-pilled thinking – a belief that life is hopeless, unfair, and unchangeable, especially in terms of love, success, or social status. The "black pill" worldview suggests that genetics and looks determine everything – and that no effort can improve one's romantic life. These can be harmful as they can lead to misogyny and isolation.

Exclusion of Others (Red-Pilled Ideology)

The red circle emoji is used as a symbol of being "red-pilled," taken from *The Matrix*, but twisted to mean "waking up" to uncomfortable truths about women and society. In the manosphere, red-pilled thinking assumes: Feminism is a lie, women manipulate men through hypergamy (dating "up"), equality is a myth, and men are the real victims.

This is harmful as it promotes misogyny and encourages men to reject empathy and social cooperation.

Chart of Emoji Hearts

Here's a more detailed breakdown of what each heart means

- ♥ (Red Heart):

The classic heart, representing love, romance, passion and strong emotions.

- ♥ (Orange Heart):

Often used to express care, support or affection for someone.

- ♥ (Yellow Heart):

Represents happiness, friendship and positive energy. It can also symbolise warmth and hope.

- ♥ (Green Heart):

Signifies nature, growth and harmony.

- ♥ (Blue Heart):

Often associated with trust, loyalty and peace, it can also represent calm and serenity.

- ♥ (Purple Heart):

Can symbolise spirituality, creativity or a connection to the colour purple. It can also represent luxury or ambition.

Introduction to Circle Plans 173

Theme 3: Unpacking Gender Role Stereotypes (Age 15–18)

Process	Resources	Facilitator notes	Expectations
Step 1 Meeting-Up The facilitator introduces the five skills and Ground Rules if needed.			
Step 1 Game – "Step In – Step Out" **Objective:** To surface and reflect on common gender stereotypes and expectations in a non-confrontational way. **Playing the Game:** Everyone stands in the circle facing inward. Explain the Instructions The facilitator will read out a series of statements. (*The statements are provided at the end of this plan.*) If the statement feels true to them, pupils should take one step into the circle. After a brief moment, they step back to the original circle. There is no discussion or judgement during the stepping – just observation. The facilitator stands inside the circle and calls out each statement. (See list below.) The beginning ones are simple, non-threatening ones to build comfort. The later statements are related to gender roles and stereotypes.		The game works because it makes invisible stereotypes visible, without shaming or calling out. It shows shared experiences and diversity in thought. It sets up a rich, respectful conversation on gender socialisation.	To help the participants to relax. Gives students the opportunity to connect with their peers and build a group identity.
The facilitator asks questions 1 and 2 and offers the sentence stem **"One thing this activity made me think of was ..."** (*Speaking Round*) The facilitator asks questions 3 and 4 and invites students who feel ready to speak.	Speaking object	1 and 2 What did you notice whilst playing this Step-In – Step-Out game? Were there any statements that made you pause? Why? 3 and 4 What gender stereotypes do we sometimes assume about other people or sometimes apply to ourselves? How do these stereotypes affect how we behave or feel?	This activity enables students to get comfortable about verbalising what they experienced in the previous game.

Process	Resources	Facilitator notes	Expectations
Step 3 Opening-Up The facilitator asks: **"Have you heard the terms toxic masculinity and toxic femininity? What meaning do they have for you?"** Students are encouraged to put their thumbs up if they wish to or are ready to speak. Some students' views are gathered. The facilitator then asks question 1 and invites responses from the pupils. (See note on Toxic Masculinity and Toxic Femininity below.) Do a speaking round using the sentence stem **"One thing we could do to stop toxic stereotyping is …"** After a few students share their views, The facilitator could ask the whole class which idea/s they are drawn to and why.	Speaking object	1. What could be ways to challenge or change unfair expectations?	This activity enables students to gather the vocabulary to deal with deeply entrenched gender stereotypes. It is likely there will be differing views from students who identify themselves across a gender spectrum.
Step 4 Cheering-Up – **A–Z Gender-Inclusive Superpowers** (See *sample list of superpowers below.*) The facilitator asks each student sitting in the circle to take turns in coming up with a superpower beginning with alphabet A, then B, C, D, etc. It needs to be gender-inclusive and positive. In case a student can't think of a word, they may "pass" and seek support from the group who can thumbs up. These must be words we would all like to be described as.	Refer to the sample list if no one can think of anything.	The facilitator appreciates the participation of the students by saying "Thank you, you have all shared so honestly and bravely." OR "You all used your five skills!"	This activity helps shift the conversation from limiting gender roles to celebrating human strengths. It encourages inclusion, respect, and positive identity development. It's simple, fast, and energising!
Step 5 Calming Down Use a breathing exercise or guided visualisation.			To help the pupils to experience a closing calm ritual that would ensure that their transition to the next part of their day is smooth and successful.

Introduction to Circle Plans 175

Note to teachers: This theme might require several QCT sessions to unpack students' perspectives on the subject – stereotypical or progressive. Primarily, because we know there are some male influencers on social media who promote toxic masculinity as a badge of honour.

Step In – Step Out Statements (Choose Any 8–10 Statements)

Warm-Up
I like playing sports.
I enjoy dancing or singing.
I have a favourite superhero.
I've cried during a film.

Gender Roles and Stereotypes

Boys are expected to always be strong, even when they feel hurt.
Girls are told to behave more "properly" than boys.
I've heard someone say "That's not something girls should do."
I've heard "Boys don't cry."
I've been told "Boys are stronger than girls."
I've been teased for doing something "too girly" or "too boyish."
I feel like I can't always express myself freely because of my gender.
I've been expected to act a certain way because I'm a boy/girl.
I've seen adults treat boys and girls differently in school or at home.

Note on Toxic Gender Roles

Toxic masculinity and toxic femininity refer to harmful societal expectations about how boys/men and girls/women "should" behave – especially when those expectations limit emotions, choices, or personal freedom. They don't mean all masculinity or femininity is bad. The word **"toxic"** refers to the rigid, exaggerated, or extreme versions of gender roles that can be damaging – to individuals and to others.

Toxic masculinity refers to socially enforced behaviours and attitudes that pressure men to display dominance, suppress emotions and avoid vulnerability – traits like aggression, emotional restraint, and discouraging empathy. Such norms can harm both men and those around them by discouraging healthy emotional expression and reinforcing rigid gender roles.

Toxic femininity involves the pressure on women to conform to exaggerated traits such as passivity, selflessness, and excessive nurturing, often to the detriment of their personal needs and autonomy. Examples include prioritising others over oneself, avoiding assertiveness or focusing heavily on appearance to gain social approval.

Both concepts highlight how rigid, stereotypical gender roles can be damaging to individuals and society, reinforcing limiting expectations and contributing to mental and social challenges.

A healthy way forward: everyone, regardless of gender, should be free to express a range of emotions, be kind and confident, strong and sensitive.

Healthy masculinity and femininity are about being true to oneself, not fitting into a narrow box.

A–Z of Gender-Inclusive Superpowers

A – Assertiveness, Adaptability
B – Bravery
C – Compassion
D – Determination
E – Empathy
F – Flexibility (mental or emotional)
G – Generosity
H – Honesty
I – Imagination
J – Joyfulness
K – Kindness
L – Leadership
M – Mindfulness
N – Nurturing
O – Open-mindedness
P – Perseverance
Q – Quick thinking
R – Resilience
S – Sensitivity
T – Teamwork
U – Understanding
V – Vision (big-picture thinking)
W – Wisdom
X – X-factor (your unique spark!)
Y – Youthful curiosity
Z – Zeal (enthusiasm and energy)

Introduction to Circle Plans 177

Theme 4: Using Social Media (Year 8–12)

Process	Resources	Facilitator notes	Expectations
Step 1 Meeting-Up The facilitator introduces the five skills and Ground Rules if necessary.			
Step 1 Game – "Real or Filtered?" social media game – The facilitator reads out one by one, any 8–10 statements given below and asks students to respond to each statement by giving a "thumbs up" sign (*for Real/True*), or arms crossed across the chest (*for filtered*). The facilitator needs to be alert and take note of how different pupils responded. And what seemed to be the majority view for certain worrying statements.			This activity is apt for keeping the interaction dynamic and thought-provoking for teenagers.
Step 2 Warming-Up The facilitator asks question 1 and asks the students to use the sentence stem: "**Social media makes me feel …**" (*Speaking Round*)	Speaking object	1. How does social media make you feel?	To give all students in the circle, the opportunity to speak and contribute to the shared experience of the circle.
Step 3 Opening-Up Based on students' responses in the earlier stage, the The facilitator can ask students to put their thumbs up to share an answer to the question, "**Do you need help with social media?**" Students respond with …. "**I need help with social media because …**" Select one focus child and then the students respond taking turns to speak by putting their thumbs up. They can suggest ideas to help, "**Would it help if …?**" After different students share their views, F asks the focus child "Which idea are you most drawn to? Why?" The facilitator may share their views on what and how the students responded	Speaking object	1. Why do you think this is so? 2. What is potentially problematic about this? 3. What can be done about this?	This activity focuses on encouraging young people to honestly share their feelings and dissonance in social media behaviours

Process	Resources	Facilitator notes	Expectations
Step 4 Cheering-Up – #GoodVibesOnly Social Media Positivity Wall Give Each student a "post" card, post-its or sticky notes that look like social media posts. (*You can pre-make them with a post box, heart, and comment icon.*) **Ask them to write:** One happy or inspiring thing they've experienced, seen, or shared on social media. Some examples: • *A message that made me feel supported* • *A creative post that inspired me* • *A funny meme that made my day* • *A cause I learnt about online* • *A compliment I received or gave online* • *A post that helped me feel less alone* **Create a "Good Vibes Wall"** One by one, students "post" their cards on the wall or bulletin board like a feed. As they read others' posts, they can add emoji reactions or heart stickers using the sketch pens. **Optional Activity** Invite a few students to read aloud a favourite post (*their own or someone else's*). **Step 5 Calming Down** Carry out a breathing exercise of guided visualisation.	Post-its/sticky notes, pens	The objective is to celebrate how social media can be a force for good – by focusing on its power to uplift, connect, and inspire. It Builds emotional connection and peer positivity.	Encourages teens to reflect on the positive use of tech. Easy to conduct, and leaves behind a visual reminder of joy and connection To help the pupils to experience a closing calm ritual that would ensure that their transition to the next part of their day is smooth and successful.

Statements: Real or Filtered? (Choose Any 8–10)

1. Everyone's life looks perfect on Instagram.
2. People take 20 selfies before posting just one.
3. Some people use social media to spread kindness.
4. Sharing creative work online has helped me grow.
5. I've seen people smile in photos even when they were feeling sad.
6. Influencers are paid to promote products they don't even use.
7. Likes and followers show how popular someone really is.
8. Most people edit or filter their pictures before posting.
9. My friend's feed shows she's always happy.
10. Some people use social media to make others feel jealous.
11. Not getting enough "likes" can ruin someone's mood.
12. People are always hanging out with friends and having fun – just like their posts show.
13. No one shares their failures or bad days on social media.
14. Seeing others on holiday makes me feel like I'm missing out.
15. Some people follow trends they don't believe in just to fit in online.
16. Online friends are just as close as real-life friends.
17. I've felt pressure to look a certain way because of posts I've seen.
18. Comments and likes make me feel more confident.
19. Sometimes I compare myself to influencers and feel less than.
20. I know someone who posts motivational quotes but bullies others offline.
21. Social media helps me stay connected with real friends
22. Everything I see on social media is true

More Circle Time Sessions for RSHE (Relationships, Sex and Health Education)

These Circle Time Sessions have been adapted from the earlier edition of *Quality Circle Time in the Secondary School* (Mosley and Tew, 2013).

Session 1: Friendship (Age 11/12)

Process	Resources	Rationale
Step 1 Game – Who Are You? First put the students into small groups. Explain that they need to find an alliterative adjective to go with their first name. If they are stuck, they can put their hand up to ask you for help. Check you are happy that the adjectives chosen are suitable. One pupil begins by introducing themself using their positive alliterative adjective such as "I am Energetic Esther."		To have been introduced to every person in the class.

Process	Resources	Rationale
The next person in the circle turns to the first pupil and says, **"This is 'energetic Esther' and I am 'Marvellous Martin.'"** The game continues around the circle and each pupil has to introduce the person before and then themselves.		
Step 2 Round Ask pupils to brainstorm all the attributes of friendship – e.g. kindness, cooperation, shared interests, loyalty, trust, generosity, caring, sharing, support. Go round the circle asking for ideas and write them on a flipchart or whiteboard.	Flipchart and coloured pens	To have considered the attributes of a healthy/unhealthy friendship.
Step 3 Opening-up The teacher facilitates a discussion using one or two of the following questions. • Why do people like to have friends? • Does everyone need friends? • Are all friendships good? • If not, when can a friendship be harmful (e.g. bad influences, domination, sycophantic relationships, online grooming friendships)? • Do different people look for different things in friends? • Can people be "friendly" to everyone, even if they're not real friends? Now ask **"Is there anybody here who would like some help to get more friends than they already have?"** Students can thumb up and then you can choose one who you think may genuinely need more friends. The focus student then answers. It is important that you say to the rest of the circle can you use the sentence stem **"Would it help if I ..."** Say to them **"What could you do to help this person?"** **"Are there any clubs you can suggest for school break times that could help people get to know more people?"**		To have learnt something new about a peer they didn't previously know well.
Step 4 Celebratory Round **"I am a good friend when I ..."** (*Speaking Round*)		

(Continued)

Introduction to Circle Plans 181

Process	Resources	Rationale
Step 4 Celebratory Activity Pupils form pairs with someone who is not a close friend. Each member of the pair in turn has a minute to tell the other as much about themself as possible, e.g. likes/dislikes, hobbies, beliefs, favourite programmes, etc. The pair then take turns to relate back to each other as much as they can remember of what they've been told. Close with a round when each person introduces their partner by name with one positive piece of information about them, i.e. **"This is ... (name) ... and they ..."** **Step 5 Calm Down** Refer to Chapter 21 for breathing exercises and guided visualisations.		Allows students to get to know their peers better.

Session 2: Loneliness (Age 12/13)

Process	Resources	Rationale
Step 1 Game – Word Association Word association around the circle with two claps in between each item, e.g. "book" clap, clap; "page" clap, clap; "letters" clap, clap; "parcels" clap, clap; "birthdays" clap, clap. If anyone falters or cannot think of a word, they begin a new sequence. See how fast the participants can get this going.		To get everyone warmed up and energised.
Step 2 Round The teacher tells the pupils that everyone experiences lonely times. They ask them to brainstorm occasions when they felt lonely. Do a round with the sentence stem: **"I felt lonely when ..."** *Examples:* When I split up with my best friend. When I had to stay with a relative. When I travelled to London on the train on my own.		To have considered what makes people feel lonely.

(Continued)

Process	Resources	Rationale
Step 3 Opening-up The teacher facilitates a sensitive discussion about loneliness, using one or two of the following questions that they feel most comfortable with: • What does it feel like to be lonely (e.g. nervous, frightened, uncared-for, depressed, miserable and resentful)? • What can happen to people in extreme loneliness (e.g. severe depression, physical and mental disorders and, sometimes, suicide)? • What type of people might be particularly susceptible to loneliness (e.g. old people living alone, people living in a foreign country, disabled people, people who have different customs, people who are neurodivergent)? • Do you think enough is done to help lonely people? • Do you ever consciously think about helping people who are lonely? Children can thumb up to answer the questions.		To have understood that loneliness is a common and normal feeling. To develop empathy for people who are lonely.
Step 3 Opening-Up Further Discussion Put the students into pairs. In pairs think of times when people may feel lonely at school. Write an example on a piece of paper and put it in a container. The teacher reads from one piece of paper at a time. No situation is attributed to a pair and the class makes suggestions on ways of dealing with it. Pupils make suggestions using the script **"Would it help if they ...?"**; **"Would it help if I ...?"**; **"Would it help if we ...?"** Any ideas that might result in changes in school policy or procedure should be noted and taken to the school council or relevant member of the senior management team.	Pens/pencils, paper and a container.	To have some strategies for combatting loneliness.
Step 4 Cheering up Game Explain that having a laugh together always help people feel happier. **Play the Bean Game** Start by calling out the name of a "bean" and demonstrating a suitable action to go with it. for example, Jelly Bean – shake and wobble your body, Runner Bean – jog on the spot, Jumping Bean – jump up and down on the spot, Broad Bean – do a star jump with arms and legs out wide, Chilli Bean – cross arms and shiver, String Bean – stretch up tall with arms above heads etc. Once the children have learnt the relevant actions, allow them to take turns to chose the category of bean. You can keep control at the end by choosing still, quiet human beans.		To end the circle on a positive note.
Step 5 Calm Down Refer to Chapter 21 for breathing exercises and guided visualisations.		

Session 3: Strengths and Weaknesses (Age 13/14)

Process	Resources	Rationale
Step 1 Game – Skill Swap Pupils sit in a circle. One chair is removed and pupil without chair stands in centre. The teacher calls out different categories of skill. Any pupil who thinks they fit into the named category stands up and moves across the circle to change seat and the pupil standing in the centre tries to sit on a vacant chair. The pupil who is left without a seat stands in the centre until the next category is called. Once the game is established, the pupil in the middle can choose the next category and think of areas of skill or lack of skill that might apply to other members of the class.		To warm up and start the circle with fun.

Examples of skills:

- anyone who can ride a bike;
- anyone who can't swim;
- anyone who can skateboard;
- anyone who can't knit;
- anyone who can bake.

Categories should be mixed to include some "fun" items.

Step 2 Strengths and Weaknesses
"One thing I am good at is ..."
"One thing I would like to improve on is ..."
(*Speaking Round*)

Step 3 Opening-Up
The teacher facilitates a sensitive discussion using on or two of the following questions.

- Do people see other people's strengths as more worthwhile than their own?
- Why should this be so?
- Are certain strengths generally held to be better than others?
- Are you always aware of and appreciative of your own strengths?
- What strengths do you consider most desirable?
- What would help people to appreciate other people's strengths, even if they don't particularly admire them personally?
- Do people always admit their weaknesses? If not, why not?
- How do people deal with weaknesses?
- Do you have any good ways of dealing with areas of weaknesses?

Get students to thumbs up and take some answers.
Now ask if there is any student here who would like some help to achieve something that feels hard for them?
Select a focus child and then the rest of the group can offer suggestions using the script:
"Would it help if you ...?";
Would it help if I ...?

Rationale (Step 3): To have learnt some strategies for building on strengths and addressing weaknesses.

(*Continued*)

Process	Resources	Rationale
Step 4 Celebratory Round Carry out a round with the sentence stem ... "I really admire people who ..." Introduce the idea that very quiet students also have a strength. They create a lovely atmosphere of calm and they role model hard work. Who in this class team do you admire because even when the whole class is calling out they quietly get on with their work? (I really urge you to use this sentence because many times quiet children have been surprised to know that they are admired and they are a role model.)		To boost self-esteem and appreciate their own qualities. To shift pupils' perspective from themselves to others and celebrate each other.
Step 5 Calm Down Refer to Chapter 21 for breathing exercises and guided visualisations.		

See Table 17.1 – you can send students home with this questionnaire to fill in. Ask them to bring it back so you can read through and find out more about them.

Table 17.1 Strengths and weaknesses questionnaire

Name:		Tutor group:		
Put a tick in the column that describes how good/bad you are at each of the following	Good	Quite good	Not very good	Bad
Being reliable				
Being honest				
Being hardworking				
Being kind				
Standing up for yourself				
Feeling confident in front of others				
Helping others out				
Getting work done on time				
Doing work carefully				
Being easy to get on with				
Keeping calm				
Thinking of other people's feelings				
Considering others' points of view				
Sorting out disputes calmly				
Sticking at difficult or boring tasks				
Finding things of interest to do out of school				
Being able to lead others				
Volunteering to be helpful				
Getting involved in clubs or societies				

(Continued)

Introduction to Circle Plans 185

Name:	Tutor group:			
Put a tick in the column that describes how good/bad you are at each of the following	Good	Quite good	Not very good	Bad
Making friends Achieving goals Coping with changes in your life Cooperating with others in group activities				

Session 4: Confidence (Age 14/15)

Process	Resources	Rationale
Step 1 Game – Who Am I? Choose a pupil to leave the room who you can rely on to be kind in their questioning. During their absence the others choose a person. The absent pupil returns and by questioning the participants must guess the identity of the chosen person. Only "yes," "no" or "don't know" answers can be given. Once the identity has been correctly guessed (perhaps players can be limited to three guesses) the process is repeated with new players.		To warm up and start the circle with fun.
Step 2 Round Teacher or facilitator says: **"Let's look at how confident we are coming back into the room to face a challenge, like in the game we just played. There are lots of things we aren't confident in such as failing, getting nervous making phone calls, talking to customers on our Saturday job etc …"** So let's now have a round of **"One thing I lack confidence in is …"**		To have understood that everyone has some crisis of confidence.
Step 3 Open Forum Having listened to that round what were the main issues for this group? **"I heard a lot of people say this …"** **"I heard some people say …"** **"I heard a few people say …"** This is a useful technique because the children who have spoken realise that their peer group have actually remembered and noted what they said. It's very validating. Now say to the whole circle is there any one person here who would especially like some help to get confident with a challenge they have ahead?		To have considered situations that commonly erode confidence at this age.

(Continued)

Process	Resources	Rationale
The sentence stem is **"I need help because I ...,"** e.g. don't stand up for what I believe in sometimes when my friends are being unkind, I need to tell the teacher that I don't understand something, when there is something wrong with my food I don't feel able to go back and get it sorted ... The rest of the class can then offer suggestions ... **"Would it help if you ..."**; **"Would it help if I ..."**		
Step 4 Celebrate Each Other Ask **"Who in this class have you noticed has become stronger in coming up with answers, speaking out loud, working in groups, coming in on time and you think deserves a shout out."** Students can thumbs up and nominate another student (not their best friend).		
Step 5 Creative Visualisations These imaginative stories are very useful with young people. They have great imaginations, and they often report afterwards that they could genuinely see it in their minds eye. If they have been used to doing some calm, breathing exercises with you then it's time for you to try this visualisation.		To calm pupils down and end on a positive note

Follow-up activity: pupils are given a piece of paper and a pencil and asked to write down one thing that people their age lack confidence about, e.g. entering a room full of strangers, speaking out loud in class, personal appearance, going on a journey alone. The papers are folded and placed in a container. The container is passed to someone in the circle (this can be the teacher themself or a member of the class) who takes out a piece of paper and reads out the statement. The class then suggests ideas of how the issue might be addressed and how confidence could be increased for this situation/activity. Once one issue is addressed, the next person in the circle can read out another issue.

This kind of activity is very useful for addressing sensitive or personal issues with a class of pupils. It is important, however, that no one is allowed to try and name the author of any statement.

At the end of the discussion, it helps to draw together a "toolkit" of the sorts of things that help people become more confident. For example, praise, encouragement, practice, positive self-belief, experience, etc. These can be kept as a resource list for the class to use the next time they have a crisis of confidence, such as leading an assembly, achieving something in class, or hosting a visitor.

The teacher asks the pupils to take one area of low confidence and write out an action plan at home, enlisting the help of others if necessary. Pupils are encouraged to put their action plans into practice.

Guided Visualisation (Please Edit as Much as You Feel Comfortable With)

Pupils can sit or lie with eyes closed. The teacher explains that they are going to talk them through an epic struggle, which they must try and visualise in their mind's eye.

You are standing at the bottom of a steep and rugged mountain which you have to climb. You look up; the peak is obscured by cloud. The rock face seems to go on forever. You feel daunted by the prospect of such a huge effort. Think of this feeling. It's the feeling you get when you have to do something really hard that you don't want to do. Imagine now this feeling. Where is it? In the pit of your stomach? In your shoulders? Imagine it really strongly – weighing you down, holding you back ...

You have to make a start. You adjust your backpack, take a deep breath and walk forward.

There is a path to start with. It's not too steep and you can walk fairly comfortably. Imagine a regular rhythm as you stride along. Picture yourself in motion one, two, one, two ... the path becomes narrower and scattered rocks litter its surface. Dusty, hard-baked mud. Notice the rocks strewn along it. Imagine avoiding them by stepping over or walking around them. Perhaps you stumble sometimes as you carefully pick your way along the path. You are not walking with a regular rhythm now, but slowly and carefully ... the path takes a steep upward turn. You begin to feel the effort of the ascent. The backpack feels really heavy; feel the weight of it on your back, the straps biting into your shoulders. Feel it pulling you down, draining your energy. Your leg muscles begin to ache; feel the pain in your calves and thighs – it's getting more and more intense ...

You feel totally exhausted. Imagine this feeling very strongly. You have to rest. You stop, take off the backpack and sit down. Imagine the relief as you stop climbing. Feel the weight of your limbs, heavy and relaxed. Think of the good feeling of removing the backpack. You sit and rest, eat food and drink. Perhaps you doze a little ...

You have to go on but are reluctant to make a start. Imagine urging yourself to get up and go on. You don't want that heavy backpack on again, but you know you must. Nag yourself, encourage yourself – you have to continue ...

At last, you are ready to move on. The path continues to climb steeply and now it is entering the clouds. You feel the damp chill falling slowly around you, enveloping you in its clammy, cold grip. It's so cold now, you can feel it right in your bones. Think of its penetrating coldness, imagine how you are feeling ...

On you trudge in your silent, grey, misty world. You feel very alone; the silence is overwhelming. Think of how alone you are in your chilly grey world. Feel the loneliness of your situation ...

Gradually, you emerge from the cloud layer. The sun warms your face. Feel its deep, penetrating rays bringing life back to your frozen limbs. At last, you can see the summit, but the path has run out. You prepare yourself mentally for the final effort ...

You now have to climb, inch by inch. You look for hand and foot holds and pull yourself slowly up. You feel nervous about slipping. Each movement is slow and careful. Your arms and legs ache from the effort. You are totally exhausted. You grit your teeth with determination and haul yourself upwards. Feel the effort and determination in every inch of your body. See the summit coming gradually closer. You know you can do it ...

At last, the final pull and you are there. Imagine the excitement, the feeling of success and achievement – you have done it. You have conquered the mountain, your fear, your exhaustion and you have won. Enjoy the exhilaration of your success. You feel happy and contented.

Session 5: Taking Risks (Age 15/16)

Process	Resources	Rationale
Step 1 Game – Silent Statements This is a sensitive and controversial topic. Pupils need to be reminded of the ground rules that make it safe to discuss sensitive issues, particularly the need to look after themselves in what they do and do not share publicly. Play silent statements to raise a range of risky behaviours or activities. Use the sentence stem "Stand up if you." • have ever come home later than you were allowed; • have ever lied about where you were going; • have been in a car that is breaking the speed limit; • have asked for a half-fare when you should have paid full price; • have run across a road without using the pedestrian crossing; • Have said something private to someone online that could be shared.		To warm up pupils and introduce the topic of the circle.
Step 2 – Activity That Leads to a Round Create an imaginary (or physical using rope, metre stick etc) line that runs from one side of the circle to the other, or through the circle from one side of the room to another. One end of the line represents "high risk" and the other end is "low risk." Ask pupils to stand and move to a place on the line in response to how risky they think an activity is: *Risky activities could include:* • Walking home alone at 2 am; • Smoking the occasional cigarette; • Smoking cannabis; • Riding a bike without a helmet;		To know the risks attached to certain activities that young people are prepared to do including online. To decided what risks they are prepared to take.

(Continued)

Process	Resources	Rationale

- Having unprotected sex;
- Drinking and driving;
- Having a body piercing or tattoo;
- Meeting friends in town late on a Saturday night;
- Leaving a party with someone you have just met;
- Getting friendly with strangers online;
- Watching violent or sexually explicit videos.

As you go through this process, explain to students that they can put their hand up at any point and say, **"I worry about ..."** Their peers can then respond with any suggestions to prevent this worry.
"Would it help if ...";
"I worry about this too but to make myself feel better I ..."
Now do a speaking round with the sentence stem **"The risk I worry about is ..."**

Step 3 Opening-Up
Give each pair of pupils one of the cards of a risky activity. Ask them to decide what could be done to reduce the risks of this particular activity. Pairs think of as many ways as they can to reduce risk.
What do they think is the biggest risk currently for their age-group?
Take feedback in the whole circle on ways of reducing the likelihood of harm from a risky activity.

Resources: Media stories of people caught in risky situations

Rationale: To consider how to protect themselves and stay safe.

- Does anyone know of someone who has been in a high-risk situation? (*Remind pupils to protect people's identity.*)
Should someone talk to a responsible adult about a friend/classmate who is involved in a high-risk situation?

- You could have a set of media stories to use in case no personal stories are offered.
- Ask the group to provide advice that would have reduced the harm in the story.

Step 4 Cheering-Up
"For my own safety I will try to ..."

Rationale: To return to having fun after talking about a serious topic.

Step 4 Calm Down
Carry out some relaxing breathing or a guided meditation.

Circle Sessions for PSHE Topics
Session 6: My Life (Age 11/12)

Process	Resources	Rationale
Step 1 Game – Initials Using the initials of their first and surnames, the pupils have to respond to questions asked by the teacher. This can be done around the circle. *Examples:* • Shamina Dohar, what is your favourite food? Shamina could answer "Soggy dough" or "Sugar donuts" or "Sizzling dumplings" or "Spam dinners." • Jason Connor, where would you like to go on holiday? Jason could answer "Juvenile camp" or "Jolly Canada" or "Jousting centres." If the teacher has a selection of six or seven simple questions, they can be rotated. Alternatively, they might ask the same question around the circle. Answers can be silly or nonsensical. If you think it would help, then ask them to get into pairs first to discuss ideas.		To warm up pupils and start the circle off in a fun way.
Step 2 Paired Activity In pairs, students are given a sheet of paper and writing implement; rulers can be shared. They are instructed to draw a lifeline and fill in the positive and negative events of their lives. Following on from this activity play … **Silent Statements** Ask pupils to move to a new chair if: • You found it easy to draw your life line; • You found happy events came to mind first.; • You found it easier to remember the sad/difficult events than the happy events; • You found it difficult to remember many events in your life; • You have moved school and found it a positive experience.; • You have moved house and found it a difficult experience.	A long sheet of paper for each pupil, pens/pencils and some rulers.	To review their lives. To consider what makes a positive/negative life event.

(Continued)

Process	Resources	Rationale
Step 3 Open Forum The teacher can draw out from the silent statement exercise that people experience the same kind of events in different ways. For some it is a positive experience, for others negative. Pupils are asked to look over their lifelines and the teacher facilitates an open forum using questions such as: • What makes life events positive or negative? • Could other people see any of the events in a different way? • What usually causes negative events? For example, chance, other people, changing circumstances, accidents, illness. • Do they think people tend to remember good or bad events? • Do some people find it really difficult to remember positive events in their life? • Can negative events ever have a positive outcome?		To understand the impact of perception on the way events are seen and experienced. To find ways to "reframe" life events in a more positive way for greater mental health and wellbeing.
Step 4 Celebration Is there anyone you admire because they manage to see difficult situations positively? (*This could be a class member or a real, fictional or TV character.*) Use the script "I admire … because they …"		To practice gratitude and appreciate peers.
Step 5 Calm Down Carry out some calm breathing or a guided visualisation.		To end the circle on a calm note.

Session 7: Being Popular (Age 12/13)

Process	Resources	Rationale
Step 1 Game – Waves This is played by having a circle of seats equal in number to the class members. One person volunteers to be in the middle. (*Make sure they are of a robust temperament and not vulnerable to exclusion by the social group.*) The whole class then moves round from one seat to the next in a continuous wave of motion and the person in the centre tries to sit on the vacant chair. Once the group gets the knack of this, it is extremely hard to get onto the chair because it is not ever really left vacant.		To warm up pupils and start the circle off in a fun way. To introduce the topic of popularity.

(Continued)

Process	Resources	Rationale

Step 2 Round

Once you finish the game carry out a round in the whole group using the sentence stem **"When I am left out, I feel …"**

Step 3 Activity – Being Popular

On sheets of paper ask the pupils to write down what they consider to be the five most important things that make a person popular, e.g. good looks, being trendy, having money, being good at sports, being cheerful, being kind, etc.

One pupil can read out his list and the others raise their hands if they also wrote that attribute on their list. This can be done several times to establish what the participants consider to be the most important attributes of being popular.

Resources: Paper and pens/pencils

Rationale: To understand what makes people popular/unpopular.

Step 3 Open Forum

The teacher facilitates a discussion on being popular by asking the following questions.

- What makes people popular?
- Does being popular make someone a nicer person?
- Does being unpopular mean people are unlikeable?
- Is popularity the same as powerful or influential?
- Do people have to change in order to be popular?
- Are you left out if you are not popular?
- How important is it to be popular?
- What do they see as the advantages to being popular?
- Is there ever a time when people look as if they are popular, but it is not a true picture? (for example if they are a bully and others are scared of them).
- Do they think that being popular has any disadvantages? (For example, unwelcome attention, having to maintain an "image," having to be a leader, others being jealous and resentful.)

Children thumbs up to give an answer but if they want to discuss something further then they put their hand up.

Now remind them not to mention anyone's name during this discussion.

Rationale: To recognise that popularity can come at the cost of integrity.

(Continued)

Introduction to Circle Plans 193

Process	Resources	Rationale
As a group lets consider this sentence, "we would like a popular person to have these attributes..." Then children thumb up to say an attribute. **Step 4 Celebration** Is there anyone in this group that you would like to thank because they always allow people into their group? The student looks at their peer and says **"Jacob I would like to thank you because ..."** **Step 4 Calm Down** Do the guided visualisation below.		To show gratitude for peers. End in a calm way

Guided Visualisation

Close your eyes, close your mouth, open your ears. Put your right hand on your tummy with your left hand over. Breathe in 1... 2... 3... And breathe out slowly 1... 2... 3. Keep this slow, calm breathing going whilst I ask you to imagine that the whole class has gone on a school outing. You are on a really peaceful, beautiful river. You are all in a coracle, which is a big round boat and you all have one oar which you are paddling together in complete harmony with the rest of your circle. It's a skill you were taught and you are enjoying it. Everyone's got a seat and everyone's feeling really safe. As you go down the river you notice there are willow trees with their branches trailing in the water. There are two beautiful swans going by. Their white feathers are almost luminous, glowing. You can feel a breeze on your face and the warmth of the sun on your back. You have been rowing for some time now and the fresh air and the warmth are making you feel tired. You all decide to pull into the riverbank, moor the boat and you help each other out to the low bank. The meadow is warm and dry. In your boat, you have a huge round picnic bag. Each one of you has a little bag of your favourite food. You lie down with your feet all touching and your heads creating an outside circle. You feel very very warm and dozy because you have now finished your food. You feel this sense of happiness. You are really pleased that you are in this class and that you can go on a journey and feel safe with these people. You close your eyes. When I say in a minute 1... 2... 3 – a memory bubble will float in front of you, put the picture of your imagined boat journey, your picnic rug and your food into the bubble. Blow it over the back of your head; it pops into your memory bank. Have a little stretch, open your eyes and by the time I count to 3, how many students' eyes can you smile into.

Session 8: Saying "No" (Age 14/15)

Process	Resources	Rationale
Step 1 Buzz Game Sitting in a circle, the children count around the circle, like so: "1 ... 2 ... 3 ... BUZZ ... 5 ... 6 ... 7 ...BUZZ ... 9 ... 10... 11 ... BUZZ..." The children must not say the multiples of four and have to say "BUZZ" instead. See how far the children can count without doing this. Whoever misses a "BUZZ" is out. You can choose different numbers depending on the age and competency of children playing. This game has been chosen because it can raise feelings of inclusion and exclusion when you get out.		To introduce the themes of inclusion and exclusion. To begin the Circle Time with a fun warm-up.
Step 1 Silent Statements Stand up if you: • are wearing earrings; • have a tattoo; • wear designer trainers; • like logos on your T-shirts; • subscribe to a particular dress code out of school; • go to parties; • have a strong preference for one type of music.		To start thinking about people's differences.
Step 2 Round Start by discussing in pairs what is involved in being part of a group. Feedback to the whole group in a round to hear everyone's view. The sentence stem is, **"Being part of a group means ..."**		To have considered the pressure other people put us under.
Step 3 Double Circle Activity Give each member of the circle the letter A or the letter B. Ask all the As to identify the B to their left. Then get them to stand up, pick up their chair and move it to face the B. This creates a double circle with the inner circle facing out and the outer circle facing in. The pairs face each other. The person in the outer circle tries to persuade the person in the inner circle to try something such as smoke a cigarette, try a joint, have an alcoholic drink, lie to their parents about where they are going, skive a lesson, meet someone they met online and so on. The person in the inner circle has to find ways of saying **"No, I don't want to do it"** without becoming aggressive or offensive. The teacher times the group for a minute and then claps or finds a way to bring the discussion to an end. The people in the inner circle stay still and those on the outer circle move on one place clockwise to create new pairs. After a couple of discussions, swap round so that the outer circle people get practice at saying "No" and those in the inner circle try their hand at persuasion.		To be able to say "No" assertively. To be able to resist pressure from others.

(Continued)

Process	Resources	Rationale
Step 3 Open Forum Put the chairs back to form one circle and hold a discussion. Ask **"Is there anybody here who needs help to resist pressure?"** The students can thumb up with the sentence stem, **"I would like to say no to …"** Choose a focus child and the rest of the group can suggest ideas to help using the sentence stem, **"Would it help if you …"; "Would it help if I …?"** **Step 4 Celebration** Who do you admire in this circle who stands up for their values? Praise by saying **"We have noticed Rashid that you are very kind and cannot be persuaded to put people down."** **Step 5 Calm Down** Carry out some calm breathing or guided visualisation.		To recognise what situations cause discomfort. To praise their peers and boost self-esteem.

Session 9: Moving to Key Stage 4 (Age 14/15)

In the lower school (Key Stage 3), pupils have often been taught in the same groups. Once they start Key Stage 4 and choose exam subjects, they may come into contact with pupils they have barely met before. This circle session can be part of the PSHE course or in tutorial time to draw attention to the need to make new relationships in the new subject groupings. It also gives pupils the opportunity to think about the challenges and demands of the next two years as they prepare for external examinations.

Process	Resources	Rationale
Step 1: Game – Sevens Everyone starts standing up. They then count in turn around the circle. Each person can choose to say 1, 2 or 3 numbers, but every time the count gets to seven that person "dies" and has to sit down. The teacher may start by saying "1,2" and the next person can say "3" or "3, 4" or "3, 4, 5" then the next person picks up the counting at 6 thus forcing the next person to sit down on 7. The counting then starts again at 1. The game should be played quickly so that those who are out early do not get bored.		To introduce the themes of inclusion and exclusion. To begin the Circle Time with a fun warm-up.

(Continued)

Process	Resources	Rationale

Step 1 Silent Statements
Ask the pupils to cross the circle if the following statements are true for them:

- You have people at home who help you to make decisions;
- Talking to friends is an important part of making decisions;
- You like to make up your own mind without being influenced by other people;
- You prefer to be part of a crowd when you try out something new;
- You don't mind being the only one who does something.

Step 2 Round
First, discuss with your partner the subjects you have chosen, how you made the decision to study these subjects and the changes that Key Stage 4 subjects make to your life at school.
Then, have a round using the sentence stem **"One change I really like this year is …"**

To review the differences between Key Stage 3 and 4 as they start their exam courses.

Step 3 Open Forum
Ask the group if they had heard any common themes during the round. For instance, there might have been relief at not having to study some subjects or sadness that they are no longer in classes with a particular friend, or anxiety about subjects they have selected or anger that there wasn't a big enough range of choice, etc.
Draw out the themes and try to reframe them as: expectations, opportunities, concerns, fears, losses.
Ask students if they want to thumb up what issues they have faced so far. Ask them to use the sentence stem, **"The biggest issue I have found with moving up to Key Stage 4 is …"**
Pick a focus student and then the rest of the group can start offering suggestions to help … **"Would it help if you…?"**; **"Would it help if I…?"**

To develop a sense of purpose for this phase of their school life.

Step 4 Celebration and Personal Reflection
Ask the students to think back to some of the best lessons or teaching approaches that your really liked. You can mention names positively here.
Students can thumb up if they want to share their reflection.

To end the Circle Time with a positive reflection.

Step 5 Calm Down
Carry out a calm breathing exercise or guided visualisation.

References

Mosley, J., 2005. *Important Issues Relating to the Promotion of Positive Behaviour and Self-esteem in Secondary Schools* (Paperback ed.). Nottingham: Positive Press Ltd.

Mosley, J. and Tew, M., 2013. *Quality Circle Time in the Secondary School: A Handbook of Good Practice* (2nd ed.). Abingdon: Routledge.

Chapter 18

Game Ideas for Step 1 and Step 4

Step 1 games are about meeting up for fun – they are a physical and emotional warm-up. It's possible to use those same games for the celebratory Step 4. Step 4 is about cheering up near the end of your Circle Time. Games are helpful because you can actually ask "what skills were you using just now?" – and because you have trained them in the Five Skills, they will identify these very easily. This can lead you on to thanking them all for the skills they have contributed to the circle session or, even better, ask the students if they would like to nominate someone (not their best friend) for the skills they have been using throughout the circle so far.

In this chapter games and activities are catalogued alphabetically. Each entry includes the basic game, the materials needed and a description of what to do, followed by ways in which it could be extended or varied. You might find it simpler to play the initial game first, then once you are confident with the way that it goes, you can begin to branch out and extend it. All games have great potential to make people feel good and equal potential to destroy morale. For instance, the game "You're positive" (p. 226) can greatly enhance the self-esteem of the person who is asked to leave the room if the comments are truly positive. On the other hand, the class could use a game like this one to "wind up" the teacher by only saying negative things. You will have to develop an atmosphere of trust in the group by using "safe" games such as "Keeper of the Keys," then move on to more "risky" ones. You will quickly acquire a sense of when a game is going well, or when it is "unsafe." If you think the group is not yet ready for any activity, drop it and do something that you know will go well.

All games can be played at any age/stage but they may need adapting to fit the older or younger audience. They work best when the teacher or group facilitator is totally committed to the game and shows no embarrassment or reserve. However, when learning to lead and play games, you need to give yourself permission to fail. Tell the class that you are learning about these games too and you don't know if they will work or not. You can encourage the group to evaluate the games and they can suggest ways of improving or developing them. Once you have more confidence, you will become very skilled at drawing out the rules, skills and learning points that emerge from your particular group in relation to a game. Any learning point that emerges can also be explored using drama and role-play techniques in pairs, in small groups or involving the whole group.

Aliens

What to Do

This is a game that has the potential to include and exclude people.

Each group member has to imagine that they have alien antennae on their heads. These are represented by using the index finger of each hand on either side of the head.

One person starts by putting up his or her antennae and calling across the circle to another person using their name. The person called has to respond by putting up his/her antennae and the two people sitting either side of him/her also put up the nearest antenna (making four antennae in all). The original "Alien" returns their hands to their lap. The new "Alien" then calls to another person, who responds by becoming an "Alien," supported by the two people either side and so on. The game goes best when it is played very fast. It requires concentration to ensure that the right people respond.

How This Can Be Varied or Developed

1. If the group tends to select some individuals and to deliberately exclude others, ask pupils to cross their ankles once they have had a turn so they can't be selected again.
2. If people are a bit reluctant to play with concentration, introduce some kind of forfeit for people who are not quick enough in the responses.
3. A sophisticated version of this is played in absolute silence. Pupils have to observe the eye contact that is made as the alien points his/her antennae at another member of the group. Those on either side also have to be alert to the eye contact in order to respond quickly.

A Star for a Second

What to Do

Each participant chooses a celebrity who they would like to be and writes the name on a piece of paper. They also write what they think they have in common with this person and/or why they would like to be this particular star. The teacher collects all the names and, one at a time, reads out the celebrity named. Participants have to guess who chose each celebrity; they are allowed one guess each. NB. Make sure that there are no negative put-downs in this activity.

How This Could Be Varied and Developed

Participants can discuss what they admire about the celebrity they chose. Do they think celebrities are chosen for the right or wrong reasons? Do they think some celebrities are paid too much, e.g. film stars, football players?

A Worry Shared

What to Do

Participants sit in an inward-facing circle. They are each given a piece of paper and anonymously write one worry that they have in the class or group.

Examples

- speaking in front of others;
- being laughed at;
- arriving late;
- feeling isolated;
- being asked questions/put on the spot.

The pieces of paper are folded and placed in a container and participants are invited to each take one and in turn, read out the "worry." They are instructed that they may say "Yes" to any worry they also experience, but they are not allowed to negate any, even if they do not share it. NB. Discourage participants from trying to guess who wrote a particular worry.

How This Could Be Varied or Developed

1. The teacher can facilitate a discussion on worries and have a round of "I feel worried when …" In the circle, participants can discuss strategies they have developed for dealing with worries.
2. Individuals can be given the opportunity to ask for help with a particular worry. The teacher could say "Does anyone need help with any particular worry that they have?" The group can then offer help, advice and support using the script "Would it help if I?," "Would it help if you?" As in all Whole Circle discussions, the person who asked for help may accept or reject the advice.

And Another Thing

What to Do

Participants stand in an inward-facing circle. In silence one person makes a simple sound. The next person copies the sound and adds another, the next copies the two previous sounds and adds a third and so on around the circle until a player forgets the sequence or gets a sound wrong. Once the sequence is broken, a new one begins, but this time, instead of a sound they initiate a movement.

Make sure that a player doesn't get too bogged down in trying to remember the sequence. If someone is having real difficulties start the game again. If you know someone is likely to find this game very hard, they can be the one to start or can be near the beginning.

How This Can Be Varied or Developed

1. This game can be played as a verbal memory game instead of a visual one, e.g. "I went on holiday and packed ..." or "My grandmother went to market and bought ..."
2. In the circle participants can discuss the issue of memory. They consider whether they think they have good/bad memories. What memories stay "bright" – which ones thankfully get lost?
3. The teacher can lead a discussion on types of memory, visual/auditory/ kinaesthetic and encourage pupils to identify their preferred learning style.
4. Do they think they can improve their memory?
5. Individuals can ask for help with certain aspects of memory and learn from the strategies other members of the group use to remember things.

Believe Me?

What to Do

Participants are given a prepared list of value statements with true and false columns in which they tick their responses.

Examples

- A doctor is a better person than a refuse collector.
- People should be judged by the clothes they wear.
- Young people should always respect adults.
- Rich people are nicer than poor people.
- People who get high grades are better than people who get low grades.
- Old people are a nuisance.
- Disabled people can't play sports

How This Can Be Varied or Developed

1. In pairs then small groups, participants compare their responses.
2. In the circle discuss what sort of value judgements people make about others, e.g. appearance, clothes, social standing, age, able-bodied, intellect.
3. Can the group come up with a set of values to admire and promote that would allow equal opportunities?

Copycat

What to Do

Participants are divided into groups of six or eight. Each group forms a small circle and a member of each group thinks of a short, but fairly complicated task to mime. Participants must not practice or talk about their mimes.

All other participants except for the player next to the one with the mime close their eyes. The performer shows their mime to the next player who then taps the third player, who opens their eyes. The second player then repeats the mime, and so on until the mime has been passed right round the circle. Each player says what their think the task was and the originator tells the group what it actually was. The next person then thinks of a task to mime and the game continues until all the participants have had a turn at miming a task.

Encourage participants to make their actions clear and to avoid deliberately changing them.

How This Could Be Varied or Developed

1. In a circle, the group members can discuss how events can be altered or distorted in the telling. How can this lead to problems in life? For example, tales can be very different from the truth by the time they reach the fourth or fifth person.
2. Develop the idea of distorted communication. Individuals can say how they feel when they are misrepresented by distortion of the truth and share strategies for dealing with such incidents. There is great scope for role-play to show ways in which information is distorted and the hurt/misunderstandings/chaos that can ensue.

Copy Me – or "Simon Says"!

What to Do

Any group member can be designated as the leader. The leader initiates an action accompanied by the words "I say" or "Simon says," e.g. "I say touch your toes." If the instruction is preceded by "I say" then the class copies it. If the action is not preceded by "I say" the class ignores it. There is plenty of opportunity to "catch people out" with this game and so look at the issues around making mistakes, how we feel when we make mistakes and the value of mistakes in the learning process. There is also opportunity to discuss the need to keep the learning environment "safe" by avoiding ridicule and "put-downs."

How It Could Be Varied

1. The leader can start an action which the group copies. When the leader changes the action, the whole group follows suit. Then one person is chosen as a detective. They go outside the room whilst a leader is chosen.

On return, they stand in the middle of the circle and have to work out which group member is changing the action. The detective has to keep turning in the middle, they cannot stand still and stare at one person. They have to keep "whipping" around to test their theory out.

2. The action can be playing a musical instrument as the leader of an orchestra. The whole group has to play the same instrument. When the detective returns to the room, they have to find the leader of the orchestra.

Dealing with Failure

What to Do

Divide the group into pairs. In turn, each participant chooses an area of failure which they relates to their partner. The partner must think of and say as many genuine positive responses as can be made. The initial participant isn't allowed to respond with "yes ... but ..." They have to say "That's one way of looking at it ..."

Give Examples of "Failure"

- low grade in a piece of work;
- failure to get girl/boyfriend/partner of one's choice;
- being left out of a sport's team;
- being excluded from a social event;
- unable to understand in a teaching situation;
- job application turned down.

How This Can Be Varied or Developed

1. In the circle discuss how failure makes you feel. Have a round "When I fail at something I feel ..."
2. Brainstorm why failure is worse for some people than for others.
3. Brainstorm effective strategies for dealing with failure.
4. Discuss any ways in which failure can be seen in a positive light.
5. Look at examples of where you can apply negative or positive thinking, e.g. my glass is half empty/full!

Nonsense Talk

(It would probably be better to do this activity after an initial warm-up round or game so that people are feeling more relaxed and less self-conscious.)

What to Do

The group is divided into pairs and each pair is given a pre-written card with a situation to initiate dialogue. (See below for situations.) The pairs can only talk gibberish. They must try to convey meaning through tone of voice, inflection, facial expressions and gestures. They need to imagine what they are saying before they "speak."

How This Could Be Varied or Developed

1. Whole group discussion on importance of body language.
2. Participants can discuss in their pairs how clearly they were able to convey their meaning to each other and how often they were misinterpreted or not understood at all. The paired work could be followed by a group discussion or round about being understood/misunderstood.
3. Repeat the exercise in groups of four with group situations.
4. In pairs, the participants could carry on a "conversation" using drawings and symbols only (no written words).
5. Participants could discuss the importance of language and how someone with language problems might be affected.

Situations for Pairs

- Person asks for directions to the football ground.
- Person seeks shop assistant's help in choosing a Fathers' Day present.
- Person teaches pupil how to make a cake.
- Person wants to find out all the details of a package holiday from a travel agent.
- Employer speaks to worker who has not completed a task satisfactorily.
- Customer in restaurant talks to waiter about menu and orders meal.
- Two people discuss and prepare a picnic meal.
- Person tells friend about dog training classes s/he has been attending.
- Person complains to shop assistant about shoddy goods.
- Patient seeks doctor's advice over ailment.

Situations for Groups

- People are in a lift which breaks down.
- Policeman interviews witnesses to an accident.
- Leader discusses organising a party with team members.
- Group discusses a chosen television programme.
- Group discusses merits/disadvantages of living in the town or country.
- Group talk about how to entertain a foreign visitor.

Electric Squeeze

What to Do

The group members all hold hands in the circle. One person starts off by squeezing the hand next door. The squeeze gets passed round the circle.

It can be sent in both directions at once and variations can include double squeezes that change the direction of "flow." A one-minute timer can be used to ensure that the "squeeze" returns to the beginning of the circle and a small group of students do not dominate the game.

Gloop

What to Do

Some imaginary slime is "thrown" from one group member to another. The "slime" always lands on the person's face and as it is pulled off, the group makes sucking, slurping noises. The game generates good eye contact and much laughter. It gives power to people who rarely have any and it can be a good energiser if the mood in the group is rather "flat."

Good Try!

What to Do

The group sit in an inward-facing circle with one person standing in the centre. The person in the middle has an object such as a ruler which s/he uses to mime a common activity such as brushing teeth, combing hair, spreading butter, etc. Group members have to guess the activity. If a person gets it right, the one in the middle says "Well done" and gives the object to the new person who thinks of a mime. If they get it wrong, the one in the middle says "Good try" and carries on miming until someone makes a correct guess.

How This Could Be Varied or Developed

1. Group members can mime their particular hobby and the others have to guess what the hobby is. Everyone who has the same hobby then changes places.
2. In the circle discuss what it feels like to be congratulated on getting something right.
3. How does it feel to get it wrong, but be told "Good try" rather than "You're wrong"?
4. Discuss the power of the way we say things to each other and brainstorm helpful and unhelpful ways of pointing out mistakes. This can lead on to role-play of helpful ways of giving and receiving feedback.

Gotcha

What to Do

Participants sit in an inward-facing circle. The teacher spins an empty bottle in the centre. Whenever the bottle stops spinning, the participant sitting opposite the bottle neck speaks on a chosen topic. The person who has just spoken then spins the bottle to identify the next person.

Topics for Self-Disclosure

- What I like about myself.
- What I dislike about myself.
- Something I worry about.
- Something I would like to achieve, etc.

How This Could Be Varied and Developed

1. Any topic can be chosen for Gotcha. It becomes a more amusing and fun way of having a round and eliciting views or opinions on the topic to be discussed.
2. Gotcha can lead on into a whole circle discussion on the chosen topic, e.g. it can be used for college applications or goal-setting in Personal Development Plans. Individuals who want help in achieving goals or overcoming fears etc. can ask for advice and support from their peers.

Guided Walk

What to Do

Participants work in pairs. The whole group sets up a short obstacle course with chairs, bags, books, bins, desks, etc. (Several obstacle courses can be used at once, or one for the whole group, depending on the availability of space.) One of the pair is blindfolded and led through the obstacle course by his/her partner's verbal instructions. They then reverse roles. The obstacle course is rearranged at the end of each turn. If the group is very boisterous, just let one pair work at a time with the whole class watching. Each pair has to aim to "get through with no bumps."

How This Can Be Varied or Developed

1. In the circle, discuss times when we need to trust one another. What makes it easy/difficult to trust people? The group could have a round of "I find it hard to trust people when ..." or "I find it easy to trust people when ..."
2. In the circle, participants can discuss how it felt to be "blind" and what it might be like for someone who is visually impaired or blind.
3. How might loss of sight affect the individual and how might it affect others around him/her?
4. When the sense of sight is missing, which other senses are used to compensate?

I Am a Chair!

What to Do

The teacher supplies a collection of everyday objects, such as a coat, vase, pen, curtain, bucket, plate, etc., to stimulate imagination. Each participant is given an object to think about. You can start with objects in the room, then branch out into objects that pupils imagine. They are to look for all the positive features of their chosen or assigned object. A round follows in which each person names his/her object (in the first person) and expands on all its qualities. They are asked to be as imaginative and inventive as possible.

Example

"I am a chair. I am strong and durable. I am attractive to look at because I am beautifully carved and my seat is covered in soft strong leather. I provide people with somewhere to rest or work. I enhance a room with my appearance."

NB. Start with a confident person so that the shy and embarrassed have time to get used to the activity.

How It Could Be Varied or Developed

Pupils are asked which object they would choose to represent themselves and why. Have a round "If I were an animal, I'd be a ... because..."

Identification Cards

What to Do

Each participant is given a piece of card and told to make it into his/her personal identification card. They are asked to include details of themselves on the card which shows their uniqueness (rather than general descriptions that might apply to many others). Ensure you guide them to only write the positive aspects.

Examples

- They can write their name.
- Attach a photograph.
- Make a thumb print.
- Detail any unique physical feature that they value.
- Detail positive aspects of personality.
- Give any special ideas only they have.
- Any special achievement.

NB. Be ready to help out any individuals who do not see themselves as unique and valuable.

How This Could Be Varied and Developed

1. In the circle discuss in what ways individuals are unique and the importance/value of each individual.
2. This activity can be extended to examine how I feel about how I see myself. How I feel about how others see me. What I would need to change in order for others to see me differently.

Keeper of the Keys

What to Do

This is a game of stealth. The group can construct the story that accompanies the game, but the essential ingredients are a chair in the middle of the circle with a pupil sat on it blindfolded and under the chair, a large bunch of keys. The idea is that the keys represent some treasure or something of value, which has been stolen and is being guarded by the pupil on the chair. One at a time, other pupils in the group are chosen to attempt to recapture the treasure. They have to be as quiet as possible and if the pupil on the chair hears any sound, s/he shouts "stop" and points in the direction of the sound. If the challenge is correct, the discovered pupil has to sit on the floor and become an obstacle to the next pupil who attempts to recapture the treasure. Once someone succeeds in picking up the keys without being detected, they can become the new Keeper of the keys. Remind the other players to keep very still and quiet whilst an attempt is made to capture the treasure.

How This Can Be Varied or Developed

1. The teacher asks the group "If the treasure was a target, what would you like to achieve at school?" Many members of the group might suggest targets of various kinds: academic, sporting, social, etc. These can be written down and pupils encouraged to identify with one or more of them.
2. One of these targets can be chosen and the whole group can examine the question, "What are the obstacles that stop us from achieving this target?"
3. The question, "Does anyone want help with a specific target?" can be asked and then the group is given the opportunity to help an individual using the script "Would it help if you …" An action plan could be written from this activity and given to the individual.

Life Line

What to Do

Participants will need large sheets of paper and pencils. Each person is given a sheet of paper and asked to draw a line. The line represents their life so far.

On one side of the line they write all the positive things that have happened in their life and on the other side all the negative things. You must consider that a student may make a serious disclosure in this exercise so be prepared to deal with this in the correct manner.

How This Could Be Varied or Developed

1. In a circle discuss whether life is an even mix of positive and negative things or more of one than the other.
2. What would you like to see on your lifeline in the future? Is there anything you can do to bring it about?
3. What do you hope will be the next major event on your lifeline? What do you have to do in order to be certain it will happen?
4. The lifeline can be drawn with peaks and troughs rather than on a straight line. This gives a pictorial representation of the "highs" and "lows" of life.

Man's Best Friend

What to Do

Each participant writes his/her name on a piece of paper and puts it into a container. One at a time, the facilitator draws out a name from the container and invites a participant to choose a dog that would suit the named person.

The person whose name is on the slip of paper can reply by agreeing or making their own statement:

"Yes, I'd like a ..." or
"No, I'd rather have a ..."

How This Could Be Varied or Developed

1. In the circle, participants can discuss what attributes they would look for in choosing a dog.
2. What would they like a dog for, e.g. companionship, protection, image, physical appearance, etc.?
3. This can be extended to the attributes and qualities the group members would look for in a friend.
4. How would they have to change in order to be a better friend to other people? This can be followed by a round "I am a good friend when ..." or "A good friend to me is someone who ..."

Moan On

What to Do

The teacher asks the group members to brainstorm all the things in life that irritate them. These can be people, places, situations, TV programmes, etc.

(No comment must be made about any of the ideas, no-one in the circle can be negatively named and they are all noted down on a large sheet of paper). Each member of the group then lists their ten greatest moans in order of magnitude with the biggest as number 1.

How This Can Be Varied or Developed

1. In the circle have a round "The biggest irritation in my life is ..."
2. Discuss why certain things annoy some people and not others.
3. In the light of the discussion, encourage pupils to evaluate how valid they now think their grumbles are. Has anyone changed their opinion? What made them change it?
4. A grumble/irritation that occurred often in the group could be discussed and an action plan produced on how to avoid, change or deal with this grumble. It may be helpful to role-play the irritation or grumble in order to clarify what exactly goes on. Doubling (as explained on page 220) can be used to discuss more helpful ways forward.

My Gang/Group

What to Do

In turn pupils are chosen to stand in the centre of the circle and invite group members to join their gang/group by naming a category for entry.

Examples

- Anyone who likes Eastenders can be in my gang/group.
- Anyone who plays hockey can be in my gang/group.
- Anyone who supports Manchester United can be in my gang/group. And so on.

Anyone who fits the category goes to stand by the speaker in the centre of the circle. A new gang/group leader is chosen, and group members move on to a new "gang/group" each time they fit in with the requirements of the category stated. Individuals keep a tally of the number of gangs/groups they "belonged" to. At the end pupils return to their seats in the circle. Those who belonged to one gang/group stand up and are applauded by the rest. Then those who belonged to two, then three up to the maximum number of "gangs/group" in the game. Each time a group of pupils stand up they are applauded by the pupils sitting down. (Minority groups should then get the maximum applause!) NB. It is important that participants do not base their choices of "gang/group" on personalities but on categories.

How This Can Be Varied or Developed

1. In the circle participants can discuss the pros and cons of belonging to a "gang"/group.
2. Do they normally belong to just one or several different groups and why?
3. Have a round of "I feel … when I am left out."
4. The activity can be followed by a round of "I feel included when …"

My Other Half

What to Do

You will need photocopies of symbols such as the ones in Figure 18.1. The symbols are cut in half and there must be enough for each group member to have one half of a matched pair. The teacher explains that each participant will be given half a symbol. On the command "Go," participants mingle and,

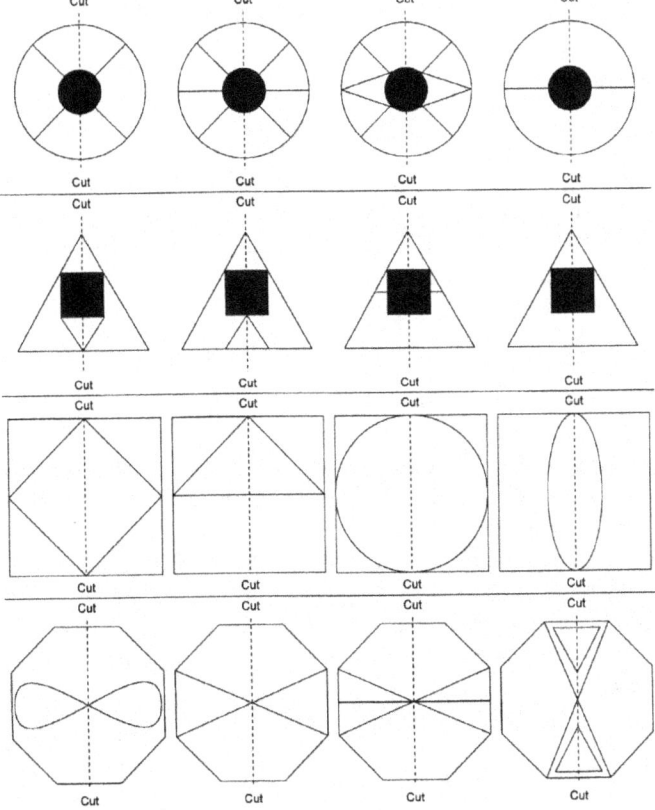

Figure 18.1 Symbols and shapes for "My Other Half."

without any verbal communication, they have a set time (2.5 minutes) to try and locate the person who is holding the matching half of their symbol. This person then becomes their partner. At the end of the set time, any participants without partners can receive help. Alternatively, they can take turns to "draw" their symbol in the air until everyone is matched up.

How This Could Be Varied

1. This activity can be used as an ice-breaker for new groups. After the pairs are formed, they are given five minutes to find out as much about their partners as possible. The group then forms a circle and each participant introduces his/her partner to the group stating three facts about him/her, e.g. "This is Hassan Ahmed. His favourite food is roast chicken. He plays rugby for a local team and he has a Cockerpoo dog called Tyson."
2. In an established group, the activity is a good way to create random pairs for further paired exercises if you want to give the participants the opportunity to work with people they would not necessarily choose as partners. One of the paired exercises on the next pages could then be used.

Negotiating

What to Do

The teacher has a selection of situations in which two people disagree about something. Participants form pairs and role-play negotiating a compromise, which is acceptable to both of them. The teacher tells participants they must only agree to something they feel happy with.

Examples

- A wants to go to the cinema, and B wants to go swimming, but they both want the other's company.
- A wants chips for tea and B wants roast, but they can only prepare one meal.
- A wants to holiday abroad somewhere hot but B cannot tolerate the heat. They want to go somewhere together.
- A has a work deadline to complete for his/her boss B, but cannot finish the work by that time.
- A and B want to buy their father a joint present. A wants to buy something useful, e.g. a jumper but B wants to buy something just for pleasure, e.g. a large cake.

Check Out

Encourage participants to try and play roles "for real."

How This Could Be Varied and Developed

1. The teacher can lead a discussion on how easy/difficult it is to listen to the other person when you want your own way.
2. Did one person just "give in" and let the other have his/her own way?
3. Did either member of the partnership get angry and aggressive in order to get his/ her own way?
4. What helped you to arrive at a compromise?
5. Can you think of any situations that require you to be able to negotiate successfully?
6. Role-play some situations such as wanting to stay out late at a party or getting an extension for a piece of school work. One pair role-play and freeze the action so that the rest of the group can "double" and explore alternative ways of handling negotiation.

Newspaper Stories

What to Do

The teacher collects newspaper headlines. The group members are then divided into pairs or small groups, each of which is given a headline. They must plan and enact a scene which they think fits the headline. Then they discuss the purpose of "headlines" and the ways in which the media attract our interest/influence our thinking.

How This Could Be Varied or Developed

1. Collect and compare different headlines about the same story.
2. Discuss why different newspapers emphasise different aspects of a story.
3. Discuss what sorts of headlines attract pupil interest and why? What aspects of our nature is the headline appealing to?
4. The teacher can read a selection of news items from a paper and ask pairs or groups of pupils to think of a headline for each one. Groups then compare their suggested headlines.
5. The above activities can be extended into the realm of teenage magazines and developed to look at the issues surrounding teenage images and stereotypes.

Number Call

What to Do

Number the class consecutively round the circle, making sure that everyone has a number and can remember it. The leader then makes strong eye contact with one group member and calls out any number between 1 and the maximum number in the group. The person who has eye contact is not allowed to look away or say "yes" or "no" until the person to whom the number belongs "rescues" him/her by calling out "yes." Be sensitive to those pupils, e.g. on the ASD spectrum who might not like making eye contact with anyone.

The game highlights the need to be kind to one another and "rescue" our class team. It also highlights the issues of comfortable and uncomfortable eye contact, the appropriateness of eye contact and its uses in social settings.

How It Could Be Varied or Developed

1. The numbers can be "thrown" across the circle. The person who "catches" the number then "throws" it to someone else, e.g. number 1 calls out "1 to 17," then 17 says "17 to 3," etc.
2. Add complications such as a rule that no number can be repeated and/or the number has to be sent to the opposite side of the circle, not to the person next door.
3. A development of this game is to add a noise by patting hands on knees. The noise makes the game much harder because it distracts the players and it is very hard to concentrate on two things at the same time. The group can then discuss the distractions that make it difficult to concentrate in lessons.
4. From variation 3 develop a discussion about distractions in class. Have a round "I can't concentrate when …" and move the discussion on to common distractions in this class and ways of resolving them.

Opting Out

What to Do

Participants are divided into groups of four. They are asked to think of a situation in which three members of the group are putting pressure on the fourth to join them in an activity/situation which the fourth does not want to do. The three persuaders use various tactics, e.g. persuasion, bullying, threats, bribes, etc. Each group role-plays their situation.

Examples

- A, B, C want D to join them in picking a fight with someone else.
- A, B, C want D to join them in playing truant.
- A, B, C want D to join them on a shoplifting spree.
- A, B, C want D to sneak out with them at night after bedtime.
- A, B, C want D to break into a scrap merchants yard with them to "have some fun."

Check Out

Encourage participants to try and really "feel" their roles.

How This Could Be Varied and Developed

1. The teacher leads a discussion on the difficulties of dealing with peer pressure. If there are lots of views, the teacher could instigate a round of "I find it difficult to resist when ..."
2. What makes them comply and what would help them to refuse?
3. Do any individuals want help with an issue involving peer pressure? Individuals in the group can suggest strategies to help deal effectively with peer pressure. Use the scripts "Would it help if you ...?," "Would it help if I...?," "Would it help if we...?" If an individual does not want help, keep the discussion more general, perhaps picking up from the initial role-plays.

Parental Concerns

What to Do

Participants work in pairs. They choose a situation of conflict that arises between them and one of their parents. They each take a turn to play the role of a parent then the child. The parent tells the child all the concerns s/he has about the child's behaviour, whilst the child justifies or excuses whatever the concern is.

How This Could Be Varied or Developed

1. Participants can discuss whether they consider parental concerns are usually justifiable. What should parents do about the concerns they have for their children's welfare?
2. How might the children allay their parent's concerns?
3. One or more of the role-plays could be shown to the whole group and "doubling" used to find a variety of ways of thinking and responding. The teacher could play the child in one of the role-plays!

Pass the Action

What to Do

Any action can be passed round the circle from one person to the next as fast and as smoothly as possible. Mexican waves are popular and develop a sense of "whole group" as the members cooperate in transferring the action. Passing a smile generates a lot of laughter.

How It Could Be Varied

1. Passing actions, e.g. a handshake can be good for introducing touch into the group. Touch is associated with being liked and accepted; it can bring acceptance and warmth into the group.
2. An action can be "activated" in the next person by gently touching them below the knee.
3. The group stands in a circle facing in one direction. The first person draws a simple design on the back of the next person. This design is then passed on round the circle and the end person draws it on to a piece of paper. A comparison is made between the end design and the initial one drawn by the first participant.

Pass the Python

What to Do

Participants stand in an inward-facing circle. The teacher tells them they are going to mime passing "objects" around the circle from one person to the next. The teacher chooses one player to mime passing a python in an appropriate manner. After the python has been passed several times, the teacher changes the "object" and the game continues with the appropriate changes.

Examples of "Objects"

- hot plate of soup;
- sticky bun;
- heavy suitcase;
- foul smelling experiment.

How This Can Be Varied or Developed

1. Participants can form small groups of four or five and improvise a scene, passing one of the "objects" as a starting point.
2. In the circle the group can discuss how we understand one another without words and the concentration required to read non-verbal signals in conversation.
3. Brainstorm times when it is essential that you can accurately read non-verbal cues.

Play the Game

What to Do

Participants sit in an inward-facing circle. Two or three participants leave the room. The remaining players decide on a "rule" to play the game by. When the rule is established, the absent players return and take turns to question everyone in the circle about anything. All answers must abide by the agreed rule. The object of the game is to discover the rule and the people who are guessing can confer. NB. Make sure that the rules do not become too complicated, especially at the beginning.

Examples

- Girls answer truthfully and boys do not.
- Anyone answering must cross their legs.
- All answers must include a specific word, e.g. "perhaps."

How This Can Be Varied and Developed

1. This game can lead to a discussion on rules and their purpose; why people keep them and why they break them.
2. What sort of rules are most beneficial and which are least?
3. Participants can consider rules in different contexts and circumstances as appropriate to the group's experience, e.g. in society, at home, at school, at work.
4. Can have a round of "If I were in charge one rule I would make is …"

Positive News

What to Do

Participants are told to mingle with each other. Each person must say one genuine and positive thing to as many other people as possible. If the group is not able to do this yet, structure the activity by giving each person in the circle the letter A or B alternately. A and B make up a pair. When you want to change the pairs, ask all the A's to stand up and move clockwise to the fourth chair along and sit down. The person to their right is their new partner. NB. Watch out for any pupils who find it particularly difficult to give a compliment and warn pupils not to pay inappropriate compliments, e.g. about private body parts.

Examples

- You have lovely blue eyes.
- I like your shoes.
- You're always friendly.
- I liked the way you spoke about …
- I really like the way you smile at me.

How This Can Be Varied and Developed

1. In the circle discuss why it is sometimes difficult to give or receive compliments.
2. Why is positive feedback important to people? For example, as an encouragement, to make them feel valued and to boost confidence.
3. Each person can set a target to give a compliment to someone every day this week and to say "Thank you" when they receive a compliment.

Problem-Solving

What to Do

Start the game by asking the group to brainstorm problems. A brainstorm requires that every suggestion is accepted without comment. No-one may say that one person's idea is not a problem, even if it would not present a problem to them!

In groups of four, participants are given problem situations, which they must resolve as a group, by discussing what each member would do to help. At the end, each group can present their solution to the rest of the class.

Examples

- The group is walking in remote countryside. It is dusk and getting cold. One member of the group falls over a cliff edge and is badly hurt. The territory is unfamiliar to the group.
- You've lost something you borrowed from a friend. You promised to return it today and can't find it.
- You've found out your brother/sister is taking drugs.
- You don't know how to finish with your boy/girlfriend.
- A friend has started shoplifting.
- You've been feeling unwell and are frightened you might have a serious illness.
- You don't understand a piece of work, but don't want to appear stupid.

How This Could Be Varied and Developed

1. Participants can discuss panic situations; have a round of "I tend to panic when ..."
2. Discuss the nature of panic. How do they think they would react?
3. Brainstorm ways of dealing with panic so that they can stay calm and think rationally.
4. Ask if any individual would like some help with a particular situation that causes them to panic. Ask the class to use the script "Would it help if ...?"

Racing Pictionary

This is a team game that can be used to revise keywords or to expose stereotypes.

Divide the circle into teams of four or five pupils. Each group has one pencil and a block of paper. The groups need to be separated in the room so that they can't see one another's papers or hear the suggestions that are made. One pupil from each group holds the pencil and comes up to the teacher for the first word from the list. You whisper the word from the list, or show it to them. They run back to their group and draw a representation of the word. They can't use hand gestures, writing or any spoken words to communicate – just drawings. When the pupils in the group guess what the drawing is, they whisper so that other teams don't hear. Once somebody in the group guesses correctly, s/he takes the pencil and rushes off to the teacher, whispers the word to check that it is correct, and receives the next word, and so on.

The winning team is the one that guesses the most words, but beware of cheating. If you suspect cheating, you can challenge the group and ask to see the drawing.

How This Can Be Varied or Developed

1. The game can be adapted to use with revision lists in any subject.
2. It can also be used to introduce a discussion in PSHE or Citizenship, particularly if the topic involves stereotypes. It helps if the list begins with easier clues and then moves on to harder ones.
3. Pictionary can be used as an introduction to exploring communication skills. In this case, a random list of words can be used such as London Eye, Hamburger, Beethoven, Celtic, Daffodils and so on.

Red Queen

What to Do

The teacher supplies a pack of playing cards. Each participant is given a card (two of which are the Queen of Hearts and the Queen of Diamonds). Players must not name their cards out loud. The object of the game is to get rid of the red queens. Players approach one another and ask if they can swap cards. If the individual feels this is safe, they comply. If they think they might be given a red queen, they can refuse. However, each player has to make at least two swaps. After several minutes the teacher stops the game and the two players holding the red queens are out and sit down in the circle. The cards are collected in. Two "safe" cards are removed and they are dealt out again. The game can continue for several more goes.

Check that players do swap and don't hang on to "safe" cards.

How This Could Be Varied and Developed

1. The teacher leads a discussion on how pupils reacted when they held the red queens. Could they "read" other players' expressions/body language to know if they held "safe" cards or the queens? How daring were they in swapping cards?
2. Discussion can continue on how daring we are in life. What kind of risks do we take? How do we feel about taking on new challenges? How secure are we in the face of change? What prevents people from being more daring – look at lack of confidence, low self-esteem, physical fear, etc.
3. The game can be repeated at a faster tempo where participants are not allowed to refuse a request to swap.
4. Change the rules so that each time the action stops, the two players holding the red queens gain a point.

Reflections

What to Do

Participants work in pairs. One of the pair copies the action of the other as if s/he were a reflection in a mirror. The pair then swap roles. It is important that the participants make the movements slow and distinct so that the pair can synchronise movements as much as possible.

How This Can Be Varied or Developed

1. Make up groups of four. One pair agrees and performs a cooperative movement and the second pair mirrors the action.
2. Return to the circle and discuss how hard/easy the game was. Could they "read" their partner's mind and anticipate the movement that would follow? What did they have to concentrate on most?
3. This can be developed into a counselling type exercise where pairs have a discussion and subtly mirror one another's body movements in order to enhance empathy, e.g. If one person looks fed up whilst recounting an incident his/her partner "mirrors" that emotion, using facial expression, body stance, etc.
4. Are there situations in life when it is important to be able to "read" what will happen next?
5. Discuss times when an ability to "read" the situation accurately would enable you to intervene and change the course of things before a crisis developed. Questions 4 and 5 may lead to some role-play of situations the pupils have raised and using the "doubling" technique to explore different ways of intervening before there is a crisis.

Ring on a String

What to Do

The teacher supplies a length of string and a ring. The participants sit close together, i.e. with their shoulders touching, in an inward-facing circle. A piece of string is cut long enough to stretch around the circle. A ring is threaded on to the string and the two ends tied together to form a continuous circle. One participant leaves the room and the remaining people hold the string with both hands palms downwards. They covertly pass the ring along the string from one person to the next. The absent player returns and must guess which player is holding the ring. Other players pretend to pass the ring to confuse the "detective." When a correct guess is made, another "detective" is chosen and leaves the room whilst the ring is passed to a different place in the circle. NB. It might be advisable to limit the number of guesses to three after which a new detective is chosen so that players don't get bored if someone has difficulty locating the ring.

How This Could Be Varied or Developed

1. Participants form two teams which stand facing each other, shoulder touching shoulder, hands behind their backs. Each team has a small object which they pass backwards and forwards along the line. Each team takes turns to guess or pass the object and every participant has a go at guessing which member of the opposite team has the object. The player is allowed two guesses and, if correct, his/her team receives a point. The game is played in silence, but participants try to confuse the person who is guessing with facial expressions, pretending to pass the object, etc.
2. In a circle, the group can discuss situations where good teamwork is beneficial. What qualities make a good team member?

Saying Sorry

What to Do

The teacher has a selection of errors and misdemeanours. Participants work in pairs. Each participant chooses a situation from the selection and "apologises" for it to his/her partner. The teacher tells the participants to choose initially a situation they might normally apologise for and then one which they would find difficult to apologise for.

Examples

- You deliberately ignored someone.
- You accidentally broke someone's window.
- You forgot you had arranged to meet someone.

- You made an unkind remark about someone which they learned about.
- You were rude to someone.

How This Could Be Varied and Developed

1. Participants can discuss why or when they might find it difficult to apologise. Suggested round: "I find it difficult to apologise when …"
2. What are the pros and cons of apologising?
3. What might make it easier for them to apologise? Suggested round: "I find it easier to apologise if …"

Setbacks

What to Do

Participants set up an obstacle course of chairs, books, bags etc. They take turns to negotiate the course, first on one leg, then backwards, etc. (This can be done in groups of two or three if there is sufficient space.)

How This Can Be Varied and Developed

1. In the circle, the group brainstorms the irritating things that make progress around school more difficult for them, e.g. no locker, heavy bags, too long a queue.
2. Individuals can ask for the group's help in coping with difficulties.
3. Circle discussion about physical disability could immediately follow this game. What negative effects does disability bring? Could there be any positive effects? How do other people treat those with physical disability?

Sevens

What to Do

This is a group cooperation game. Everyone starts standing up. They then count in turn round the circle. Each person can choose to say one, two, or three numbers, but every time the count gets to seven, that person "dies" and has to sit down. So the teacher may start by saying "One, two" and the next person in the circle can say "three" or "three, four" or "three, four, five" then the next person picks up the counting at "six" thus forcing the next person to sit down on "seven." The counting then starts again at "one." The game should be played fast so that those who are out early on do not get bored.

How This Can Be Varied or Developed

1. If the group tends to gang up on individuals to ensure they are out early, you can choose the person who will win before the game begins, thus

getting everyone to play cooperatively to ensure that chosen person is not out.
2. Introduce "Guardian Angels." These are the pupils on either side of you. They can volunteer to become heroes and sacrifice themselves rather than letting the person next to them die. This can lead to interesting discussions about protecting others from risk or harm.

Similarities and Differences

What to Do

The teacher starts off by choosing some aspect of the group which is common to several members such as, "All those who have laces in their shoes change places." The statements can change from totally non-threatening, observable similarities to more personal disclosures such as "Everyone who likes chocolate change places" or "Everyone who dislikes their middle name." Once the game is established, a chair is removed from the circle so that one person is left in the middle. The person left in the middle then chooses the next similarity or difference.

Rules

- To get as far across the circle and away from your chair as possible.
- Not to push into anyone.
- To be honest about your preferences or dislikes.
- Not to be left in the middle.

How It Could Be Varied or Developed

1. In the circle, discuss the importance of having things in common with other people.
2. Extend the discussion to belonging to families, social groups, communities. What are the benefits and what are the responsibilities of being part of these different groups?

Tease

What to Do

The teacher has a selection of situations in which someone is teased. In groups of four, participants are given a situation which they role-play, each member taking on a different character, e.g. A – teaser, B – victim, C – observer, D – friend of either A or B. They can then swap roles. The repetition of a scenario with different people taking the different roles tends to release more imagination and a richer role-play. NB. Encourage participants to try and feel empathy with "victims."

Examples

- A teases B about new hairstyle.
- A teases B, because B has spots.
- A teases B about their name.
- A teases B about being stupid.
- A teases B about the way they talk.

How This Could Be Varied and Developed

1. The teacher leads a discussion on teasing. Is it always malicious or sometimes affectionate?
2. How can the victim respond effectively to stop the teasing? Brainstorm effective methods of dealing with unwanted teasing. One of the earlier role-play situations can be used as a basis for exploring different ways of dealing with teasing.
3. Discuss why some people are persistent teasers/victims?

Things in Common

What to Do

Four fruits are chosen and participants are each given the name of a fruit in order round the circle, e.g. apples, oranges, pears, bananas, apples, etc. Everyone sits down in the circle and the teacher calls out a fruit. All the people who have that fruit name must change places. When "fruit bowl" is called, everyone changes places.

How This Could Be Varied and Extended

1. The names given to each class member can be from any group of objects, e.g. vehicles such as cars, lorries, motorbikes, vans and all traffic, or countries, such as England, Scotland, Wales, Northern Ireland and United Kingdom. The possibilities are endless and the group can create their own categories.
2. The group mixes freely and the teacher calls out a category. Any person who fits that category has to find a partner in the same category, e.g. anyone who has a birthday in September, anyone with brown eyes, etc. When a pair has been formed, they both score a point and participants keep a tally of their score.
3. In the circle discuss the importance of sharing things in common.
4. Discuss the groups of people you belong to where you share something in common, e.g. your family which may share the same name, or the same house. Your community may live in the same area, use the same community hall, etc. Your school has the same teachers, the same building etc.
5. Are there responsibilities that are attached to being part of a group?

Touchdown

What to Do

Divide the group into pairs. Depending on the size of the group, divide the pairs into several teams, e.g. four teams with three pairs in each team. The teacher explains that s/he will call a number and the pairs in each team have to devise different ways of placing that number of body parts on the floor, e.g. if the number is three, one pair could stand with three feet touching the ground between them. The next pair in the team might kneel with three knees touching the ground between them. The next pair might have one person standing on one foot holding their partner's feet off the ground as in a wheelbarrow race. The first team to achieve three different positions wins a point.

How This Could Be Varied or Developed

1. The teams have to negotiate the different methods of touching the ground without speaking, using non-verbal communication skills.
2. The team designates one leader who has to make the decisions and everyone else must do as they are told, no matter whether they agree or disagree. The role of leader is rotated round the group.
3. Follow activity 2 with a discussion about how it feels to be responsible for the decision-making and how it feels to have to follow instructions even when you think you have a better idea.
4. Whole Circle Activities and discussions can offer opportunities for members to look at situations when they have to follow instructions even when they disagree and strategies for coping with the accompanying feelings.

Who Are You?

What to Do

The group stands or sits in a circle and, in pairs, they think of a positive adjective that begins with the same letter as their first name, e.g. "Smashing Shakira" or "Wonderful Wayne," etc. It is important to ensure that positive adjectives are used. Once everyone has thought of a positive alliterative adjective, each person, in turn says his/her name preceded by the positive adjective. Warn the group that no-one may make a derogatory comment or gesture about someone's choice of adjective.

How It Can Be Varied or Developed

1. Each person says his/her name accompanied by a verb and an action, e.g. "Mountaineering Maya" said whilst the person performs a mime of mountaineering.

2. A ball or beanbag can be thrown across the circle to different people. The person who catches it has to say his/her name either with or without the adjective. Or once the group gets to know one another's names, the thrower has to use the name of the person they throw to.
3. A ball or beanbag or soft toy can be thrown across the circle from one person to another accompanied by the script "Hi, Smashing Shakira," "I'm Wonderful Wayne" If anyone forgets the name of another group member, they can say "Hi, I'm Wonderful Wayne, what's your name please?"
4. A ball of string or wool can be thrown to named people, so that it unravels and creates a web. The wool ensures that every person is included and there is a visual picture of "group" at the end when everyone is joined together.

You're Positive

What to Do

Participants sit in an inward-facing circle. One person is asked to leave the room and the teacher asks for several positive statements about that person from any member of the group. When the person returns, the teacher repeats each statement asking him/her to guess who said each one. The teacher must ensure that no negative reactions occur if the person makes an incorrect guess, e.g. "I wouldn't say that about you because I think you're ugly!" You can only play this when the group has built up a good rapport and ethos.

How This Can Be Varied or Developed

1. If group members are as yet unable to make three positive statements about individuals, discussion can take place so that the whole group comes up with positive statements which are written down and given as a present to the person outside the room on their return.
2. In the circle discuss how hearing positive statements affects people.
3. What effect do positive statements have on self-confidence, relationships with others and work?
4. Targets can be set to look for positive things to say to people in the next week.

Waves

What to Do

This is played by having a circle of seats equal in number to the class members. One seat is removed and one person volunteers to be in the middle. (Make sure they are of a robust temperament and not vulnerable to exclusion by the social group.) The whole class then moves round from one seat to the next in a continuous wave of motion and the person in the centre tries to sit on the vacant chair. Once the group gets the knack of this, it is extremely hard to get into the chair because it is not ever really left vacant.

Zoom – Eek

What to Do

One pupil starts a car going around the circle by saying "Zoom" and turning his or her head quickly to the person on the right. The next person repeats this action and it continues around the circle until a pupils says "Eek." The car then changes direction and the "Zoom" sound goes the other way until the next "Eek." At first the teacher can say "Zoom" and "Eek" and once the game is established, the pupils can determine the direction of the car's movement themselves.

How This Can Be Varied or Developed

1. Sometimes one section of the circle will monopolise the action by their use of the "Eek." If this happens, it can be highlighted with a discussion on consideration and how to be considerate with one another.
2. Another strategy is to issue each pupil with an "Eek" card. Once they have used their "Eek," they must put the card into the centre of the circle. They can learn to use their "Eek" card strategically and eventually all the "Eeks" will be used up.

Chapter 19

Step 2 – Rounds

The round, already described in Chapter 12, is used to make sure that everyone has the opportunity to speak and be listened to. In this model of Circle Time, a speaking object is used as a visual symbol of respectful listening. When someone holds the object, they have the opportunity to speak and everyone else listens. The rule is that no one may interrupt the person holding the speaking object. Even the teacher must get up, move across the circle, touch the object and apologise to the person who is speaking before they may interrupt the process. The round gives a very strong message about the respect afforded to someone when they speak. It is also a democratic process as everyone has a turn. The right to say "I pass" means that an individual can choose whether to take part or to sit quietly. At the end of the round the last person to speak says "Does anyone who passed want a turn?" If someone who has not already contributed to the round has now thought of something they want to say, the object is taken to them and they have an opportunity to speak.

Members of the group are always encouraged to take responsibility for what they say and whether or not they contribute. Very often a round has a scripted sentence stem which begins the statement pupils are invited to complete. Sometimes the statements begin with "I," e.g. "I feel happy when…," "In my spare time I like to …" The use of "I" and "My" can be important to assertive communication and encourage ownership of and responsibility for thoughts, feelings and actions. Sometimes, however, the topic being discussed is too sensitive or controversial, and it is safer for pupils to use a sentence stem that distances the issue. Sentence stems can then begin with "People find it hard when …," "Some people might take risks by …," "It would make someone happy if …" and so on.

Getting to Know You: Paired Discussions and Rounds

Discussion: Where did you live at the age of 7? How many brothers and sisters did you have?

Round: "When I was 7, I lived in ... I had ... brothers and ... sisters." Or "This is ... When he/she was 7 he/she lived ... and he/she had ... brothers and ... sisters."
Discussion: What was the happiest moment in your life?
Round: "The happiest moment of my life was ..."
Discussion: What is the greatest regret of your life?
Round: "My greatest regret is ..."
Discussion: Which room in your house do you like best and why?
Round: "My favourite room is ... because ..."
Discussion: What is one thing you want to do next week?
Round: "Next week I will ..."
Discussion: If you had a time machine that would work only once, what point in the future or in history would you visit?
Round: "I would use my machine to visit ..., because..."
Discussion: If you could take a tablet that would enable you to live to 1000 years, would you take it and why/why not?
Round: "I would/would not take the tablet because ..."
Discussion: What was the best/worst experience of your week?
Round: "The best thing that happened this week was ..." "The worst thing that happened this week was ..."
Discussion: If you could go anywhere in the world for three days, where would you go and why?
Round: "I would go to ..., because ..."
Discussion: How do you relax?
Round: "I relax by..."
Discussion: What is your favourite type of music/song?
Round: "My favourite music is ..."
Discussion: If you could not fail, what would you like to do?
Round: "If I could not fail, I would ..."
Discussion: Name a present you will never forget.
Round: "A present I will never forget is ..."
Discussion: When was the last time you made a mistake? How did you feel?
Round: "When I make a mistake, I feel ..."

Rounds About Feelings

There has been much research in recent years on what makes people do well in life. The traditional view is that bright people – those with a high IQ – do well and those with a lower IQ score do less well, and since intelligence is genetically fixed there is nothing we can do about it. More and more research demonstrates this to be untrue. We could all cite examples of those with high IQ who have foundered and those with modest IQ who have done exceedingly well. Other factors seem to be at work. These factors have been called emotional intelligence, and include self-control, zeal, persistence and the ability to motivate oneself. These skills can be taught to pupils, giving them a better chance to use whatever intellectual potential their genetic make-up may have given them.

The following rounds are designed to encourage recognition and ownership of emotions. They involve "I" statements and connect an emotion with a situation that engenders those feelings.

The group is given the sentence stem and a minute or two to think about the feelings and situations. The speaking object is given to the first person or a volunteer who is brave enough to start, and the round begins.

"I feel happy when …"	"I feel sad when …"
"One thing that makes me angry is …"	"I get scared when …"
"The most frustrating thing for me is …"	"I am always excited when …"
"I feel really safe when …"	"My favourite person is …"
"The possession I love the most is …"	"Silence makes me feel …"
"The person I admire the most is …"	"I hate it when …"
"I feel pushed when …"	"I like to be alone when …"
"A sound that makes me happy is …"	"I hate being alone when …"

The list is endless and can be designed to suit any topic when it is important to access feelings.

Chapter 20

Step 3 – Open Forum Drama and Role-Play Ideas

Step 3 is the heart of Circle Time. When I am training teachers, I tell them that if they are in a rush or have a very short period of time then leave Open Forum out. It's a vulnerable step as you are asking children to nominate themselves to request help from their peers. You're also asking them at times to reflect on very sensitive issues. You're harnessing the goodwill and energy of students to practise honesty and inclusion. That is why, earlier in the book, I say never finish on a Step 3. Otherwise, the children will go out in a fragile way unable to cope with the hurly-burly of the corridors and playgrounds. If you finish on a fun game, a very positive activity or a mindfulness which strengthens their resilience and inner sense of strength … then that is fine.

Often, to stimulate a good discussion, it might be necessary for a teacher to role-play a character who has many of the problems that the class is currently experiencing. The teacher then becomes the person whom the students try and support with their ideas – so by social observational learning they are still being enriched with possibilities of ways forward. Even better would be to ask a sixth former to come and role-play one of their peers asking for help.

Children love drama. A few of these following ideas you can adapt to bring into Step 3 – some of the others are a lovely reward for your group at the end of term! (Figure 20.1)

Committees

What to Do

You will need a prepared list of different types of committees. In groups of 4–6, participants are told they are committee members of a meeting. Each group is given a "situation" to role-play. Participants must try and think of all the difficulties, needs, circumstances, possibilities and concerns. They can elect a chairperson to oversee proceedings. NB. Encourage participants to adopt a character type and act/react accordingly.

DOI: 10.4324/9781003679615-24

	Cooperation	Concentration	Imagination	Listening	Speaking	Observation	Creativity	Thinking	Self-affirmation	Self-esteem	Assertiveness	Appreciation	Laughter/fun	Empathy	Self-disclosure	Confidence
Adverbs			•	•		•	•		•						•	•
Committees	•			•	•			•			•	•				•
Defusing anger	•			•	•								•	•		
Dramatic scenes	•		•	•	•	•										
Emotions			•		•		•			•				•	•	•
Factories	•	•					•					•				
Freeze		•	•	•		•		•								•
Guess the scene			•										•			
If the cap fits			•						•	•	•			•		•
Improvisation 1	•	•				•				•	•				•	•
Improvisation 2	•	•				•				•	•				•	•
Instructions					•			•								•
Muscial scenes			•	•		•										
Opposites	•		•	•	•	•	•	•					•			
Party-goers			•	•	•	•							•	•		•
Proverbs		•	•													
Racing charades		•	•										•			
Scene change	•	•	•				•									
Scenes					•	•		•	•				•	•	•	•
Sign language		•	•			•	•									
Silent movies		•	•			•	•									
Social gatherings			•	•	•	•						•		•	•	•
Story roundabout	•	•		•			•	•					•	•		•
The journey			•		•		•					•	•			
The waiting room			•	•	•								•			•
Theme pictures	•		•	•	•		•	•								
Yes and no			•	•	•									•		•

Figure 20.1 Key to drama and role-play for Circle Time.

Examples

- members of the school council with £500 to spend on extra equipment;
- members of a committee discussing which venues to take foreign visitors to.

How This Could Be Varied and Developed

1 Participants can discuss the problems they encountered. What qualities do they think make a good and effective team of committee members? For example, being able to cooperate, being able to listen, being able to negotiate.
2 Are any school situations similar to a committee? Are there times in school when we need the same skills as committee members?
3 Have a round of "I am a good team member when I ..."

Defusing Anger

What to Do

Prepare a list of confrontational situations. The teacher has a selection of situations that have provoked anger. Pupils work in pairs A and B role-play how the angry person would behave and how the partner might respond, first in a negative way and then in a positive way to resolve the situation. Pupils then choose a new situation and reverse roles. NB. Encourage participants to try and respond as they would if they really were angry.

Examples

- A is spreading untrue rumours about B.
- A has copied B's idea for a piece of work.
- A has tried to steal B's girlfriend/boyfriend.
- A has "told tales" on B, resulting in B getting into trouble.
- A is angry with B for not tidying up as agreed.
- A has borrowed something from B and ruined it.

How This Could Be Varied and Developed

1. Have a round "When I get angry I ..." This will encourage an understanding of a range of responses to anger.
2. Pupils discuss the best ways of dealing with someone else's anger.
3. What might escalate anger and what defuses it?
4. Pupils discuss ways of defusing their own anger so that it becomes less destructive to self/others.

Emotions

What to Do

The teacher needs a prepared list of emotions. Pupils are divided into small groups, and each group is given two emotions. The groups are asked to think up and enact a "scene" that involves both emotions. NB. Encourage participants to use both emotions plausibly.

Examples

- panic–anger
- grief–weariness
- embarrassment–impatience
- amusement–triumph

How This Could Be Varied and Developed

1. On a large sheet of paper or the board, pupils can list emotions under the headings "negative emotions," "positive emotions" and discuss what effect they have on us.

2. Do some emotions fit into both lists?
3. Can negative emotions be made into positive ones?
4. What factors/situations make it difficult for group members to control their emotions? This could be followed by a round "I find it difficult to control my emotions when …"
5. What strategies can members of the group suggest for managing their emotions?

Factories

What to Do

In groups of four to six, the participants are told that they work on a production line in a factory. Each group decides on its "product" and manufacturing process, so that every member has a job to do on the production line. The groups then mime their factories "at work." They can give a commentary on the process, as it happens. NB. Encourage participants to divide up the "action" evenly.

How This Could be Varied and Developed

1. Participants can discuss the benefits of working together to achieve a goal.
2. How are people uncooperative?
3. Why might people not cooperate with others? Suggested round: "I find it difficult to cooperate in groupwork when …"
4. What helps people to be cooperative? Suggested round: "I find it easier to work in groups when …"

Proverbs

What to Do

You will need a prepared list of proverbs, perhaps written individually on slips of paper. Working in small groups, participants are given a proverb to build a scene around. They are instructed that their scene must portray the meaning of the proverb, but must not be a direct play around the words of the proverb. Groups perform their scenes to the other participants who are then invited to guess what the proverb was.

Examples

- All that glitters is not gold
- Don't count your chickens before they've hatched
- Blood is thicker than water
- A stitch in time saves nine

How This Could Be Varied and Developed

1. Participants can discuss the value of proverbs.
2. Why do they think they are seldom used today?

Racing Charades

What to Do

The teacher has a prepared list of well-known books, films and television titles. The class is divided into two teams which go to opposite ends of the room. The teacher sits in the middle with the list of titles. A player from each team goes to the teacher who whispers the first title to them. They race back to their team and mime the title (they can state or mime whether it is a book/film/TV show). As soon as the team has guessed a title, another player goes to the teacher to say the correct answer and receive the next whispered title. The winning team is the one which guesses all the titles first. No verbal clues are allowed.

If a team gets really stuck, they can go to the next clue and come back to the problem clue at the end.

How This Could Be Varied and Developed

1. Two teams can play challenge charades where they sit in rows facing the opposite team. Players from each team take turns to challenge a named opponent to guess the mimes they perform. If the "opponent" answers correctly, his/her team receives two points. If s/he needs help from other team members, they only receive one point. Players must choose a different named opponent each time to prevent them from continuously choosing someone who is not very good at guessing.
2. Pupils discuss how they found the first or second game. Did they find it difficult to communicate or to think of appropriate mimes? Did they feel embarrassed or nervous about performing the mimes? Are there situations in life where they have to "perform" in front of others? How might they cope better with the fear of performing?

Sign Language

What to Do

The teacher gives each participant a prepared question. The participants are put in pairs and each person looks at their questions then, in silence, takes turns to mime the question and a response (players can check verbally afterwards to see if they have properly understood the question and response). Both members of the pair can mime their questions then move on to another player and repeat the process. NB. Make sure that shy participants do join in.

Examples

- Can I have six eggs please?
- Where is the restaurant?
- What time does the cinema open?
- Would you like to come to the disco with me?

How This Could Be Varied and Developed

1. Participants can discuss how difficult/easy they found the game.
2. Did their mimes improve with practice?
3. What other "signs" did they use? For example, facial expressions.
4. What do they think it would be like to rely on sign language as deaf people do?

Yes and No

What to Do

You will need a prepared list of subjects. Participants work in pairs. They are given or they choose a subject about which they must argue, one for and one against. The teacher explains that, regardless of personal opinions, they must really try to think and feel as the role demands. After a time, the teacher tells them to reverse roles (trying to reverse their thoughts and feelings as well) and continue the argument.

Examples of Subjects

- homework;
- single-sex schools;
- competitive sports;
- smoking in restaurants;
- school uniforms;
- violence on television.

How This Could Be Varied and Developed

1. Participants can discuss the value of changing roles.
2. Discuss whether acknowledging other people's opinions and how putting themselves in other people's shoes could help resolve disputes.

Chapter 21

Step 5 – Calm Down Ideas

This chapter focuses on Step 5, the final step of Circle Time. This is the Calm Down, which helps children transition from activity to peaceful reflection through guided visualisations and mindfulness. It offers four detailed visualisations ("Into Africa," "Mountain Stream," "The Sea" and "Morning Birds"), each designed to promote relaxation, imagination and emotional calm. Guidance is given on preparing the environment, selecting music and using calming scripts to develop focus and inner stillness. Through sensory imagery and gradual re-orientation, participants learn self-regulation, resilience and mindfulness. The chapter emphasises safe facilitation, emotional grounding and using calm down rituals to nurture confidence, wellbeing and readiness for learning.

Calm downs can be short and simple like the example in Chapter 12. However, if you want to spend more time on Step 5 or feel the class benefits from learning how to engage more deeply with mindfulness, then the following Guided Visualisations are great.

There are four Guided Visualisations here:

- Into Africa
- Mountain Stream
- The Sea
- Morning Birds

Before You Begin

- Dim the lights if at all possible.
- Offer eye masks if that is possible too. You can buy them very cheaply.
- Ensure that distractions will be kept to a minimum – put do not disturb on the door.
- Make sure that everyone is aware of the benefits of guided visualisation so that they begin with a motivated and serious attitude. Tell them that this technique is used by athletes, actors and business people to help them achieve success.

DOI: 10.4324/9781003679615-25

- Decide which visualisation you are going to use and find some calming music on YouTube or on Spotify that relates to the visualisation, e.g. for Into Africa – Calming African Jungle Sounds, for Mountain Stream – Mountain Stream – Relaxing Nature Sounds, for The Sea – Calming Wave Sounds and for Morning Birds – Calming Bird Song.
- When you are speaking, turn the music down low, and when you pause, turn it up a bit.

Introductory Phase

Use the following script to settle and calm the children.

Sit with both feet on the floor. Make sure you are comfortable, warm and relaxed.

Close your eyes and let your body feel soft and relaxed.

Listen to your breathing. Can you feel the air going in and out? Just listen to your breath for a moment and let it become slow and calm. Slow and calm.

Let your mind become very still as you take a long, slow breath.

Now let the breath out very gently.

Your breathing is slow and calm.

Slow and calm.

Your mind is very still

You feel warm and relaxed and comfortable.

Your eyes are closed and your body is relaxed and warm and still.

Jenny Mosley's Guided Visualisation: Into Africa

Play the music for a minute to accustom the children to the sounds of Africa.

You feel warm. Warmth wraps itself around you. You feel calm and safe.

Wiggle your toes and feel the warm air all around them.

The warm air relaxes your toes and makes them feel comfortable and soft.

Pause.

Feel the warm air on your legs and knees. Tense them so that they feel tight and then relax them so that they are soft and relaxed. The warm air relaxes your legs and knees and makes them feel comfortable and loose.

Pause then continue this process, moving up the body until you reach the head. Pause for each part of the body.

Turn up the sound so that it fills the children's minds.

The air is warm and steamy. You can feel the dampness in the air, but it is warm and cosy and comfortable.

A drop of warm water drips down onto your cheek and runs down your face. Wipe it away with your hand. It smells rich and exotic like expensive perfume or aftershave. It is spicy and flowery.

You like the smell. You breathe it in and enjoy the perfume as it fills your lungs with happiness and contentment.

Spend a little time imagining the rich, wonderful smell.

Pause.

You look around and see that you are in a jungle. Plants grow all around you. They are so huge and tall that you can hardly see the sky.

Look around and see the crowded jungle plants. See how shiny and green they are. Look at their enormous leaves, shiny and dark green in the dimness of the jungle.

Pause.

Turn the sound down a little.

There are flowers all around you. They are strange flowers. They have strange petals of many different colours. Look at some of the flowers and imagine them clearly in your mind. Touch them and feel their delicate petals.

Pause.

You get up and begin to walk through the jungle. The ground is very soft beneath your feet. It is spongy and bouncy. Warm, wet mud oozes between your toes. Feel the mud squelch between your toes as you walk.

Pause.

Turn the sound up so that it creates a feeling of slight tension.

There are no pathways in the jungle. With every step you take, leaves brush up against your body. They are damp in the warm air and they slip and slide against your skin. You feel them, warm and damp and slippery as you move through the jungle.

Pause.

You hear many jungle sounds. Animals and birds are all around you. You can hear them clearly. Some are close by and some are further away.

Pause.

Turn the sound down a little.

You hear many animals calling but you are not afraid. You feel strong and capable. This is your jungle and you have nothing to fear. You hold your head up high because the jungle is your home and you are happy there. You are safe and your breathing is calm and steady as you walk along.

Pause.

You look at your skin. You are a real jungle person and your skin is covered with body painting, feathers and beads.

The body painting shows that you are the leader of your tribe. It makes you proud to have these patterns painted on your skin.

Stop for a while and look at the feathers and beads and patterns. Look at them closely.

Pause.

Turn the sound down very low.

You are fit and clever and strong. You are the fastest runner in your tribe. Your arms are muscular and strong. It is easy for you to push the thick jungle branches aside as you move along. You are the strongest, fittest, cleverest person in the whole jungle. You feel strong and happy and relaxed.

Pause.

The jungle is full of secrets. It is a mysterious place, but you are at home here. You know all of its secrets, and that makes you feel confident and happy.

You know the secret places where fruit grows. You are hungry, so you move through the leaves and branches to a special place that only you know about.

Pause.

You arrive at the secret place. The trees are full of fruit. Reach up and pick whatever you want. Rest for a while as you enjoy the fruit. Rest in your special place and taste the sweet juice on your lips.

Pause.

You are safe here. You are safe and happy. You can rest here for a while feeling content and calm and happy whilst the noises of the jungle go on all around you. You are warm and strong and happy.

Pause.

Slowly turn off the sound.

Closing Ritual

Now it is time for you to bring your mind back to the classroom.

Your mind is clear and you feel calm and relaxed.

You feel strong and clever and you leave all of your fears behind you as you return to the classroom.

Take along, deep breath and begin to notice the sounds around you.

Shake your shoulders and arms.

Wiggle your fingers and toes.

Wiggle your knees and elbows.

Open your eyes when you are ready and sit quietly for a moment.

Remember the warm, calm, feeling and keep it inside your head and touch it whenever you feel tired or cross or unhappy.

Jenny Mosley's Guided Visualisation: Mountain Stream

Turn on the music and give the children time to accustom themselves to the sounds. Play the sounds quietly.

You are walking along a path beside a stream. The mountain towers above you. You are walking up the side of the mountain and you are carrying a backpack on your back. The path is steep but your legs are strong and the walking is easy. Stand still for a while and take a long, deep breath of the crisp, clean mountain air. Look around you. What can you see? What can you hear?

Pause.

The sky is bright and clear. It's a beautiful day to be out on the mountain. You can see for miles and miles. All around you the sun is shining down on the hills and moorland and the mountain. You can hear birds singing.

Pause.

You look down at the stream. The water is very clear. It sparkles in the sunlight. It is moving fast, down the mountainside. Look into the water and watch it as it glints and shines in the sunlight.

Pause.

You have a long way to go if you are going to reach the top of the mountain, but you are fit and strong. You have strong boots on your feet. Feel how firm and strong they are. They support you. Wiggle your toes and feel the roughness of your socks and the firm leather of your boots.

Pause.

Turn up the volume to create a small sense of tension.

You clamber up a steep path next to the stream. It is hard work but you are not tired. You concentrate on your walking. You need to look where you are going because the path is craggy and there are rocks to climb over. You keep moving onwards over the jagged rocks. You are climbing higher and higher and you hear the stream as it tumbles down the side of the mountain.

Pause.

Your muscles are aching from all the hard climbing but you are fit and strong and you know you will get to the top of the mountain. You climb on, up and up. Your mind is clear and empty. You have nothing to think about. Your mind is calm and empty and determined. You just climb and climb and your fit, strong body moves easily from rock to rock as you climb the mountain.

Pause.

With one last push you reach the top of the mountain. You sit down. You feel happy and alive and satisfied. You have done a difficult thing and you feel proud of yourself. You have made it to the top. You have earned a rest. You lie back and look at the wide, blue, beautiful sky and feel relaxed and happy and at peace with the world. You half close your eyes and rest for a while feeling pleased and triumphant.

Pause.

Now you are rested and relaxed and you look around you. You can see for miles. You can look around and see in every direction. What do you see? Can you see hills and farms? Can you see the sea in the distance or a big city far away below you? Take your time. Take a good look around and see what you can see from your resting place high up on the mountain top.

Pause.

Turn down the volume a little.

You take off your strong boots and dangle your feet in the stream. The water is very cold and it soothes your tired feet. It fills them with energy. The water is moving very fast and it massages your feet and refreshes them. You feel the crisp energy of the stream moving through your toes and into your ankles. You make circular movements with your ankles and look at the wide blue, beautiful sky whilst the sharp, bright water refreshes and relaxes you. You feel happy, energetic and strong.

Pause.

You pick up the backpack you have been carrying. There is something very precious inside. It is an important, valuable thing. You undo the backpack and look inside to check that the precious thing is safe inside. What is it that you are carrying? Is it an important letter? Is it some kind of treasure or is it a magic book? You decide. It is your important thing. Look inside the backpack and see what it is that you are carrying so carefully.

Pause.

You put the backpack on again. You move to the other side of the mountain and find another stream. This stream will guide you to where you need to go. Ah, there it is. You have found the stream that will take you where you need to go. You climb down towards your destination.

Pause.

Where are you going? Only you know. It is your secret. Are you taking a letter to someone important? Are you heading for a city or down towards the sea? You are the only one who knows where you are going. You are the keeper of the secret. Think about where you are going and what will happen when you get there. Keep climbing down the mountain, getting closer and closer to your destination. You can feel your excitement rising. What will happen when you arrive there?

Turn up the volume a little to create the mood of excitement.

Long pause.

Closing Ritual

Now it is time for you to bring your mind back to the classroom.

Your mind is clear and you feel calm and relaxed.

You feel strong and clever and you leave all of your fears behind you as you return to the classroom.

Take a long, deep breath and begin to notice the sounds around you.

Shake your shoulders and arms.

Wiggle your fingers and toes.

Wiggle your knees and elbows.

Open your eyes when you are ready and sit quietly for a moment.

Remember the warm, calm, feeling and keep it inside your head and touch it whenever you feel tired or cross or unhappy.

Jenny Mosley's Guided Visualisation: The Sea

Turn on the CD and slowly increase the volume so that it is playing quietly in the background. Allow the children time to relax and accustom themselves to the sounds.

You are lying on a beach. The sun shines down on you. You are feeling comfortable and warm and very relaxed. You are happy on the beach. You hear the sound of the waves not far away and you listen to them as you lie on your towel, with your body stretched out in the sunlight.

Pause.

As you listen to the waves not far away, you feel your body changing. It is curling up and forming itself into a round smooth shape. All of your body curls up into itself and becomes very still and strong.

Pause.

Increase the volume a little.
You realise that you are becoming a pebble. You are becoming a strong silent round pebble. You feel very calm. Your pebble is very old and it is calm and thoughtful. Its thoughts come slowly and calmly as it feels the waves wash over it. You are a beautiful pebble. You are a pebble of many colours. Use your imagination to see yourself – round and smooth and shining as the water laps over you.

Pause.

You feel the waves as they gently lap over your surface. The water is cold, but you are a pebble and you like the shining coldness of the water as it laps over you, going first one way and then the other. You feel the grittiness of the sand underneath you. It shifts and moves with the flow of the water. You enjoy the tickly feel of the sand as it moves on the surface of your pebble.

Pause.

Turn up the volume a little more.

The waves are getting stronger and the tide is rising. The water is getting deeper and deeper. It lifts you up and carries you out to sea. You roll and bounce across the sand as the sea takes you into deeper and deeper water. Feel yourself rolling and bouncing as you drift across the seabed further and further out into the ocean.

Pause.

Now you feel your body changing. You are becoming loose and flexible again. You can feel your muscles loosening as your body changes and becomes light and energetic. It is easy to move now. You can twist and turn and move quickly through the water. You realise that you have become a fish.

Pause.

Now you are a fish in the bright blue ocean. You can swim quickly. Your body moves easily and you swim gracefully through the water. You enjoy your graceful movements as you dart and flash through the clear pure water.

Pause.

You bend your body and take a look at yourself. What kind of fish are you? Are you big or small? Are your fins big and wavy or are they small and sharp? Take a long look at yourself and see what kind of fish you are.

Pause.

Look around you. You are in the middle of the ocean. What can you see? Can you see plants around you? How are they moving? Swim among the plants and take a good look at them.

Pause.

You are full of energy. You decide to swim fast just for the fun of it. Swimming is easy for you and you can move very quickly through the water. Where do you want to go? You can swim upwards and look at the sky or you can swim downwards and look for buried treasure. You are free and happy and relaxed to be a fish in the enormous ocean. You can swim anywhere you want to go. Swim fast for a while and go anywhere that you want to go.

Pause.

You swim up to the surface of the ocean. You can see the bright light of the sun as it sparkles through the water. You are getting closer and closer to the surface of the sea. You feel your body changing again. You are becoming lighter and lighter. Your body is growing rounder and you realise that you are becoming a bird. Feathers grow all over your body and just as you gasp for breath, you stretch your huge wide wings and crash out of the water and up into the sky.

Pause.

Turn down the volume so that it continues quietly in the background.

You are a huge seabird. You are very strong and you fly with strong wide wings. Feel how strong and wide your wings are as you soar higher and higher above the bright blue ocean.

Pause.

You are happy up in the sky. It is easy for you to fly. You feel the sun on your back and you dip and dive and soar above the wide wonderful ocean. You feel strong and happy and relaxed up in the sky on this lovely sunny day. You feel free. What can you see when you look down? You fly in a huge circle as you look down on to the sea. What can you see so far below you? Take a good look.

Pause.

Slowly, turn off the sound for a while.

You fly towards the land. You soar up high and spread your wings in slow lazy beats that capture the warm air and make you feel free and happy. You are flying towards the beach. You look down and you can see the sand and pebbles on the beach. You fly lower and get closer and closer to the sand.

Pause.

Play the music very quietly.

As you quietly fly down, you can clearly see someone sunbathing on the beach. You gently fly towards them. As you fly closer, you feel yourself changing. You are gently losing your feathers and turning into another creature altogether. You feel happy to be changing. You feel yourself changing into a person on the beach. You feel the warmth of the sun on your skin and you hear the sound of the waves lapping nearby as they move gently up and down across the sand. You realise that you have turned into yourself again and you lie on your towel feeling warm and relaxed and happy to be on the beach listening to the waves.

Pause.

Slowly turn off the music.

Closing Ritual

Now it is time for you to bring your mind back to the classroom.

Your mind is clear and you feel calm and relaxed.

You feel strong and clever and you leave all of your fears behind you as you return to the classroom.

Take along, deep breath and begin to notice the sounds around you.

Shake your shoulders and arms.

Wiggle your fingers and toes.

Wiggle your knees and elbows.

Open your eyes when you are ready and sit quietly for a moment.

Remember the warm, calm, feeling and keep it inside your head and touch it whenever you feel tired or cross or unhappy.

Jenny Mosley's Guided Visualisation: Morning Birds

This guided visualisation is divided into three parts. Each part can be used separately or you can use it as a single, longer session. The choice is yours, but you need to remember that all visualisations, whether short or long, MUST begin with the introductory phase and end with a closing ritual because these ensure that participants are in the right frame of mind to benefit from the guided visualisation and to return to the complexities of "real" life feeling refreshed and positive. When you first start, children won't be able to use their imaginations for too long, so just use a short "visual story" in-between the opening and closing rituals.

Before You Begin

- Have a good CD player ready with the disc inside.
- Dim the lights and close the blinds (if at all possible!), or give everyone a small "airline" blindfold.
- Ensure that distractions will be kept to a minimum (do not disturb on your door?).

- Help children feel positive about the visualisation by telling them that this strategy is used by athletes, actors and business people to help them achieve relaxation and also help them to learn how to focus their minds.
- Some children cannot close their eyes yet. Often their lives are so chaotic they can't trust things to be the same when they open their eyes. Just say to them that they can choose a blindfold and, using an iPod, they can listen to the same music you are using, or you can give them a beautiful picture of whatever you are talking about, which they can then look at whilst you are speaking through the visualisation.

Introductory Phase

Use the following script to settle and calm the children.

Get comfortable in your chair, try and get your back upright and supported by the chair.

Sit with both feet slightly apart on the floor. Make sure you are comfortable and relaxed.

Close your eyes and let your body feel soft and relaxed (at this point children can put on blindfolds if using them).

Listen to your breathing. Feel yourself breathing in slowly and out slowly. Just listen to your breath for a moment and let it become slow and calm. Slow and calm.

Let your mind become very still as you take a long, slow breath through your nose to the count of 3.

Now let the breath out very gently through your mouth to the count of ... (find a number that suits you).

Your breathing is now slow and balanced.

Slow and calm.

Your mind is very still.

You feel warm and relaxed and comfortable.

Your eyes are closed and your body is relaxed and warm and still.

You are happy to listen to the following story and make believe you are in it.

Part 1

Start the CD and slowly increase the volume so that it is quiet but strong.

You pretend you are in bed. You are waking up, but you are doing it slowly. There is no need to rush. You can relax and take your time because today you have nothing to do except enjoy yourself.

You feel the warmth of the covers and your body is relaxed and still sleepy. It is still a little bit dark outside. Your curtains are open and you can see that it is nearly time for the sun to rise. You don't have to hurry anything. The day is just beginning and you can snuggle up in your bed for as long as you like. You are warm and cosy. You feel relaxed. Your whole body is warm and comfortable and still just a little bit sleepy. Feel the sleepy, soft warmth of your bed and enjoy the feeling of being safe and snug for a little while.

Pause.

Turn up the sound.

The birds are already awake. You can hear them singing in the garden outside your window. They make a welcoming, cheerful sound as they sing to one another. You lie in your warm bed and listen to them. How many different birds can you hear? Listen carefully and see if you can hear the different songs they sing.

Pause.

The sun is rising; you watch it as the light begins to fill your bedroom. It is a silvery light. It is early morning so the sun isn't warm yet but the light is bright and crisp and lively. It is full of energy and hope and strength. The light shines on your body, as you lie warm and comfortable in your bed. The light fills you with energy and hope and strength. You feel the light on your forehead. It fills your head with strong morning light, crisp and clear and full of joy. You lie still for a while and let the wonderful morning sunlight stream into your head.

Pause.

The light streams into your head and gradually moves through your whole body. It moves down your neck. You feel it crisp and warm as it fills your neck with morning brightness. It moves into your chest. You feel the clear silver light of morning fill your chest with life and energy. The light moves down into your legs and finally reaches your toes. Your whole body is full of energy and light and happiness.

Part 2

Turn the sound down a little.

You look out of the window. The sky is pale blue in the morning light. Clouds make soft shapes in the sky. Look at the clouds and watch them move slowly and gently across the sky. What shapes do you see in the clouds? Are they long and stringy or are they round and fluffy? Look at them carefully. Use your imagination to picture the clouds and the shapes they are making.

You feel very awake now. You get out of bed. You put on a warm dressing gown and walk downstairs, through the house and out into the garden. You are wide awake now and you feel full of happiness and expectation.

Pause.

You look around the garden. All around you, birds are singing. You look at the beautiful garden. It is very still and quiet in the morning sunlight. What do you see? Picture your garden in your imagination. It is your garden. You can make it in any way that you like. Is there a lawn? Do trees grow in your wonderful garden? Can you see the flowers and plants in your peaceful, beautiful garden? Is there a pond? You decide. Explore your peaceful garden in your imagination.

Pause.

You look up at one of the trees. There is a little bird sitting on a branch. It looks back at you. It seems to be quite tame and it watches you with its beady bright eyes. You carefully walk towards it but it doesn't fly away. You stand quite close and listen to it singing in the bright morning sunshine.

Part 3

The bird hops onto another branch. It looks back at you. Does it want you to follow? It hops from branch to branch, singing and looking back to make sure that you are following. Where is it taking you? Why does it want you to follow? It seems to want to show you something. It hops and sings as it moves across the garden from tree to tree. You follow the little singing bird. How do you feel as you follow it? This is a very special moment and the little bird wants you to follow. Take a moment to think about how you feel about this amazing, secret experience.

Pause.

The little bird takes you to a magical, astonishing place. There is something wonderful there. What has it taken you to see? Imagine it in your mind. Think about it. How do you feel when the bird shows you this amazing, secret thing? Feel the amazement in your body and think about what the bird has shown you.

Pause.

You sit down in the special place and watch the bird as it flutters around. The sun is getting very warm now. It is going to be a lovely hot day in your wonderful garden. You feel happy and relaxed and peaceful as you sit in your special place with your friend the little bird.

Pause.

Sit still for a while and enjoy the sunshine.

Slowly turn off the sound.

Closing Ritual

Now it is time for us to come back into the classroom.

The easiest way to do this is to imagine in front of you a huge, beautiful bubble. We call this the memory bubble.

Put the picture of yourself smiling happily after your lovely journey into the bubble.

Blow the bubble "ppphhh" – and now the bubble floats over the top of your head and pops into your memory bank. It will sit there ready for you to get it out at any other time when you want to go on a lovely nature journey and feel happy and relaxed.

Keeping your eyes closed, start to stretch your legs and your arms.

Make little tiny circular movements with your wrists first one way and now round the other way.

Make little tiny circles with your ankles first one way then the other way.

Give a little wiggle of your toes and fingers. One more stretch.

Now when I count to 3, open your eyes and by the time I have counted to 6 see how many children's eyes you can smile into whilst I am quietly counting.

Well done everyone.

The Last Word

Thank you, dear reader, for choosing this book – and getting to this end page.

For me it has been a huge journey. This is the last book I will write for secondary schools. Same for its primary "mirror" book which is also coming out this year (2026).

I am happy to keep working with teachers and young people. I think it is a huge privilege to be well at this age and to be able to support and help others. So many older people would love to meet and chat to young people – they still have so much to offer: wisdom, fun and delight in the children. Please explore similar projects like Leeds Local Authority did when Sean Duggan, one of their brilliant Learning Mentors, took secondary pupils into older people's homes. They all need each other.

Maybe the above is one step too far for you at the moment, so just put your energy into creating circles. How can humanity go on this endless digital route unless it's balanced by children experiencing the nurture, care and safety or belonging to a circle.

If people listen to you over time, never interrupt, offer solutions, have fun with you, share feelings honestly and openly, turn up most weeks and treat you with respect and empathy, then you have finally found a "home" where your spirit can rest a while, away from the emotional and academic pushing and shoving that can exhaust you. Circles refresh, welcome and inspire.

As I said at the beginning of the book, if treated warmly and mindfully, over a period of time you begin to love in a quiet, trusting way, those that give you the experience.

Good luck, you wonderful unsung heroes. I can do this bit of life, i.e. writing and training, but I can no longer do what you do: come in every day, work your socks off, often rocked by endless pressures and meetings, and still care strongly about the young people. I can sparkle occasionally but not every day; you are in for the long haul. I genuinely believe if you create a regular circle, small or large, with young people, it will begin to pull you together eventually and it will help you to last the long journey as it will revive and restore you.

Training Available from Jenny Mosley Consultancies

Jenny Mosley has been training in schools for 50 years and her Whole School Quality Circle Time model is now well established and welcomed by thousands of schools throughout the UK and internationally.

There are two options for Jenny to work with your staff and/or children:

1. Closure Inset Days

Jenny is used to working with large numbers. In her happy world, all members of staff would be invited from each school that she is working with. Recent titles for these training days have included "Supporting Wellbeing and Emotional Resilience So We Have the Energy to Help Others" and "A Whole School Approach to Positive Relationships in the Classroom, Playground and Staffroom."

2. Working In School Days

Jenny will come in and work with classes of challenging students through the Circle Approach. Staff will observe the sessions and debrief on the strategies that they too can use in the classroom.

Different workshops can be requested that can be run throughout the day including staff meetings at the end of the day.

Separately, some schools request Jenny to work with the lunchtime supervisors' team and the senior managers to create more productive, happier lunchtime experiences.

Resources and Books

Jenny's key books are being republished by Taylor & Francis in 2026 so will be available to buy. These include:

101 Games for Social Skills: Exploring Positive Relationships and Healthy Interactions
101 Games for Self-Esteem: Building Confidence and Motivation
101 Games for Better Behaviour: Supporting Feelings and Building Emotional Awareness
101 Activities to Help Children Get On Together: Building Co-operation and Belonging
A Primary Circle Approach to Supporting Oracy, Wellbeing, and Inclusive Relationships: Making Time to Listen
Early Intervention Through Circles of Support: An Inclusive Approach to Building Self Confidence, Communication Skills and Peer Relationships

If you would like to book Jenny for training, purchase any of her resources or find out more please contact Jenny Mosley Consultancies:

Telephone: 01225 767157
E-mail: circletime@jennymosley.co.uk
Website:
www.circle-time.co.uk

Index

Note: Page numbers in *italics* reference figures.

ACEs *see* adverse childhood experiences
active groupwork 4, 10
activities: Double Circle Activity 194; Good Vibes Wall 178; *see also* games
add-on interventions 39
adverse childhood experiences (ACEs) 14, 83
agency 15
Aliens game 199
alternative education programmes 113–114
"always" child 64
And Another Thing game 200–201
anger, defusing 233
anxiety 11
Atherton, Carolina 106–107
Attachment Theory 14
auditing lunchtimes 80–81
autonomy 15
A–Z of gender-inclusive superpowers 176

bags that pulsate guilt 45
Bean Game 155, 182
behaviour 38, 82; acknowledging 64; disruptive behaviour 82–83; dysregulated behavior 82–85; hostile behaviour 88; *Ofsted's Education Inspection Framework* 29–31; withdrawn behaviour 88
Believe Me? game 201
belonging 15, 24, 38
black-pilled ideology 171
Boardman, Ann 110–112
breathing techniques 44
bridges 37

Bright, Mary 113–114
bullying 53, 78
Burgh Thomas, Esther de 107–108
Burley, Jennie 108
Burstow, Claire, Circle Time progress report 121–122, 130–131
Butler, Sam 112–113
Button Sculpture 55
Buzz Game 194

calming down 103–104, 237; Emojis and Emoticons (Age 13–16) 170; Teasing/Bullying (Age 13–15) 167; Unpacking Gender Role Stereotypes (Age 15–18) 174
calming rituals 44
Carr Manor Community School 17–19; One-to-One Coaching 53
case studies: Carr Manor Community School 17–18; Chat Time 53–54; cross-phase teaching school project 114–127; incentives 65–68; Shoeburyness County High School 112–113; South Essex Health Authority 110–112; Tameside Community Care Trust, South Essex 110–112; Trafalgar School 18–19
celebrating positivity, success and fun 103
Chads, emojis 171
Changes Happen 151
Chat Time 15, 53–54
Choice Theory model (1998) 14
Chudley, Sue 108
Circle Approach 4, 9–10
Circle Coach 18

Index

Circle of Friends 86
Circle of Respect 4
Circle of Support 86, 95
Circle Time procedures survey, Train the Trainers programme *117*
Circle Time progress report, Fallibroome Academy 130–131
circles, and spirituality 16
coaching circles 18
codes of conduct 60–61, 72; *see also* rules
committees 231–232
communication, rules for 38–39
Community Council, sample Circle Time session plan (Year 7) 128–130
community rewards 68–70
confidence, lesson plans 185–186
consequences 71–73; examples of 75–76; tellings-off 73–75; withdrawal of privilege 75; yellow cards 73
containment 90–91
Copy Me – or "Simon Says" 202–203
Copycat 202
COVID-19 pandemic 130–131
Cox, Norma 110–112
Cranford Community School 106–107
cross-phase teaching school project, Fallibroome Academy 114–127

Dealing with Failure game 203
deepening relationships through circles 31–32
defusing anger 233
digital pressures 83
Dinner game 135
discipline 30, 32
disruptive behaviour 82–83
Don't Say Yes or No! 157
Dorset 108, 110
drama and role-play 231–236
dysregulated behavior 82–85; support for pupils 85; tiny, achievable tickable targets (TATTs) 86–88

ecosystemic model 37–39, 41, 51; codes of conduct 60; consequences 71; incentives 63; lunchtimes 77; students 'beyond' 82; *see also* Whole-School Quality Circle Time (QCT) Approach to Wellbeing
educational psychologists, perspectives on whole-school quality Circle Time 39

Electric Squeeze game 138, 204–205
Elephant, Palm Tree and Aeroplane game 144
emojis 168–172
emoticons 168–171
emotional dysregulation 83
emotional intelligence 229–230
emotional safety 15
emotions 233–234
empathetic ethos 54
empathy 154–158
Empty Chair 154
Exchanging Places game 164
exclusion of others, emojis 171
expectations for behaviour 30
external locus of control 32
Extra Circles of Support 15

factories 234
failure 203
Fallibroome Academy 106; Circle Time progress report 121–122, 130–131; cross-phase teaching school project 114–127; participant comments 122–126
false self-esteem 74
feelings: managing 161–163; rounds 229–230
femininity 175–176
Five Steps to Quality Circle Time 5; calming down 103–104; celebrating positivity, success and fun 103; meeting for team fun 99–100; opening up issues that matter 100–103; warming up to speaking 100
"Five Wells for Wellbeing" 45–48
foot tapping 153
Forrest, Edith 109–110
Freedom Writers (2007) 54–55
friendship, lesson plans 179–181
Friendship Feelings 157
fun: celebrating 103; Choice Theory model (1998) 14; steps to quality circle time 99–100

games 107–108; Aliens 199; And Another Thing 200–201; Bean Game 155, 182; Believe Me? 201; Buzz Game 194; Copy Me – or "Simon Says" 202–203; Copycat 202; Dealing with Failure 203; Dinner 135; Electric Squeeze 138, 204–205; Elephant, Palm

Tree and Aeroplane 144; Exchanging Places 164; Gloop 162, 205; Good Try! 205; Gotcha 205–206; Guided Walk 206; I Am a Chair! 207; "I Like It When …" 161; I Love You Honey But I Just Can't Smile 143; Identification Cards 207–208; Initials 190; Keeper of the Keys 198, 208; Knots 149; Life Line 208–209; Man's Best Friend 209; Moan On 209–210; My Gang/Group 163, 210–211; My Other Half 211–212; Name Exercise 134; Negotiating 212–213; Newspaper Stories 213; Noise 141; Nonsense Talk 203–204; Number Call 213–214; Opting Out 214–215; Our World 147; Parental Concerns 215; Pass the Action 215–216; Pass the Python 216; Play the Game 216–217; Positive News 217–218; Problem-Solving 218; racing charades 235; Racing Pictionary 219; Rainbow 140; Real or Filtered? 177, 179; Red Queen 219–220; Reflections 220; Ring on a String 221; Sausage 162; Saying Sorry 221–222; Setbacks 222; Sevens 195, 222–223; "Silent Statements" 188; Silly Answers 135; Similarities and Differences 223; Sitting on the Long Grass 161; Skill Swap 183; Sleeping Spell 168; A Star for a Second 199–200; "Step In - Step Out" 173; Tease 223–224; Things in Common 224; Touchdown 146, 225; Two Things 160; Waves 191, 226–227; Who Am I? 185; Who Are You? 179–180, 225–226; Word Association 181; A Worry Shared 200; Yes and No 236; "You're Positive" 198, 226; Zoom – Eek 227
gender roles 175–176
gender stereotypes 173–176; emojis 171
gender-inclusive superpowers 176
"generalised other" 19
Glasser's Choice Theory model (1998) 14
Gloop game 162, 205
goals 160
Golden Moments 44
Golden Rules 15, 62
Good Friends 156
Good Try! game 205

Good Vibes Wall 178
Gotcha game 205–206
group management 30
growth 16
growth mindset 68
guided visualisations 187–188, 193, 237–238; Into Africa 238–242; introductory phase 238; Morning Birds 248–252; Mountain Stream 242–245; The Sea 245–248
Guided Walk game 206
guilt 45

heart emojis 172
Hierarchy of Needs Model (Maslow 1943) 13
higher self-esteem *87*
home-school agreement 37
hopelessness, emojis 171
hostile behaviour 88
house systems, incentives 69
human needs 38

I Am a Chair! game 207
"I Like It When …" game 161
I Love You Honey, But I Just Can't Smile game 143
Identification Cards 207–208
identifying dysregulated pupils 85
identity 38
If I Was an Animal 158
Ignore and Distract strategy 75
importance of Circle Time 9
In My Opinion 158
incentives 63–65; "always" child 64; case studies 65–68; community rewards 69–70; individual rewards 68–69
inclusion 53
individual rewards 68–69
Initials 190
INSET day 111, 113
intelligence 229
interventions, add-on 39
Into Africa, guided visualisations 238–242
introductory phase for guided visualisation 238
Inverkeithing High School 108–109
IQ 229
Islington Comprehensive 107–108
It's OK 158

Jenny Mosley Whole-School Quality Circle Time Model for Wellbeing *36*
John of Gaunt School, incentives 65–68
John's Day-- Boost Ups and Put Downs 155–156

Keeper of the Keys game 198, 208
kindness 21–22
Kindness Test 22
Kindness UK 22
Knots game 149

learning about me 161–163
Learning Brain Europe 114
Left and Right Hands 153
lesson plans: Being Popular (Age 12/13) 191–193; Confidence (Age 14/15) 185–186; Emojis and Emoticons (Age 13–16) 168–171; Friendship (Age 11/12) 179–181; Loneliness (Age 12/13) 181–182; Moving to Key Stage 4 (Age 14/15) 195–196; My Life (Age 11/12) lesson 190–191; picking and mixing 132–133; Saying "No" (Age 14/15) 194–195; Secondary Transition First Day/Lesson 1 134–135; Secondary Transition Lesson 2 136–138; Secondary Transition Lesson 3 139–140; Secondary Transition Lesson 4 141–143; Secondary Transition Lesson 5 144–146; Secondary Transition Lesson 6 147–149; Strengths and Weaknesses (Age 13/14) 183–185; Taking Risks (Age 15/16) 188–189; Teasing/Bullying (Age 13–15) 164–167; Tutor Circle Session 1 150; Tutor Circle Session 3 152–153; Tutor Circle Session 4 153–154; Tutor Circle Session 5 155–156; Tutor Circle Session 6 157; Tutor Circle Session 7 158; Tutor Circle Session 8 159–160; Tutor Circle Session 9 160–161; Tutor Circle Session 10 161–162; Tutor Circle Session 11 162–163; Twenty-Minute Tutor Circle Session 2 151–152; Unpacking Gender Role Stereotypes (Age 15–18) 173–176; Using Social Media (Year 8–12) 177–179
Life Line game 208–209
listening, non-verbal 15, 54–55

listening systems 37, 51–52; example of listening system by Bethan Sioned Rogers-Jones 55–59; one-to-one listening 53; peer listening systems 53
locus of control 31–32
loneliness, lesson plans 181–182
lower self-esteem *84*
lunchtimes 77–80; audits of 80–81

Man's Best Friend game 209
masculinity 175–176
Maslow's Hierarchy of Needs Model (1943) 13
McFarlane, Isobel 108–109
mental health 1, 11; impact of school on 11
mindfulness 103–104; *see also* guided visualisations
Moan On game 209–210
moods, taking responsibility for your mood 45–48
moral values 61
Morning Birds, guided visualisations 248–252
motivation 159–161; *see also* incentives
Mountain Stream, guided visualisations 242–245
Moving Changes 151
My Gang/Group game 163, 210–211
My Other Half game 211–212

Name Exercise game 134
Negotiating game 212–213
Newspaper Stories game 213
Noise game 141
Nominations 152
Nonsense Talk game 203–204
non-verbal listening 15, 54–55
Northwood College for Girls 99
notes from teachers, praise 75
Number Call game 213–214

Ofsted's Education Inspection Framework 28–33
one-to-one listening 37, 53; non-verbal listening 54–55; *see also* Chat Time
open forum drama and role-play ideas 231–236
opening up issues that matter to us 100–103
Opting Out game 214–215

Index

Our World game 147
other 19
Our Gifts to You 159–160

paired discussions 228–229
Parental Concerns game 215
participant comments, Fallibroom Academy 122–126
Pass the Action game 215–216
Pass the Python game 216
peer listening systems 53
peer support groups 87–88
personal notes from teachers 75
perspectives on Circle Time: Atherton, Carolina 106–107; Boardman, Ann 110–112; Bright, Mary 113–114; Burgh Thomas, Esther de 107–108; Burley, Jennie 108; Butler, Sam 112–113; Chudley, Sue 108; Cox, Norma 110–112; Forrest, Edith 109–110; Headteacher's view of 33–34; McFarlane, Isobel 108–109; Robinson, Mandy 110
Perth and Kinross 109–110
picking and mixing Circle Time lesson plans 132–133
pivotal management circles 37
places to learn 150–153
play, lunchtimes 81
Play the Game 216–217
popularity, Being Popular (Age 12/13) 191–193
Positive News game 217–218
positive relationships 15
positivity 94; celebrating 103
praise 94; personal notes from teachers 75
privileges, withdrawal of 75
problematic behaviour 38
Problem-Solving game 218
proverbs 234–235
PSHE 23–25, 32–33, 92–93, 112, 130–131, 133; Being Popular (Age 12/13) lesson 191–193; Moving to Key Stage 4 (Age 14/15) 195; My Life (Age 11/12) lesson 190–191; Saying "No" (Age 14/15) 194–195; tricks for making things run smoothly 25–26
psychological safety 15
public tellings-off 73–75
punishments *see* consequences
pupil voice 1, 123
pupils *see also* students

QCT *see* Whole-School Quality Circle Time (QCT) Approach to Wellbeing
Quality Circle Time model (1980s onwards) 15, 35–37; five steps to Quality Circle Time 99–105
Quality Circle Time *see* Whole-School Quality Circle Time (QCT) Approach to Wellbeing
questionnaires: for pupils 118–120; staff feelings about school 118–119, *118*; strengths and weaknesses 184–185

racing charades 235
Racing Pictionary 219
Rainbow game 140
Real or Filtered? game 177, 179
Red Queen game 219–220
red-pilled ideology 171
reflection 163
Reflections game 220
Relationship Guidance 23
relationships 3, 16, 113; deepening through circles 31–32
Relationships, Sex Education and Health Education (RSHE) 22–26, 163; Confidence (Age 14/15) 185–186; Emojis and Emoticons (Age 13–16) 168–171; Friendship (Age 11/12) 179–181; Loneliness (Age 12/13) 181–182; Moving to Key Stage 4 (Age 14/15) 195–196; Saying "No" (Age 14/15) 194–195; Strengths and Weaknesses (Age 13/14) 183–185; Taking Risks (Age 15/16) 188–189; Teasing/Bullying (Age 13–15) 164–167; Unpacking Gender Role Stereotypes (Age 15–18) 173–176; Using Social Media (Year 8–12) 177–179
repair 16
respect 30; speaking objects 228
Respect Rules 61–62
responsibility, taking responsibility for your mood 45–48
responsiveness 30
restoration 16
Restorative Justice model (2000s onwards) 14
rewards 63–64; *see also* incentives
Ring on a String game 221
risks, Taking Risks (Age 15/16) 188–189
Robinson, Mandy 110
Rocket Launch 150

role-play 231–236
Rota System 53
rounds 228; about feelings 229–230; Getting to Know You 228–229
routine rules 61
RSHE *see* Relationships, Sex Education and Health Education
rules 59–62; based on moral values 61; Golden Rules 62; Respect Rules 61–62; routine rules 61; for safety 93–94

safeguarding 53
safety: *Ofsted's Education Inspection Framework* 29–31; rules for 93–94
sample Circle Time session plan (Year 6) 127–128
sample Circle Time session plan (Year 7) 128–130
Sausage game 162
Saying Sorry game 221–222
SC *see* School Council
school, impact on mental health 11
School Council (SC) 52
school discipline 30
school-based community circles: Carr Manor Community School 17–18; Trafalgar School 18–19
screen time 9
The Sea, guided visualisations 245–248
SEAL (Social, Emotional Aspects of Learning) *see* Social and Emotional Aspects of Learning, 10
Secure Base model (2009) 14
SEL *see* Social and Emotional Learning
self-care 43; bags that pulsate guilt 45; breathing techniques 44; calming rituals 44; taking responsibility for your mood 45–48; visualisation techniques 44
self-control 32
self-esteem 19, 85; false self-esteem 74; higher self-esteem *87*; vicious circle of lower self-esteem *84*; whole-School Quality Circle Time (QCT) Approach to Wellbeing 41–43
SEND children: community rewards 69; consequences 72; incentives 69; rules for 62
SEND teams 53
Setbacks game 222
Sevens game 195, 222–223
Shoeburyness County High School 112–114
sign language 235–236

Silent Statements 100, 188
Silly Answers game 135
Similarities and Differences game 223
Sitting on the Long Grass game 161
Skill Swap game 183
skills reminder, sample Circle Time session plan (Year 6) 127–128
Sleeping Spell game 168
SMSC *see* Spiritual, Moral, Social and Cultural
Social and Emotional Aspects of Learning (SEAL) 10, 21; kindness 21–22; Relationships, Sex Education and Health Education 22–23
Social and Emotional Learning (SEL) 11
social media 11, 83; Using Social Media (Year 8–12) 177–179
social skills: Tutor Circle Session 4 154–155; Tutor Circle Session 5 155–156; Tutor Circle Session 6 157; Tutor Circle Session 7 158
South Essex Health Authority 110–112
speaking objects 228
specials 65
SPICE *see* Spiritual, Physical, Intellectual, Creative, and Emotional
Spiritual, Moral, Social and Cultural (SMSC) 29
Spiritual, Physical, Intellectual, Creative, and Emotional (SPICE) 45–48
spirituality 16–17
Spot Leader 152
staff: questionnaire about feelings about school *118*–119; support for 33, 91; *see also* teachers
A Star for a Second 199–200
Step 1, games *see* games
Step 2, rounds 228–230
Step 3, open forum drama and role-play ideas 231–236
Step 5, calming down *see* calming down
"Step In - Step Out" game 173
Step In - Step Out statements 175
strengths, lesson plans 183–185
stress 78
students: comments about Circle Time (Fallibroome Academy) 120–121; questionnaires 118–120; and spirituality 17; *see also* pupils
students 'beyond' *82*, 94–95
success, celebrating 103
support: for adults 86; for dysregulated pupils 85; for staff 33, 91

survey: of Circle Time procedures *117*; survey of preferred incentives, John of Gaunt School *67*; on rewards and consequences, John of Gaunt School *66*

Tameside Community Care Trust, South Essex 110–112
TATTs *see* tiny, achievable tickable targets
teacher training 10–11, 24
teachers: arguments as to why they can't set it up 92–93; dysregulated pupils 86; lunchtimes 78–79; personal notes from 75; role of 31; support for 33; *see also* staff
Teaching Schools, Fallibroome Academy 115–116
Tease game 223–224
tellings-off 73–75
Things in Common game 224
time outs 44
time-out zones 90
tiny, achievable tickable targets (TATTs) 86–88
Touchdown game 146, 225
toxic femininity 175
toxic gender roles 175–176
toxic masculinity 175; emojis 171
Trafalgar School 18–19
Train the Trainers programme; Circle Time progress report 121–122; Teaching Schools 116
training 10–11, 123, 254; Train the Trainers programme 116

trauma-informed approaches 14, 83
trust 85
Two Things game 160

UK Teacher Training courses 24

vertical tutoring 24–25
vertical tutoring groups 23
violence, emojis 171
virtual tutoring 24
visualisation techniques 44, 103–104; *see also* guided visualisations
warming up to speaking 100
weaknesses, lesson plans 183–185
wellbeing. *see* self-esteem
Who Am I? game 185
Who Are You? 179–180, 225–226
Whole-School Quality Circle Time (QCT) Approach to Wellbeing 5, 35–37, 39, 109; ecosystemic approach 37–39, 41; perspective of an educational psychologist 39; self-esteem 41–43
withdrawn behaviour 88
Word Association game 181
work-life balance 45–48; *see also* self-care
A Worry Shared 200

yellow cards, consequences 73
Yes and No game 236
"You're Positive" game 198, 226

Zoom – Eek game 227

For Product Safety Concerns and Information please contact our EU
representative GPSR@taylorandfrancis.com
Taylor & Francis Verlag GmbH, Kaufingerstraße 24, 80331 München, Germany

www.ingramcontent.com/pod-product-compliance
Lightning Source LLC
Chambersburg PA
CBHW071405300426
44114CB00016B/2188